What All Americans
Need To Know About Economics

Frank DeFelice, MBA, Ph. D.

FINANCIAL ECONOMIST

Entrepreneur, Millionaire & Presidential Advisor

Frank DeFelice, Ph.D.

FIRST EDITION

Publisher: Frank DeFelice, Ph. D., Inc.
Lake Norman, NC

Email: DeFelice.Frank@yahoo.com

Cell Phone: 704-928-7660

ISBN: 0615634494
ISBN-13: 978-0615634494

FOREWORD

This little book is designed to present the most important fundamental economics concepts in a way that they will be understandable by high school students. This type of presentation will also be understandable by the public at large. The goal is to make all U. S. citizens informed participants in the economy. Our point of view is the big picture, what economists call "macro-economics."

Instead of hypothetical situations, we will use the U.S. 2008-09 economic malaise to show what went wrong and why, and how to fix the problems causing the malaise: short-term, long-term and permanently.

Actually, the permanent fix of such problems is the objective of this book. What's required is no less than the eradication of economics illiteracy in the land. We are presenting this material at the high school comprehension level with the hope that all high school students in the nation be required to take and pass a course that guarantees they will have the knowledge to participate in the economy as informed citizens.

We do not expect the public schools to ever have qualified economists teaching these concepts, but if we have a theoretically sound textbook, we then have a chance to have the problems identified in the 2008-09 malaise permanently solved.

We can not do much to change the thinking about economics of very many mature adults (We have tried for forty years.) for several reasons: First there is a high political philosophy elasticity for economics concepts. For example, there are those who think debt, per se, is bad; and if people only saved more to pay cash for everything, the economy would be much better. Then there is another large segment who say (internally, at least), "Don't confuse me with the facts, my mind is made up." Legions of people say that all economics problems are caused by government: too many regulations, too much spending, and too much debt. There is widespread misconception that the stock market is the economy. And very little understanding of what the role of the stock market in capitalism is correctly limited to (even by the regulators!).

Kids come to school with these incorrect ideas and limited understanding and leave with them largely intact; therefore, perpetuating all the misinformed thinking that allows the economy to operate in boom and bust cycles that hurts millions of people economically.

With an understanding of the information provided in this book, we have the opportunity to have an informed citizenry that will know what goes wrong and how to fix it, and hopefully prevent things from going wrong.

The first thing anybody reading any textbook about anything should do is check out the credentials of the author. Is he qualified as an expert in the subject matter of the book?

You answer that question for yourself from the following page: "About Us."

ABOUT US: We both finished high school in 1950; Frank in Lexington, and Ellie in Concord (MA); and were married that year. Our first home was on Cape Cod where we lived year round for five years and summers for ten while Frank did his Ph.D. Since, we have lived in North Carolina: Chapel Hill, Charlotte, and on Lake Norman, which is our principal residence. However, we live summers in Linville in the N.C. mountains, and winters in a park model trailer near Frostproof, Florida. We have three children (Frank P., our oldest, died of lung cancer in 2008), four grandchildren, two step grandchildren (both Marines), and one great-grandchild.

Dr. DeFelice earned a BA magna cum laude from Honors College at Michigan State University, an M.B.A. and a Ph.D. in Economics from UNC-Chapel Hill; is AACSB terminally qualified in both Economics and Finance; held NDEA, FORD, and NSF Fellowships; did post-doctoral work in Econometrics at Duke, Computer Science at Colorado, and Finance under the late great Henry Latane'; published articles in The Journal of Finance, The Economics Journal (Cambridge, England), The Wall Street Journal, and others; authored A Primer on Business Finance; was an SEC Registered Broker/Dealer & Investment Advisor; is an Entrepreneur, Millionaire and Presidential Advisor.

Frank DeFelice, Ph.D.

DEDICATION

This book is dedicated to Our Friend, Barack Obama, the 44th President of the United States for his inspiration and encouragement to continue our efforts to define "a better way to do business post-bubble," with the ultimate goal being the permanent cure for the recurring financial panics and recessions that have plagued our democracy for over 200 years. Chronological communications between us and his Administration going back to the presidential campaign of 2008 comprise the Appendix of this book.

To his credit, he was quick to realize that we have no political agenda or "axe to grind," but are simply willing, as good citizens, to give back from the public funding of our entire 20 years of education and wisdom garnered over a lifetime of study of economics.

However, this book should in no way be defined as a political polemic that "white-washes" Obama and his policies. Quite to the contrary, Obama is cited in the book and in an (unpublished) piece we wrote for the Journal of Political Economy (JPE) in the Fall of 2008 as a prime cause of the 2009-10 recession when he used the stock market crash and housing sector debacle, in no small measure, to defeat John McCain, who at the time, correctly said, "the (economics) fundamentals are fine." In addition, we told him and several members of his Administration in economics positions (mostly the Council of Economics Advisors and Ben Bernanke, (the FED Chairman) several times that some of his economics policies were flat out wrong.

The JPE (unpublished) piece appears in its entirety in the Appendix to the book, that also includes numerous communications from us to President Obama and his Administration along with ten replies from The White House over President Obama's signature.

TABLE OF CONTENTS

Frank DeFelice, Ph.D.

CHAPTER 1:
INTRODUCTION, DEFINITIONS AND TERMINOLOGY

When learning any new science, half the battle is understanding the terminology. (So, it might be that this chapter is half the book!)

Before we get to that, let's look at the "forest" before we begin to look at just one "tree." All knowledge can fit into three classifications: humanities, arts, and sciences.

Economics is a science. But there are two kinds of science: physical science and social science. Economics is a social science like sociology, psychology, and political science (though we tend to agree with Richard Nixon, "There is no such thing as political science." (He thought it was an art: the politics of the possible.)

What social sciences have in common and how they differ from physical sciences is that they are about human behavior. Economics is the "Queen" of social sciences because it is quantitative. But it is not exact because you can not put people in a lab and do controlled experiments, as you can with the physical sciences.

Physical sciences, physics and chemistry for example, are about things and can be much more exact because experiments are done in controlled lab environments.

The reason there is such a thing as the science of economics (raison d'etre in French) is because economic resources are RELATIVELY SCARCE when compared to man's wants for economic goods and services. In economics we assume that man's wants are unlimited, and we know that resources are limited. Therefore, we need some way to decide which of man's wants will be satisfied with limited resources. An economy is the system by which these decisions are made.

In economics we put all <u>resources</u> into just three categories: land, labor and capital. But the economics definition of these three kinds of resources differs markedly from the everyday usage of these words. For example, "land" is defined as all natural resources and therefore includes oil, natural gas, coal, copper, iron ore and even water. That's right, in economics water is in the "land category. (Now you see why a Harvard graduate we were tutoring in economics said, "Economics has no father!"; i.e., is difficult to learn.)

Labor is all human effort: physical and mental. Therefore, managers and CEO's of big corporations are part of the resource called labor. It is not management vs. labor, as in common parlance: management IS labor in economics!

Capital, as an economic resource is manufacturing plants and equipment, but it also includes all the goods used to produce other goods or services. Sometimes a good can be called either a consumer good or a capital good depending on the use. For example, a lawn mower, if bought and used to cut the grass in the buyer's yard is a consumer good. If used to cut other people's grass for money, it is a capital good. It is producing an economic service. In economics, capital is NOT money.

One easy way to understand what <u>an economy</u> is all about is to develop a simple circular flow model of the resources and money flows. Make the following assumptions, which can be relaxed later on to make the model more realistic: 1. There are just two sectors in the economy – households (HH) and business (BUS). 2. Households own all the resources. 3. All production takes place in the business sector. 4. "Real" flows – resources and economic goods flow in one direction ("real" in economics means the money value is not included). 5. Money flows in the opposite direction of the "real" flows. Illustration 1-1 is a 2-sector circular flow model of an economy.

Where the money flows intersects with the "real" flows from the household sector to the business sector is where prices for inputs are determined. Supply and demand forces determine prices, which are costs to business. Where the "real" flows out from the business intersect with the money flows from households is where output prices get determined.

There are various kinds of market structures in both input and output markets. None of them are "perfectly" competitive, so the prices arrived at are not perfect either. Study of the different market structures and what happens to price and output is the essence of micro-economics, and not our concern here.

ILLUSTRATION 1-1
2-SECTOR CIRCULAR FLOW MODEL OF AN ECONOMY

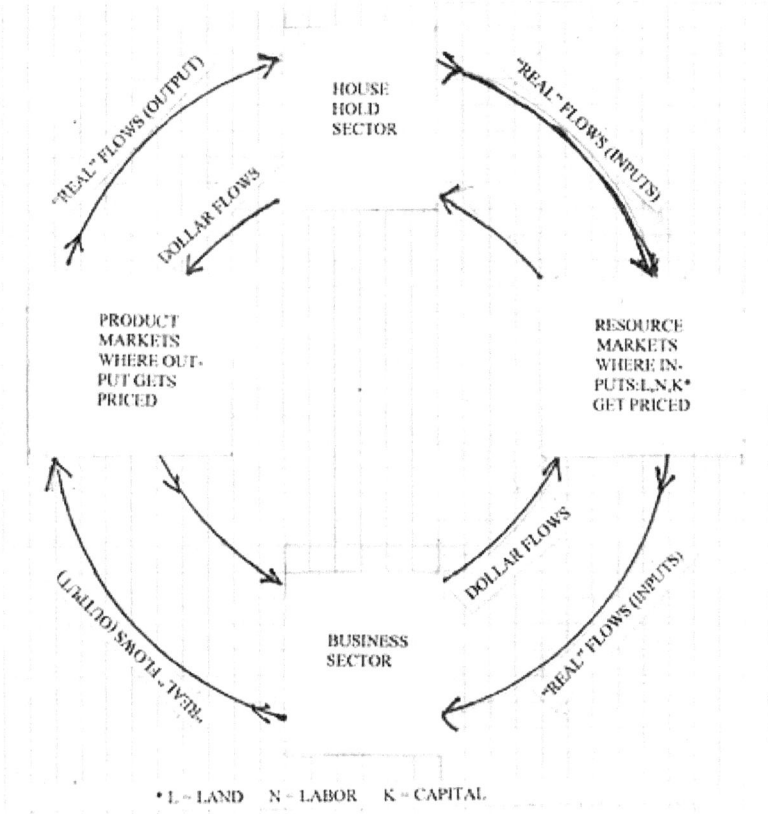

"REAL" FLOWS (OUTPUT)

DOLLAR FLOWS

HOUSE HOLD SECTOR

"REAL" FLOWS (INPUTS)

PRODUCT MARKETS WHERE OUT-PUT GETS PRICED

RESOURCE MARKETS WHERE IN-PUTS:L,N,K* GET PRICED

"REAL" FLOWS (OUTPUT)

DOLLAR FLOWS

BUSINESS SECTOR

"REAL" FLOWS (INPUTS)

* L - LAND   N - LABOR   K - CAPITAL

We can add saving and investment into the model – Illustration 1-2, a 2-sector circular flow model of an economy plus saving and investment. Both the HH sector and the BUS sector do not spend all of their income. By definition – money not spent is saved. It goes into banks who loan it (and more! as we will see in Chapter 3) out to either sector. But the important point is that the money flow is not diminished by saving as long as banks loan it out.

ILLUSTRATION 1-2
2-SECTOR CIRCULAR FLOW MODEL OF AN ECONOMY
PLUS SAVINGS AND INVESTMENT

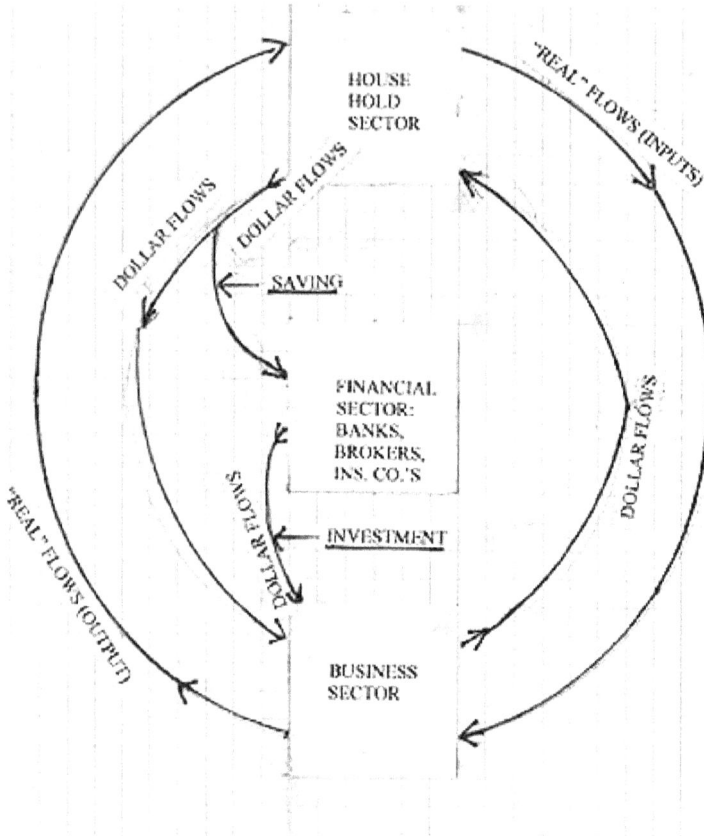

We can add a government sector – Illustration 1-3 is a 3-sector circular flow model of an economy, government sector added, which fits into the money flow taking money (taxes) from the HH sector from the income they receive, and from the profit of the BUS sector. But the economy does not lose from this government action because it puts the money back into the flow as it buys resources and output. There is nothing bad for the economy by government taxing and spending policies.

ILLUSTRATION 1-3
3-SECTOR CIRCULAR FLOW MODEL OF AN ECONOMY
GOVERNMENT SECTOR ADDED

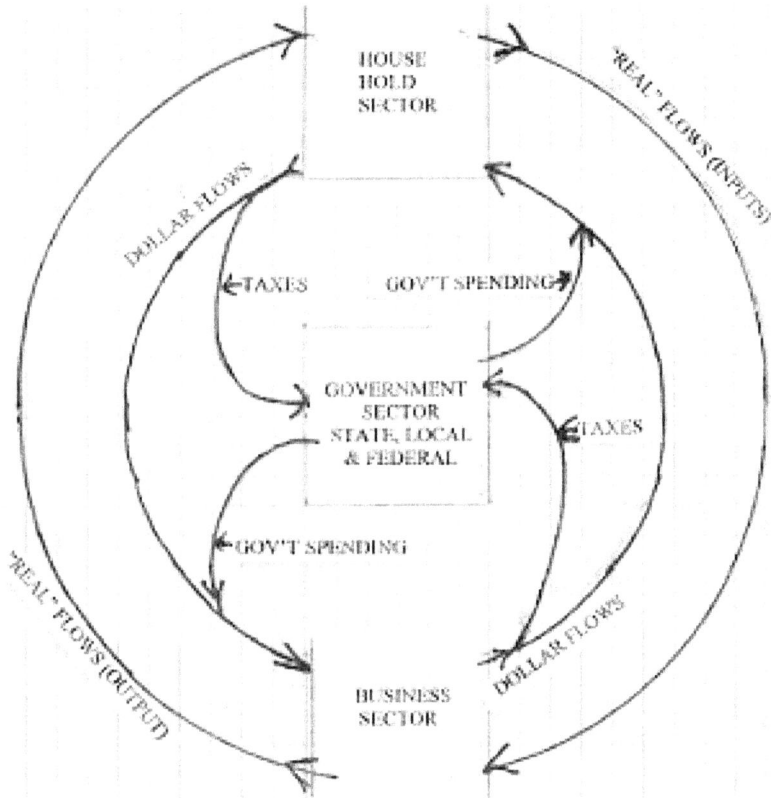

So now you know the economics meaning of "what goes around, comes around." More importantly, you can see, conceptually, how National Income equals national output, which we call Gross Domestic Product (GDP).

Here's an important conclusion to draw from these simple models: If there is full employment at the given money flow, there should be no change in the money supply. If there is unemployment, the money supply should be increased. If there is inflation, the money supply should be reduced. (We will see in Chapter 3 how changes in the money supply come about. (It is NOT by the government printing money!)

All economics systems have the same economic goals: growth of output, full employment, stable prices, an increasing standard of living, and equitable distribution of income. All have some aspects of economic freedom, defined as freedom to work at whatever job you can get, freedom to spend your money any way you want, and freedom to go into business for yourself.

In regards to equitable distribution of income – "equitable" does not mean "equal." Fairness is what the test is. In the news of November 11, 2009, we read that Goldman-Sachs, a Wall Street brokerage firm, made "record profits" in the last quarter, and will be paying an average bonus of $691,000 to all its employees, while at the same time the median income of all Americans is $50, 303/year. Is this fair? If not, we are not meeting our goal of equitable distribution of income.

From the above figures, we can demonstrate the <u>quantitative methodology</u> used in economics and also give a simple first lesson in statistical analysis. The figure for income for all Americans is the MEDIAN figure in the entire distribution. Median is a measure of "central tendency." It is the figure that is in the middle, whereas the figure of what Goldman-Sachs employees will get is called the mean, which in common parlance is called the "average." It is also a measure of central tendency, but it is calculated. The total dollar amount of bonus to be paid by Goldman is $21.9 billion, which gets divided up among the number of employees. Let's use the symbols used in statistical analysis and the simple formula to calculate the mean. The formula for the mean is: $\bar{X}= \Sigma X/N$. (Read as follows: "$\bar{X}$ bar equals the sum of the X's divided by the number of X's.") where $\bar{X}$ = the mean, X = a bonus, and N = the number of bonuses. (Σ is the Greek letter sigma and means "sum of.")

Now we use simple algebraic re-arrangement of the variables to set up the equation to calculate the number of employees at Goldman: $N=\Sigma X/\bar{X}$, and putting numbers in for the variables we know the value of:

N=$21.9 Billion/$691,000
N=31,693 employees.

Now we have to analyze and interpret the data. What do the numbers tell us? If we are comparing the average bonus with the median income, the average far understates the inequity in income distribution between Goldman employees and the "average" American because we know that many Goldman employees draw bonuses many times greater than the average. For example, for 2008, a Mr. Hall, who runs a hidden "energy trading unit" at Goldman was paid a $100 Million bonus. This was for $667 Million trading profits Goldman made on the commodities futures exchange.

"Trading" is just buy and sell, buy and sell, buy and sell, all day long, which Wall Street characterizes as "pump and dump;" i.e., they just keep driving up the price to unsustainable levels, which were $150/barrel for oil that resulted in $4-$5/gallon gasoline prices.

Hall complained that he was underpaid (!) because $100 Million is only 15% of $667 Million, whereas hedge funds (THAT DO THE SAME PUMP AND DUMP STUFF) pay 30%.

So now you have seen in a real situation with current data, the equitable distribution of income problem. And you have also seen how oil and gas prices are determined; NOT by supply and demand (which is almost heresy for an economist to say!).

There are different kinds of economies: the U.S. is capitalistic; Sweden is socialistic. Some economies are "market" economies – where market forces determine what is produced – others are planned economies – where government decides what will be produced. But no economic systems are pure examples of the theoretical models. When you read pieces comparing different economies, read critically because many of such comparisons are done on the basis of "our (theoretical) model vs. their muddle."

All economies contain elements of other types. Who owns the means of production is the basic determinant of what kind of economic system it is. In the US most of the means of production – capital – (NOT MONEY!) is privately owned, but not all.

An interesting sidelight here is the story about Ben Bernanke, FED Chairman, who said that since the government owns the means of production for money – the printing presses – if it wanted more money, all it had to do was run the presses! When asked how this money would get into the economy and do some good, the story goes, Bernanke said fly over the country with it in a helicopter and throw it out the door! That's why we economists refer to Bernanke as "helicopter Ben." When we explain how money is really created in Chapter 3, you will realize how ridiculous this all was.

Governments do own productive facilities of many kinds; so there is a good bit of socialism in the U.S. economy. All governments provide social services: more in Sweden than in the U.S., but not 100%. No economy is 100% socialism, or 100% capitalism.

Sweden has privately owned means of production, too. But no matter what kind of economic system it is, economics goals are universal. The differing systems are just different means to the same ends. All are trying to produce as much as they can, attain full employment (required to maximize output), raise the standard of living, and avoid inflation.

Just as there are different kinds of economic systems, there are different kinds of economists. The largest group by far are the Keynesians – named for John Maynard Keynes, an English economist, former Chancellor of the Exchequer (equivalent to the U.S. Treasury Secretary), and wealthy businessman (therefore, NOT an "ivory tower" theoretical academician) who wrote the basic "textbook" for modern macro-economics, The General Theory of Employment and Output in 1936, from which developed most of the modern monetary and fiscal policies. Most economists believe, as Keynes did, that only the national government has the ability to affect the economy significantly to correct aberrations from the desired path of growth, full employment and price stability. Therefore, fiscal policy tools of deficit spending and surpluses are viewed by modern economists as much more effective than monetary tools such as interest rate changes and changes in the money supply.

Another group of economists are identified as "monetarists." They believe that monetary policies are far more important in moving the economy than fiscal policies. This group is known as "Chicago School" – after the University of Chicago where most of the economics faculty is of this persuasion. The most extreme of this group call themselves "Friedmanites" after Milton Friedman, the prominent Chicago economics professor of the 20th century. They allege that Friedman made some important contributions to the monetary theory, but that his most important contribution to economics is the idea that "markets know best." What this translates to is that government's role in the economy should be very limited: the less government regulation, the better, they say. Monetary policy: changing interest rates and the money supply is all that's needed to right the economy if it goes wrong. Some of them do not even admit there is such a thing as macro-economics!

A prime example of the Chicago School, the Friedmanite group, that economists call "Brand X", would be Alan Greenspan, the FED Chairman responsible for monetary policy, bank regulation and control of the money supply, who was at the helm when all the bad things took place that precipitated the 2009-10 recession. He believed, like all of that group, that "markets know best"; i.e., the market forces for the banks and brokers to be profitable would make the financial sector self-regulating, but had to admit, when banks and brokers faced bankruptcy, "I was wrong."

When asked why the financial sector fiasco happened, he declared it was because mankind is basically greedy, and since you can not change human nature it was bound to happen again. On the surface, this sounds much like the standard assumption about man's unlimited wants, except for one thing. There is no moral characteristic to unlimited wants, whereas, it is immoral to be greedy. So, we reject Greenspan's prediction of future financial fiascos, because we do not believe that immoral behavior is inherent in man's behavior and regulations can be put in place to remove the major mechanisms by which such immoral behavior takes place.

The current (2009) Council of Economic Advisors (CEA) are all Chicago School. President Obama is from the University of Chicago, so brought with him to Washington Chicago School Friedmanite economists, who were only willing to go to fiscal policy after all they could do with monetary policy was tried and was an abysmal failure.

There are socialist economists and even Marxists – named after Karl Marx, the German author of <u>Das Kapital</u>, which predicted the decline and fall of capitalism as workers became more and more exploited by capitalists and income inequality became severe. He was wrong in his predictions about the future of capitalism, but one of his ideas is an underlying principle of U.S. taxation: progressive income tax whereby higher income people pay higher rates. This is well accepted in Western capitalism, but we also have regressive tax rates such as sales taxes whereby the poor pay a bigger part of their income than rich people because rich people do not spend all their income. Additionally, some very expensive luxury items that the rich buy – such as yachts and high end autos have reduced sales taxes.

The most regressive tax we have is the Social Security (SS) tax because SS taxes are "capped" at $100,000, which means that all who have incomes over 100K pay a smaller percentage of their income for the SS tax. When higher income people pay a lower percentage of their income – that is the definition of a regressive tax. Let's use some easy-to-follow numbers and calculate how badly regressive the SS tax is. Let's say that the rate is 10%, which means a person w/$100K income pays $10,000 (.10 X $100K). A person w/$200K income pays the same - $10K, but $10K is only 5% of $200K! How about those Wall Street fat cats that have $1 Million incomes? They pay only $10K, too. $10K is only one tenth of one percent of $1 Million – IMMORALLY REGRESSIVE! From this analysis, we can solve the SS financing problem without lowering benefits or increasing the tax: NO CAP ON TAXABLE INCOME. We will have to increase capital gains tax rates to more than ordinary income tax rates so that the Wall Street fat cats can not continue to avoid payroll taxes by getting their income as capital gains.

This change in the SS tax base will bring in so much revenue that we will be able to adjust payments to retirees for their increased cost of living, which is far greater than the BLS CPI because retirees spend a much higher percentage of their income for health care, and health care costs increase far faster than the BLS CPI, which is the current method of adjusting SS benefits. In fact, this change in the SS tax base will bring in so much revenue that the entire "entitlements" problem will be solved forever.

And it will also ameliorate the terribly inequitable distribution of income problem we have, which has been getting worse for decades, whereby the rich get richer and "Only the little people pay taxes," said Leona Helmsley.

Economists can also be fit into a liberal-conservative dichotomy. But there is a big gray area between the two and it does not help the understanding of the differences between them to affiliate them as either Democrats or Republicans.

We think "progressive" and "regressive" is a better dichotomy, but it is always good to know economists political leanings because economic theory has a high political philosophy elasticity.

("Elasticity" is an economics concept that is employed generally to measure the change in quantity demanded relative to a change in price, but the concept can be used for the change in any variable related to the change in any other variable. It is used in micro-economics to describe demand curves. Our use here is change in economic theory relative to political philosophy.)

Sometimes positions in government and business that you would assume have economists in place do not. For example, Paul Volker, FED Chairman under Reagan, is not an economist. How do we know who is and who is not an economist? Check out his (or her) credentials. Does he have a Ph.D. in economics from an accredited university program? Tim Geithner, the current Treasury Secretary, whom President Obama has put in charge of the economic recovery program is not an economist. Geithner has a B.A. from Dartmouth and a Master's in international studies, but no Ph.D.

(We had an insurance man on Cape Cod, who was an economics major at Dartmouth, who confided to us that he never understood the graphs!)

So what difference does it make that he is not an economist? He is a banker, former president of the New York Federal Reserve Bank, and therefore believes the bankers' bias that money "is the lifeblood of the economy." For economists money is merely a <u>numeraire</u>, (Fr., numbering system). He thought and said, "You have to fix the financial sector to fix the economy." Economists know that the entire financial sector: thousands of banks, brokers, insurance companies and other financial firms constitute only 10% of the economy in normal (pre-bubble) times. So he threw $Billions into banks and brokerages and convinced businesses to buy or become banks (e.g., Goldman-Sachs and GMAC <u>inter alios</u>) and threw $Billions into them under the mistaken notion that credit dried up because banks did not have reserves to loan, whereas the facts are that they had plenty of reserves, but with the stock market and housing market crashes there were not credit-worthy borrowers. He cited that things were so bad, that banks would not even loan to other banks. The facts of the matter are that the balance sheets of banks were loaded with valueless assets, actually bad loans they made mostly to real estate developers and mortgage brokers (called "toxic assets" to disguise the fact that they were loans that properly regulated banks should not have been allowed to make by a properly run central bank). This is to say that the bad loans are evidence of the abject failure of the FED, our central bank. So next he thought if he got rid of the bad loans on the banks' balance sheets the banks would start lending again. Did it, but banks still did not revive their lending to the detriment of the economy. So, his banker's bias was wrong again.

Any mainstream economist knows that banks' incentive to loan is not how much reserves they have to lend nor how few bad loans they have on the books; rather it is the credit-worthiness of the borrower. With the economy down and unemployment rising fast, it is not rocket science to know that not many businesses nor individuals were sure bets to make money from loans to pay back the loan and the interest. So the $Billions put into the banks are now fueling another boom-and-bust cycle in commodities, the stock market, and is making arbitrageurs worldwide wealthy. "Arbitrage" is buying any asset in one market where it is relatively cheap and simultaneously selling it in another market at a higher price. With interest rates being held very low by the FED, speculators worldwide are borrowing $Billions in the U.S. and buying government debt and other financial assets in countries where the interest rate is higher, which is practically everywhere these days.

Another example of a non-economist in a position where you would assume there would be an economist would be David Wessel, the economics editor of the Wall Street Journal, who authored In Fed We Trust. In a promo interview on NPR on August 4, 2009, he was asked the question: "Can't the FED with just a keystroke (on the computer) create money?" His immediate and INCORRECT answer was "yes." This immediately disqualified him from ever making any theoretically sound answers to economics questions because all economists know that this is not how money is created. The interviewer then went on to a follow-up question: "If that is so, why did the banks have to go to the Treasury for Billion dollar bailouts?" David Wessel did a lot of fast talking quickly after that question, but did not and could not answer it, because his ignorance on the first question put him in an impossible position. We knew he was not an economist from that point, but since he is the economics editor of the Wall Street Journal we had to check his credentials. How? "Googled" him – a BA and a Master's in writing business and economic news. No Ph.D. Not an economist.

An important lesson to learn from this is do not assume the WSJ is authoritative, always right. They are flat wrong at times, and biased all the time. Have to be pro-business to sell papers!

An example of their bias can be found in an editorial we responded to in 1967. Our response was nothing more than what any competent economist could have said, but they still run editorials to this day with the same bias, and our critical reply is just as correct today as it was in 1967! This classic answer to WSJ's bias was reprinted in Glen Mills' Reason in Controversy along with the editorial, and we include both in Chapter 2, Government and Debt, which is the heading on the piece we wrote – still theoretically as sound today as in 1967, and as it will be right through the 21st century.

Non-economists making economic decisions is a recipe for disaster as it was in the Soviet Union. They did not have economists. Engineers and politicians made all the economics decisions, and this is the number one factor that lead to the failure of the Soviet economic system. (Did not fail because it was socialism.)

So, when you hear some economics "news," you have to ask who is saying what, and what are his credentials and possible bias.

Economics competition is very different from the common definition of competition, which, for example, would be an NFL game between the N.E. Patriots and the N.Y. Jets. In economics such games would be classified as "rivalry." There are very specific requirements for competition to be "perfect" in economics. First, the market must be made up of a relatively large number of buyers and sellers so that no one has the ability to raise or lower price by his actions alone. The product being sold and bought by all sellers and buyers must be virtually identical. In economics we call this a "homogeneous" product. There must be free entry and exit into the industry, and all buyers and sellers must have "perfect" knowledge about all relevant market factors.

Obviously, no such market ever did or ever will exist. So why study such strictly constructed theoretical models? Two reasons: some markets do approach perfect competition; for example, some agricultural products markets: let's say wheat. There are some very big wheat farmers (as measured by output), but relative to the total size of the market (as measured by total output), the biggest producer by itself could not affect the market determined price. Same thing on the buy side; no single buyer, no matter how big absolutely could affect price by itself alone. (This is a good place to inform you of DeFelice's Law of Absolute Numbers, which is that absolute numbers means absolutely nothing. They have to be related or compared with another number to make any worthwhile meaning of them.) And No. 2 Kansas red wheat is No. 2 Kansas red wheat no matter who grows it – and is therefore a homogeneous product, which means that no buyer has a preference for any particular grower's output. So economics competition, unlike football rivalry, is very impersonal.

Free entry and exit into markets is required for competition to work by clearing out the inefficient – high cost – producers (that is to say, they must be allowed to fail), and to bring in more producers to wipe out excess profits. Economics is not opposed to producers making profits. Profit is necessary to pay for the use of the business owners' investment in the firm. There has to be payment for all resources used in the production of anything. Dividends pay the firms' costs for the use of the firms' owners' investment. Anything beyond that is excess profit. All other resource costs are paid as tax deductible expenses before profits are determined.

Modern farming is highly mechanized – economists say "capital intensive," and all the machines are very expensive. Such heavy capital requirements inhibit free entry. But this heavily mechanized highly efficient technology in modern farming made the over-supply of many commodities push down prices to the extent that farmers can not be successful businessmen at market determined prices. Here, exit is impaired by government subsidy programs. Prices for a number of commodities are set by government at a level required for the farmers to remain in business and if market prices do not come up to the set prices, the government buys up the surplus. Therefore, a market that would adjust output based on market signals is thwarted from doing so by politics. Politics? Congressmen from many states have large numbers of farmers as constituents. If they want to be elected and re-elected they must keep this nice government subsidy for the farmers going to the detriment of the economy and the public at large. This is bad economically because those extra resources employed in farming should be used to produce other outputs, plus the public pays higher prices for the output to subsidize the farmers. Then we have to pay storage costs for the surplus and figure out how to get rid of it all. One time they painted potatoes blue and dumped them in the ocean (Blue paint so fishermen would not pick up and sell them – potatoes float in salt water.) This is but one small sample of politics in economics.

Another market that economists used to cite as approaching the perfect competition model is the stock market. Even though there always have been some big buyers and sellers; relative to the market no one by itself could affect price. Shares of stock from one seller are virtually identical – a homogeneous product – with shares from any seller. And capital requirements to get into the market were not prohibitive, but that has all changed now. Huge one-bank holding companies that contain within them huge brokerage firms are big enough alone to affect prices and do so. For example, Goldman-Sachs, a broker/dealer became a one-bank holding company in October, 2008 when the Treasury Secretary, a Goldman-Sachs ex-CEO, put in $10 Billion of our money.

Now when Goldman goes into stock and commodities markets it can by itself drive up prices. After they have moved up a little, they sell. This technique is called "pump and dump," and is so successful that Goldman is currently making $100 Million/day! "So what," you say? That is not competition, not a competitive market, not a "fair and orderly market" – WHICH IS AN SEC MANDATE! It is how we get boom-and-bust cycles, "bubbles" that burst causing downturns and unemployment in the real economy. The stock market is not the economy.

That kind of market structure is called an "oligopoly" by economists – from two Greek words: "olig," meaning a few, and "poly," meaning seller. A few large firms dominate the stock market. They are, in addition to

Goldman-Sachs, Bank of America, Citigroup, and JP Morgan Chase. These companies are in violation of Antitrust Laws put into place to preserve competition. They are also in violation of banking regulations that prohibit any bank from holding more than 10% of the nation's deposits. All three are over the 10% limit.

The other reason for understanding the "perfect" competition model is, as already implied, it produces the best level of output at the lowest price. We need that efficiency because we (nobody, actually) has enough resources to meet all the wants of consumers.

There is a "pecking order" in the economics profession beyond the quality of the university where the economist earned his Ph.D. Econometricians are at the top of the list because they are the most quantitative. That is, they express their hypotheses and theories in mathematical and statistical terms. That's what econometrics is all about. You do not have to go beyond simple algebra (maybe differential calculus) in math, and statistical analysis uses only simple algebra. The statistical tests do require understanding of the theory involved in their application, but there are so many statistical tests nobody knows them all. Statistics has its own terminology and carefully defined formulas to calculate the values. We already introduced a few with the data relating to the equitable-distribution-of-income goal earlier in this chapter.

Here's another example of the quantitative approach in economics using just simple algebra to solve an economics question. The question is: How big is the U.S. labor force? Here's what we know: unemployment is currently at 10.2%, and 15 million are unemployed. (Even though this is a problem that you can solve in your head without setting up an equation, we will do so to show the methodology so that when the numbers are not easy to manipulate mentally, you will know how to proceed algebraically.)

Let X = the unknown size of the labor force,
and $.102 X$ = the unemployed percentage,
then $.102X = 15,000,000$.
Solve for X. Divide both sides of the equation by .102.
$X = 147,058,820$ (rounded – a fraction of a person is not possible.)

The final step in this procedure is to make a rough approximation of the answer based on the data to see if your answer makes sense. That goes like this: If unemployment was 10%, then 10% X 150 million would be 15,000,000. Your answer makes sense.

The following page is a good example of econometrics. It starts with the relevant historical theories (sometimes called "received doctrine"), posits a hypothesis, and describes a test, (or tests) to determine what conclusions can be made from statistical tests of the relevant data. (You always have to cite the source of your data.)

Everything is put into equation form; i.e., dependent variables go on the left side of the equation and the independent variables are on the right side. We used an equation from the Wharton School of Business' econometric model because it fit our needs. (No need to re-invent the wheel.) Only the first page of the article is printed here, but it shows the web site where you can get the whole article and follow through to see the kinds of statistical tests of the hypothesis were made and how the independent variables affect the dependent variable and then decide what conclusions about the hypothesis are right or wrong.

This article is also a good demonstration of what the <u>scientific method</u> is all about: You start with a hypothesis (a "guesstimate") about the relationship between some economics phenomena that has some plausible connection to reality, then decide how to formulate the idea in equation form, where to get the data, and what statistical tests are required to test the hypothesis. If the hypothesis is confirmed by the tests of the data, and it was a sufficient size sample, and it can be replicated, then it can be added to theory.

Frank DeFelice, Ph.D.

JSTOR: The Journal of Finance, Vol. 25, No. 4 (Sep., 1970), pp. 803-807

SECURITY AND INVESTMENT: MORE EVIDENCE

FRANK DEFELICE*

INTRODUCTION

IN CLASSICAL economic theory, the firm's stock of physical capital is adjusted toward the optimum as capital productivity is greater or less than cost. A thread of this thinking is woven into the investment equations of most of the major econometric models by inserting, in independent variable(s) form, the stock-adjustment idea.

In modern (Keynesian) macroeconomic theory optimum investment is where the marginal efficiency of capital just equals "the" interest rate. The marginal efficiency of capital is the rate of discount that equates expected dollar flow to the present cost of the investment. Since the expected dollar flow is a function of effective demand and the stock of capital, investment again is seen to be an adjustment as the stock of capital is either more or less than optimal. Thus, both classical and modern investment theories contain the stock-adjustment idea.

But in addition, modern investment theory places heavy emphasis on "the" interest rate, expected dollar returns, and dollar cost of investments, all financial variables. Therefore in the typical econometric investment function, the classical "real" variables are synthesized with the modern financial variables. For example, in the basic investment equation (4a) of the Wharton model, investment in manufacturing plant and equipment is a function of the "real" variables: capacity utilization, gross output, the stock of manufacturing capital; two financial variables; and anticipations. Distributed lag weights are applied to those variables where required. Equation 4a is:

$$I_{pm} = -11.43 + 15.62\, C_{p-1} + 0.0892 \sum_{i=0}^{7} A_i\, Xm_{-i-2}$$

$$+ 0.1069 \sum_{i=0}^{7} A_i\, Lm_{-i-2} - 0.0271 \sum_{i=0}^{7} A_i\, (Km)_{-i-2}$$

$$+ 0.3954\, ANP_{m} - 0.3201 \sum_{i=0}^{7} A_i\, (i_L)_{-i-2}$$

I_{pm} = investment in manufacturing plant and equipment,
C_{p-1} = Wharton school index of capacity utilization,
A_i = distributed lag weights (Almon weights),
X_m = gross output originating in the manufacturing sector,

* Associate Professor of Economics, Queens College, Charlotte, North Carolina. The research for this paper was done while the author was on a Ford Faculty Fellowship in the Duke-UNC Cooperative Program in International Studies during the 1968-69 year. Thanks are due to Professors Henry Latané and Charles Richter for their help and inspiration and to Lloyd Davis for programming assistance.

803

Theory is everything in science. If you do not know the theoretical relationships in economics, you do not know the questions to ask. "Theory" is another of those words that have very different meaning in ordinary converse. For example, in law, lawyers often say, "Our theory of the case is _____." This is actually a hypothesis – a "guesstimate" of what happened. And people who argue that evolution is "only a theory" are also using the non-scientific meaning of the word. The evolution theory that springs from Darwin's Origin of Species has thousands of tested hypotheses to back it up. It used scientific method. Biology is a science just as is economics.

There are two major measures of how the economy is doing and they are opposite sides of the "same coin." National Income is all the money received by all in all sectors of the economy. Gross Domestic Product (GDP) is the dollar value of all output in all sectors of the economy (except the foreign trade sector). GNP, Gross National Product, included Net Foreign Investment (NFI), but doing that reduced National Income because we always have more imports than exports; so, government economists charged with doing national income accounting revised the process to exclude that sector. Doing so actually does not change things much because the U.S. is not a big trading nation. Basically, we are self-contained – buying and selling our own output from our own producers.

Connected with the subject of foreign trade, is an old, hard to kill fallacy about the "balance of trade": you prefer to sell more to others overseas than you buy from them. There are two problems with this thinking. First, others can not buy from you unless you buy from them. Second, a so-called "favorable balance of trade" is only favorable in financial terms. Before the gold standard was abolished, differences in foreign trade were settled with gold movements, but you can't eat gold; i.e., the real economic results of a "favorable" balance of trade are unfavorable. If more of our output is going abroad than foreign goods being brought in, we are worse off in real terms; i.e., we have less output for ourselves.

It is worthwhile to go back in time to understand how and why the balance-of-trade nonsense started. There is a group of economists that do this for many economics topics. They are called economic historians, and their output forms a body of study in economics called History of Thought.

Before Adam Smith, who wrote The Wealth of Nations in 1776, the wealth of nations was generally conceded to be how much "specie" – gold and silver – were in the kings' coffers. In 1492 when Columbus discovered America (which was named for Americus Vespucci!?) he was actually out looking for specie for King Ferdinand of Spain. The "cover story" was that he was looking for a short cut to India (which is why American natives are called Indians) to get into the spice trade. It was thought such a dumb thing to do, because everybody at the time knew the world was flat, and he'd go right over the edge, no dummies could be found to man his ships; so, Ferdinand (or Queen Isabella) unloaded prisons to get crews for Columbus. That's right, the first people to set foot in America were criminals from Spain. Smith said that specie was NOT the wealth of nations; productive capability is. And for this is considered the father of economics.

"Favorable balance of trade" is but one of several <u>fallacies in economic reasoning</u>. The "fallacy of composition" is that it is wrong to think that what is good for one is good for all. For example, if one farmer grows more crop, he will get more income, but if all farmers grow more crop, they will all be worse off because the increased supply will drive down the price. (You need to study micro-economics to see how this comes about.)

Years ago, the GM CEO was Charles Wilson, called "Engine Charlie" at the time, who, at a Congressional hearing said, "What's good for GM is good for the country." He was, of course, laughed right out of the hearing. Sometimes something that is good for one particular business is good for the economy of the country, but it's wrong to think that this is always the case. In the business sector there are a lot of what we call "zero-sum games"; i.e., the gain by one firm in an industry is just the loss of other firms in that industry so that if you sum up the gains and losses, the total is zero. Say that the total demand for U.S. cars is 15 million. If GM has a good advertising campaign that increases its sales, GM's gain is Ford and Chrysler's loss. So the economy (the country) is no better off even though GM is.

Another fallacy goes by the Latin words <u>post hoc ergo propter hoc</u> (sometimes by just <u>post hoc</u>) which translates to "after this therefore because of this." This is the kind of fallacious reasoning perpetrated on unsophisticated Americans every day on TV when the stock market report is given. For example, a news reporter says "the FED lowered interest rates and the stock market rallied." Because one thing followed the other is no reason to conclude that one caused the other. This is not science; it's <u>anecdotal data</u> or we could call it comparative static analysis in which we make the unwarranted assumption that everything except interest remained static (unchanged) and therefore the stock market rally had to be caused by the interest rate change. Ridiculous? You bet! But this sort of nonsense goes on every day all day long on TV.

We can throw in some more Latin here. When anyone does comparative static analysis, he is making an implicit <u>ceteris paribus</u> assumption. <u>Ceteris paribus</u> means "other things equal"; i.e., unchanging. That is very unrealistic assumption to make about the real world where many things are changing all the time. We have Latin words to describe that too: <u>mutatis mutandis</u>, which means "everything is changing all the time." (The English word "mutations" is derived from this Latin.) A description in English of this type of analysis is "dynamic." Here again we have a word that has a very different scientific meaning than what it means in common parlance. People who want to compliment another person will often describe him as "dynamic."

In the science of economics, <u>dynamic analysis</u> is the only analysis that is realistic. Comparative static analysis is too limiting, but is used sometimes because graphs are often used to show relationships between economics variables and graphs are two-dimensional; i.e., you can only have two variables on a plane surface. (You can put on a third, but you have to imagine it coming up off the plane surface.)

Graphs are used extensively in college courses in economics, in both micro-economics and macro-economics, but we can introduce all the ideas verbally and in the Appendix to this chapter you will find simple equation definitions of how to calculate values for all of the macro-economics variables. You can graph pairs of values on two axes and fit a straight line to them using the equation for a straight line from Algebra I: $Y = a + bX$ where a is the Y intercept and b is the slope of the function described by your pairs of values. And to make this more sophisticated (some would say "to obfuscate") we can use Greek letters in place of the English; "a" becomes α (alpha) and "b" becomes β (beta).

<u>Risk and return</u> is a good place to use this Y-intercept and b (slope) analysis:

Let Y = return and X = risk. Then we can describe the risk-return function: $Y = a + bX$. Since we have just two variables, it is quick and easy to show the relationship between the two variables graphically, which looks like this:

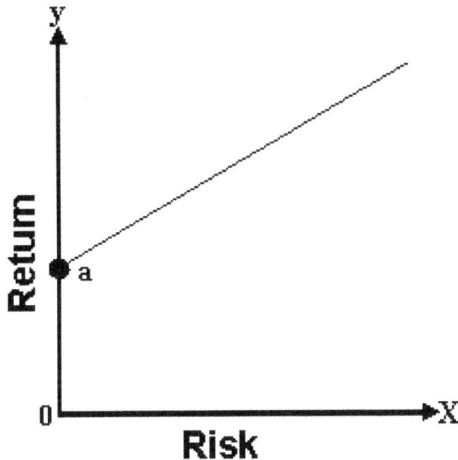

Since $Y = a + bX$, you can see that there is a possibility to invest in some security with zero risk – at point a, there is no risk. There is only one security in the world with zero risk: U.S. Treasury Bills. This conclusion comes about because the quantitative determination of risk is the standard deviation of the return (σ). Only T-Bills have no deviation of the return. Return on an investment is the combination of interest paid (or dividends) and a gain or loss of the principal involved (the amount paid for the investment). T-Bills are sold at a discount from face value. The interest return is simply the discount the buyer collects when they are redeemed at maturity. They are always redeemed at face value; there is no deviation of the return; there is therefore no risk.

But you can see that the risk-return function is a positive sloping function; i.e., that higher risks require higher returns. Investors seeking higher returns have to take higher risks. What is good about this analysis is that economics science has theoretically sound methods to quantify the variables. All investments offered to the public via registration with the SEC and/or state regulators should be required to disclose correctly calculated risk and return.

"Investment" is the single most misunderstood word in the entire economics lexicon. In macro-economic analysis it is the spending for capital goods by business. In economics we call this "real investment," which is not the money but the actual capital goods. The term is badly misused in business by sales people who claim whatever they are selling is a good investment. "Buy a house; it's the best investment you will ever make," real estate people say. "Buy this new wing-ding car; it's a great investment."

Neither is real economic investment. They are not capital goods that will help the economy grow. They are consumer goods – consumption of economic resources – good only to satisfy consumer wants. Neither are houses or cars personal financial investments. They do not qualify. In economics we have definitions of terms that have to be applied. To be a financial investment requires that it must meet two tests: the principal must be secure and a periodic payment for use of the investor's money must be paid. When people buy houses, they assume that not only is the purchase price (principal) secure, it would grow in value over time ("Always has," they say.) The housing market collapse of 2008-09 proved that assumption wrong. But even if that bubble had not burst, a house would not qualify as an investment because there is no periodic payment for the use of the investor's money.

Automobiles have neither security of principal nor periodic payment for use of the investor's money. So what does qualify? A savings account at a bank if it's a member of the Federal Deposit Insurance Corporation (FDIC), which most are. Your principal – deposit – is insured up to $250,000 and they pay interest periodically. "Real low interest," you say? Real low risk – just a little way up the risk-return function from T-Bills. Want more return, you have to take more risk. Buy a utility stock. Everybody has to have electricity, and state utilities commissions set rates that guarantee profitability. (This is in return for the states granting them monopolies over certain geographical areas which is necessary for the electric companies to operate a big enough plant to get economies of scale that you can not get if there were a large number of small scale producers.) Your investment is subject to market forces that make all prices go up and down (though there is now evidence that the huge broker/dealer bank firms put together by Paulson and Geithner can and do manipulate prices), and you do get regular dividends. The return is better than savings accounts because you can not get an increase in principal from a savings account equivalent to the increase you can get from the price of your stock, and the dividends are at a better rate than savings accounts. But you have moved up the risk-return curve because there is no guarantee – like FDIC insurance – to protect your principal.

Applying the rule further, you can find stocks of very successful companies – Microsoft is one – that do not qualify as investments because they do not pay dividends. They do not give you anything periodically for the use of your money over time. They put their profits back into the company and you hope that they use it in such a way that the price of their stock goes up. When you are hoping the price of the stock goes up, you are just speculating; not investing. You can buy lots of assets and hope the price goes up: gold, silver and land. But prices do not always go up. With so many so-called investors engaged in these bets for increased prices, they do go up for awhile – until the market value bears little or no reflection of the actual economic value, then they do what they did in 2008, 1929 and a dozen times in between - crash.

Speculation is good for the speculators if they get in and out at the right time, but bad for the economy because the inevitable stock market crash is incorrectly interpreted as a failure of the real economy that causes negative changes in the real economy: reduced output and unemployment that hurts all "the little people" while the speculators make so much money they can buy sports franchises as did John Henry, who bought the Boston Red Sox for "change."

There is no room to argue that Mr. Henry did a good thing to buy the Red Sox, and that the end, therefore, justifies the means, because the "means" includes that his $Billions were made in the commodities futures markets, where oil prices were pumped up to $150/barrel and gasoline to $4-$5/gallon. All Americans paid, in higher energy costs, for Mr. Henry's fortune. Just another example of a zero-sum game: all Americans lost the Billions of dollars he gained. Also an example of the SEC's failure to provide "fair and orderly markets" as the law requires. Also an example of the "turf war" problems in the regulatory structure, because a Commission was set up to regulate the Commodities Futures market called the Commodities Futures Trading Commission (CFTC), which takes it away from the SEC in spite of the fact that all the trading done there is securities trading. But even if the

SEC had regulatory authority, they would make it a <u>Self Regulating Organization (SRO)</u> just as it does with the NYSE and NASD, which is what it is anyway. The CFTC makes the rules for the CFTC: the traders regulate the traders – a no-brainer conflict of interest. Repeating for emphasis: self regulation does not work. And what makes the pump and dump operations on the CFT exchange so profitable is that the margin requirements are way down around 10% and lower. The FED is responsible for setting margin requirements, but maybe it's part of the turf wars that their authority does not extend to the CFT market.

We know of no sound economic rationale why there should be margin trading for any securities. And since we know that leveraged speculation is the root cause of the boom-and-bust cycles, no leveraging – no margin trading – is a no-brainer solution that should be imposed by the central bank whose major function is to control the terms of all loans for the good of the economy. Our central bank, the FED, is not run for the good of the economy, but for the good of the bankers. Bankers make money making loans, and since they regulate themselves, they are not going to stop margin trading. Thus we have another sound economic rationale to have a new central bank.

Through 50 years of "teaching" economics we have found a constant response from students and others to our discussions along these lines: they all want a "hot tip" on what stock to buy. They are speculators that generally do not believe in the immutable veracity of the risk-return curve. They all want a high return and a low risk, and when informed there is no such thing, think we know of some but are refusing to tell them.

We will, therefore, at this point give the only personal investment advice you will find in this book: look for stocks that have a Dividend Re-Investment Plan (DRIP) with at least a ten year record of consistently paid dividends. Of the 50,000 or so issues in the market, there are perhaps 200 of such stocks. Calculate the risk and return for a few that you are interested in, plot them on a risk-return graph and then select the one(s) that meet your risk-return trade-off.

Let's go slowly through a "hypothetical" situation (so as not to be giving investment advice nor by naming a specific issue). First, look in the New York Stock Exchange (NYSE) listings for a utility stock (virtually all of them have DRIP plans). The annualized dividend will be given. "Annualized" means it is four times the latest quarterly dividend. With this figure and the current price, calculate the current yield, which is D/P, where D = the annual dividend and P = the current price of the stock. Let's make up some numbers that approximate current (early 2010) values: D = \$2.20, and P = \$45. Then D/P = .04 = 4%. This is like putting \$45 in a bank savings account that pays 4% interest/year. Dividends and interest are equivalent measures of return. But with bank savings accounts there is no opportunity to get a return from an increase in the principal equivalent to the increase in the price of the stock you may get over time. And when the yield on stocks of this class is down to 4%, bank savings rates are less than 2%. Bank accounts are insured, stocks are not; lower risk, lower return. Whether the price will go up or down depends on where "the market" is currently. You determine this by checking the current value of "The Dow" vs. what it has been.

"The Dow" is shorthand for the Dow Jones Industrial Average (DJIA), which is the average price of 30 industrial stocks. The fact that the number doesn't make sense as a price per share is due to the fact that over the many years of its existence many adjustments have had to be made in the denominator to account for stock splits, etc. We include the DJIA list of stocks here, so you can see what stocks are being used. It's only theoretically sound use is as indicated: to get a read on the general level of stock prices. It is no good as a statistical sample – too small and too narrow.

The NYSE listings in the daily paper show what the price range has been for the previous 52 weeks for each stock, which is also a read on where the market generally is.

You can start a DRIP by buying one share of stock. (A good Xmas present for grandchildren – maybe not from their point of view!) As soon as you are a registered shareholder of a DRIP stock, the issuer will send you a Prospectus (required by the SEC to sell stock) detailing the DRIP plan. You can buy additional shares directly from the issuer with no brokerage charge (probably the reason brokers hardly ever advise their purchase!) You can have the quarterly dividends sent to you or re-invested in additional shares with no brokerage charge, and you can sell shares with just a minimal fee. With re-investment of dividends you are getting compound "interest"; i.e., dividends on the dividends that have bought more shares. Compound interest is the way you can accumulate sizable value at some future time – say for college, travel or retirement.

The amount of the future value (FV) is determined by the present value (PV) of what you put in, the time period (t) and the interest rate (%i). Hand held financial calculators contain the formula linking these variables. You just put in your numbers to compute the future value by pressing the CPT FV button.

There is a simple approximation method called the Rule-of-72 that can be used to approximate the calculated values. You can estimate how many years it would take to double your money, or what interest rate it would take to double your money. Simply divide 72 by the interest rate to get the number of years to double. Assume i% = 8 (4% dividends + 4% stock price increase), then years to double = 72/8 = 9 years.

Here is the list of the 30 companies that constitute the Dow Jones Industrial Average (DJIA), which is commonly called "The Dow." This listing was done to demonstrate quantitatively how these companies have fared, in terms of change in the price of their stock since the low point of the Dow on March 9, 2009. (Unfortunately, we did not date this clipping so we can not bring the time factor into the analysis). However, we defer our analysis of the data to Allen Sinai, a world famous economist on the Harvard faculty. (Remember that we told you that you must check out the credentials of those who are doing the analysis and interpretation of the data.)

So, when Allen Sinai says that the "booming stock market and rich financial firms situation is (in part) because of the massive job losses," we believe it is a correct conclusion. He explains this conclusion by citing the simple fact that "massive job losses preserve the profits of (the Dow) companies," which makes perfect sense since we know labor costs are a big percentage of business costs and profits are one of the fundamental determinants of stock prices.

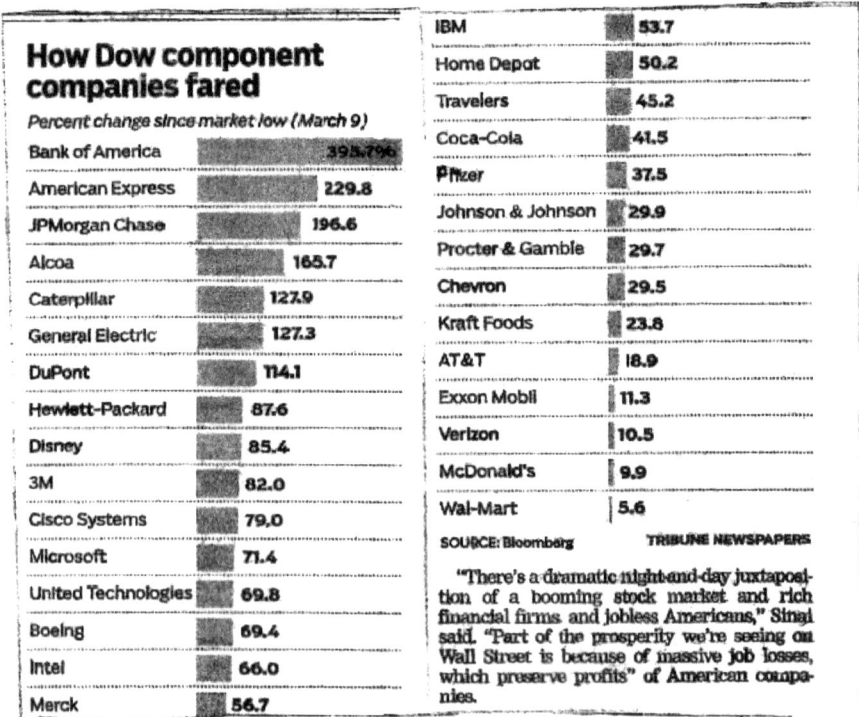

How Dow component companies fared

Percent change since market low (March 9)

Company	Percent
Bank of America	395.7%
American Express	229.8
JPMorgan Chase	196.6
Alcoa	165.7
Caterpillar	127.9
General Electric	127.3
DuPont	114.1
Hewlett-Packard	87.6
Disney	85.4
3M	82.0
Cisco Systems	79.0
Microsoft	71.4
United Technologies	69.8
Boeing	69.4
Intel	66.0
Merck	56.7
IBM	53.7
Home Depot	50.2
Travelers	45.2
Coca-Cola	41.5
Pfizer	37.5
Johnson & Johnson	29.9
Procter & Gamble	29.7
Chevron	29.5
Kraft Foods	23.8
AT&T	18.9
Exxon Mobil	11.3
Verizon	10.5
McDonald's	9.9
Wal-Mart	5.6

SOURCE: Bloomberg   TRIBUNE NEWSPAPERS

"There's a dramatic night-and-day juxtaposition of a booming stock market and rich financial firms and jobless Americans," Sinai said. "Part of the prosperity we're seeing on Wall Street is because of massive job losses, which preserve profits" of American companies.

Or assume you want to double in 6 years; then $72/6 = 12\%$ = the rate you need to get for that to happen. You could pick a stock with a higher current yield, but always remember to think of return and risk simultaneously.

We are in this simplified example just using a single starting investment amount (PV) and compounding dividends to some fixed point in time (FV). In reality, you keep buying shares periodically (they will even debit your bank account if you want) so that the amount of dividends keeps increasing. Dividends are paid quarterly so you are compounding quarterly (which is better than annual compounding) an ever increasing amount. It's like compounding the compounding!

We heard some Wall Street wag say when the market went down, "Who wants to see the market go down!" The implicit answer to his rhetorical question is "only dummies." But if you are in a DRIP, which is a long-term investment, you like to see prices go down because you get more shares for your dividends – compounding goes higher quicker. DRIP stocks hardly ever reduce dividends – when the stock price goes down. Therefore, your yield goes up when prices fall.

That Wall St. wag reflects what people generally think investing is all about – buy low now; sell high next week. This is not investment; it is just speculation for capital gains – an increase in the price of the stock enough to cover the brokerage and interest charges. Interest charges? A regular account in brokerage firms is a margin account. This means they loan you all the money above the margin – down payment required – and you have to pay the interest on that loan and the brokerage charges to make any profit. That's why the financial community wants to keep interest rates and capital gains taxes low.

And it is just flabbergasting to us that hundreds of colleges and even some high schools teach courses labeled "investments" by giving each student, say, $10,000 at the beginning of the semester in a brokerage account (sometimes even real money!) and testing their knowledge by seeing how much the account is worth at the end of the semester. Those whose account value has increased the most are called the smartest in the class! What a travesty to call that investment education. It's just perpetuation of the same old Wall St. trading clientele whom Wall St. makes $ Billions from brokerage fees and interest charges, whether or not if the "investor" makes anything. Would not surprise us one iota to find that those so-called investment courses at some colleges get their money from the big Wall Street firms. What would it matter to Goldman-Sachs whose "hidden energy trading unit" made $667 Million in 2008 to give a few thousand to some colleges for propagation of the faithful? Probably write it off as a charitable contribution!

Students in those courses may have been taught the two most widely used techniques of analysis: "Fundamentals" and "Technical," but application of those techniques is not how success is determined because those techniques are for making buy or sell decisions with long term results the goal. It is quite different really – to be trading stocks to maximize the account value over such a short time span.

Nothing about real investing is imparted in these games. Some of them are financed by big brokerage firms with real money because that is a great way to suck in customers.

Of the two analytical techniques mentioned, only the Fundamentals approach has any scientific validity. Using such fundamentals as earnings-per-share (EPS) and the price-earnings ratio (P/E), one can do valuation so as to determine possible discrepancies between market values and what your calculations come up with. Let's say stocks in a certain industry are selling at 10 times earnings (P/E = 10), and you calculate for a comparable stock in that industry a P/E of 8; then your stock is undervalued by the market, which is buy signal for you. If, on the other hand, the P/E is 20; it is over-valued; you should not buy. Other fundamentals would be the payout ratio – dividends as a percentage of EPS (D/EPS), but you always have to relate income statement figures to balance sheet figures. Ratios that do this better fundamental analysis would be return-on-investment (ROI) and return-on-equity (ROE). This follows from DeFelice's Law of Absolute Numbers: Absolute Numbers Mean Absolutely Nothing. In this case the income statement number by itself has very little meaning; so, too, the balance sheet number; but when the income statement number and balance sheet number are considered RELATIVE to each other, you have real meaning.

A couple of words of caution are in order here: all the figures used in analysis for investment come off firms' financial statements, which consist of an income statement and a balance sheet. So, if you are going to get into fundamental analysis, you do need to know a little about accounting. Second, standard accounting is not done on a cash basis; it is done on an "accrual" basis, which means that many of the figures used are not cash. Profit is not cash; income is not cash; earning is not cash; the reason being that in standard accounting there are non-cash charges against revenues (mostly depreciation) that lower the earnings before tax (EBT, another fundamental), and therefore, taxes to such an extent that many large corporations do not have any taxable income but Billions of dollars in cash!

Economics analysis is on a cash basis. We do not like the misleading information imparted when a corporation has no profit but still has Billions of dollars of cash. Also, we do not like the inconsistent treatment by standard accounting of the cost of different sources of funds in corporations. The cost of borrowed money – loans or from sale of bonds – is the interest paid, which is accounted for as a tax deductible expense, but the payment for equity money – dividends – is not accounted for as a tax deductible expense. Economists do not believe anything of economic value is free. (That would be an oxymoron: "free money"). Even if firms do not pay out dividends from profits, the retained earnings R/E are not "free."

There is very little chance that an individual using Fundamentals (or any other kind of analysis) could find and buy under-priced securities profitably because the big brokerage houses have super fast computers that execute buy and sell orders in nano-seconds worldwide before any individual even finds out the facts. Goldman-Sachs specializes in this kind of trading and now (2010) accounts for 25% of all short-term trading on the NYSE. When any one firm accounts for this high of a percentage of trading, this is not a "fair and orderly market," which is an SEC mandated responsibility. When one firm is that big relative to the market, it can and does affect price. They engage in "pump and dump" trading, because they can affect price. Individuals can not do this; therefore, individuals can not be successful traders.

The other mentioned analysis scheme known as "technical" or "charting" is nothing but some long-standing nonsense that relies on lines on a graph forming particular patterns that predict which way the market is going to go, and therefore, whether buying or selling is in order. This is not science. Economics is a science. Pay no attention to those scammers that will sell you a course in this crap for thousands of dollars.

We would be remiss in our duty to pass on distilled wisdom if we failed to mention the best investment advice we ever got. The 'original' Frank DeFelice, who was born in Catagnano, Abruzzi, Italia in 1891 (the same year Ben Bernanke's grandfather was born!), and came to America as a 15-year old illiterate immigrant told us, "Steady rain gets you wet." That's exactly what a DRIP is, PLUS COMPOUNDING!

He also explained to us, before either he or we knew the economics term, what opportunity cost, a very important economics concept, was in very practical terms. When we first bought a house on Cape Cod in 1953, we took out a 20-year mortgage and told him that in 20 years we would have no more rent to pay. "Not so," he said. "You always have to pay rent even after the mortgage is paid off. The interest you could be getting if the money you put into the house had been put in the bank is just like paying rent." He's right; the interest you do not get from the bank is the opportunity cost (lost) by buying a house, regardless of whether you have done so <u>via</u> a mortgage or paid cash.

We have gone from macro-economic investment to the micro investment principles. Let's go back to macro-economics, and start with <u>aggregate demand (AGG D)</u>. This is the total spending in all three sectors of the (domestic) economy: Consumption spending C, Business Investment (I), and Government (G).

AGG D = C + I + G.

There is a "correct" level of aggregate demand, which is where it is high enough to get full employment, but not so high that prices are rising at an unacceptable rate, – inflation. We use the symbol N for employment; so, to show full employment, we add a subscript: N_F, and to show the correct level of AGG D we add the subscripted N_F to aggregate demand:

$$AGG\ D_{N_F} = C + I + G.$$

If aggregate demand goes higher than this (AGG D > AGG D_{N_F}) the result is inflation – a rise in the general price level. Since economics is a quantitative science, we must define how much of an increase in the price level is "inflationary." That figure is set by economists at 2% because part of the increase in price of most products is due to increases in quality. On a year-to-year basis such small increases in quality are hard to see, but if you take a longer time span you have to agree with the validity of the approach. For example, it's difficult to see much difference between a 2001 Volvo and a 2000. But let's go way back and take a much longer time period – say the difference between a 1939 and a 1959 Buick. No question about the increase in quality. It might be more or less than 2%/year, but you have to build in something for change in quality to make the inflation measurement realistic.

Although inflation refers to the general price level, we use the Bureau of Labor Statistics' (BLS's) Consumer Price Index (CPI) to measure inflation. They use a "market basket" of goods and services that the average person buys, and track what happens to prices of those items month to month. The index sets a particular year as the base year at 100, and increases are a percentage of the base year. After a few years, they re-set the base and start all over again. This is so we won't say, "Geez, prices are 250% of what they were 50 years ago!" It's a very rough estimate of what the general price level is doing because it does not include wholesale and other producers' prices. And when you look at specific groups of people in the economy, it is a very inaccurate measure of changes in the cost of living. For example, it is used to adjust Social Security (SS) payments, which is very unfair because the "market basket" of goods and services seniors buy differs markedly from what the average person buys. This is especially noticeable in the purchase of health care services, and the cost of health care has risen far faster than the general price level. To be fair to our senior citizens, we should calculate the SS increase using the correct market basket of goods that for them includes more of a far faster rising cost item – health care. This is an easy adjustment to make actually; it is just changing the weights in the weighted average calculation used for the index (explained in all elementary statistics textbooks).

Now you can see that when we have either inflation or unemployment, the cause of the problem is AGG D is incorrect – too high or too low. We have two sets of macro-economics "tools" to try to fix those problems: monetary policy and fiscal policy. But before we get into those details, we should first quantitatively define "full employment," just as we did quantitatively define inflation. ECONOMICS IS A QUANTITATIVE SCIENCE.

"Full employment" is defined down to around 3-4% unemployed, because there is always that small percentage of the labor force that is transitional - changing jobs – or are structurally or frictionally unemployed as industrial structure changes. When the automobile replaced the horse and buggy, buggy whip makers were structurally unemployed. When steel mills shut down, workers in that industry were structurally unemployed. When coal mining declined…ad infinitum – this is what economic growth and development is all about: structural changes in the economy. And people who are not looking for work are not counted as unemployed.

Monetary policy is changing interest rates and/or the money supply so that those changes will affect the business investment component of AGG D : I. That has been the dominant thinking in 20th century macro-economics, but it is now abundantly clear in the 21st century that lowering interest rates to zero does not spur investment spending by business. Business investment spending is much more influenced by the expected profit for doing so rather than the cost of borrowed money to do so, plus many businesses can finance their investments, called capital budgeting in business finance, with internally generated sources of funds: retained earnings and depreciation. The authorities are not able to control the supply of money because of a fatal flaw in the make up of the Federal Reserve System (which we will explain in detail in Chapter 3, Money and Banking.)

Fiscal policy "tools" are tax and/or government spending changes. If taxes are lowered, those whose taxes are cut have an increase in income. We measure the increase in consumption spending from this income increase by calculating the marginal propensity to consume (MPC). MPC is the ratio of the change in consumption to the change in income (MPC = $\Delta C/\Delta Y$). It is always less than 1; i.e., some of any increase in income is not spent. Income not spent, by definition, is savings – in macro-economics terminology: $Y - C = S$. (We recently heard Hank Paulson, ex-Treasury Secretary, say, in explaining underlying causes of the recession, "Americans do not save enough," when the facts are that the increase in savings was a prime cause of the recession! But Paulson is not an economist, so he doesn't know that an increase in saving is a decrease in Consumption spending, ($-\Delta C$), which causes a multiplied reduction in AGG D ($- \Delta$AGG D = k ($- \Delta C$) which makes the recession worse!) Additional income is not spent just once by the recipient. There is a velocity of money flows that makes the final effect on AGG D a multiple of the original amount. (This is just another way of looking at the multiplier effect.) The higher the MPC, the higher the multiplier (k). The formula for the multiplier is k = 1/MPS, where MPS is the marginal propensity to save. Here's the simple derivation of the MPS: a change in income is either spent or saved. Therefore, MPC + MPS = 1, and

MPS = 1 − MPC. Let's put in some easy to follow numbers: let's say that MPC = .90 (90 cents of a $1.00 increase in income gets spent.) Then MPS = .10 : (1 - MPC), and the multiplier = 10 (1/.10). This means that the theoretical maximum amount AGG D can change when MPC = .90 is 10 times the change in income. It is important to point out that this is a theoretical calculation based on an infinite geometric progression, and we are in reality not in infinity. There are numerous "leakages" in addition to the time constraints that prevent the maximum from occurring. But what we do know for certain is that some multiple of the income changes will be the final effect on AGG D. In symbols we say: ΔAGG D = k (ΔC). Δ is the Greek letter delta and is used in economics to denote "change."

Instead of lowering taxes to give more income to the consumption and business sectors of the economy, the government can just increase spending beyond what it has from tax revenues. The reduction in spending caused by the MPC in the C sector of the economy does not apply to increased government spending. There is no government savings to subtract out. Therefore, the effect on AGG D is greater for any amount of government spending equal to tax cuts. There is a theoretical infinite multiplier with increases in government spending equal to tax cuts, but there are time constraints and "leakages" that cut back the final effect on AGG D. But the final effect still remains greater than what tax cuts could do.

Both tax cuts and increased government spending (beyond tax revenues) result in government budget deficits. These deficits are financed by the government borrowing money. The government borrows money by selling bonds – U.S. Treasury bonds (NOT by "printing money," as many uninformed people think!). There is no problem to sell U.S. Treasuries. They are the lowest risk securities in the world. Every week $Billions are sold in the open market to whomever wants to buy them. Currently China buys a lot, and people incorrectly think this poses some political or economic threat to the U.S. Not so. It's just a standard business transaction between buyers and sellers. There's needless concern that with ever increasing deficit financing that interest rates will go up and that will cause inflation. The FED controls interest rates and is doing a good service to the Treasury – and to the American people - to keep them low so that our interest costs will not be burdensome. There is no empirical evidence that the size of deficit spending will cause inflation.

Prices start going up as we approach full employment (not only for labor but also for capital), but we are a long way from that currently (February 17, 2010).

Those who oppose deficit spending in principle also oppose increases in government spending. Deficits caused by increases in government spending are less than those created by tax cuts because of the different MPC affect on C vs. G. So, those who want lower deficits and lower government spending are in an impossible position. They have to choose which they dislike most. They generally choose tax cuts over increased government spending; so, therefore, have to accept bigger deficits.

There is needless concern over re-payment of the loans to finance deficit spending. Every week $Billions are repaid as bonds come due by the simple process of re-funding the debt, which is the way all well run businesses handle payment on their bonds when they come due. In corporate finance this is called "floating a re-funding issue." Brokerage firms almost daily put $Billions of bond issues in the market for corporations to raise money to pay off bonds that are due. They also put $Billions of Treasuries in the market to refund those coming due plus additional amounts to finance current deficit spending. So, nobody – neither businesses, nor government, NOR OUR CHILDREN OR GRANDCHILDREN WILL EVER HAVE TO PAY OFF BONDS sold to cover deficit spending. We just keep re-funding the debt, just like well run businesses do! The facts are quite different from the politicians continuing lament of how we are going bankrupt. Being against debt and for a balanced budget is great to get elected and re-elected, but it is political demagoguery, and an example par excellence of how politics sticks its ugly nose in, to the detriment of the economy. Politicians making economics decisions is a recipe for disaster.

A balanced budget is good politics, but bad economics. When the recession hit with production down and unemployment up, government revenues declined requiring all those states (32) with "balanced budget" laws to cut back spending and/or increase taxes, which they did; making the recession worse. If there was such a federal law, then contra-cyclical fiscal policy – deficit spending in recessions – could not be done, and there would be no way for the government to carry out its responsibility to fight unemployment as is required by the Employment Act of 1946.

Contra-cyclical fiscal (and monetary) policies can also be employed when AGG D is too high, which causes inflation. Monetary policy in that situation is much more effective than trying to decrease AGG D. We make an analogy in economics about the FED's capabilities that says, "You (the FED) can pull down a balloon by a string, but you can not push up a balloon by a string." The "balloon" is the economy, and when it gets "flying too high" – overheated – inflationary AGG D – the FED can and does raise interest rates to cool it down = "pulling it down by the string." Unfortunately, the FED can not control the money supply so it has to raise rates very high – up to 16% in 1982 – when Paul Volker ran the FED under Reagan – to pull down the balloon. Since prices are pretty generally "on a ratchet" (go up only), inflation is stopped by creating high unemployment – over 10% in 1982-3. It's only nut case economists that talk about "deflation."

In modern macro-economics, the opposites in economic cycles are inflation and unemployment – not inflation and deflation.

Contra-cyclical <u>fiscal policy</u> can also be used to cool down an overheated economy when AGG D is too high with much more acceptable results than the high unemployment caused by monetary policy. What's called for is a surplus – more money being taken out <u>via</u> taxes than is put in <u>via</u> government spending. Rather than a conscious discretionary policy, surpluses just happen when the economy gets going "too good." But there are two important consequences of the surplus fiscal policy: First, it answers the criticism of those opposed to modern macro-economics fiscal policy that it is just deficit spending, and it reveals another reason why a balanced budget is a bad idea. Let's define our terms here. A balanced budget is defined as revenues (tax-takes) exactly equal to government spending. Most balanced budget advocates look at it as one-sided; i.e., spending must be kept down to revenues, but when you have a surplus, that is not a balanced budget either. To balance the budget at a time of surplus requires that the surplus be spent, thereby adding fuel to the inflationary pressures of AGG D that is already too high. From this we must conclude that the goal of a balanced budget is wrong – bad economics.

The level of AGG D is never perfect – where it does not need to be increased or decreased. If we did not have fiscal policies of deficit and surplus, we would have no way to make changes to help the economy to get to the right level of AGG D – non-inflationary full employment.

Another place where <u>politics is in economics</u> to the detriment of the economy is in the continual refunding of National debt via U.S. Treasuries. It would make great economic sense not to engage in the re-funding operation to manage the debt, which could be done by issuing "Perpetuals", which are bonds that have no due date. However, the big underwriting fees we pay the big Wall Street brokers and law firms are a major factor in their ability to pay multi-million dollar bonuses. These fees probably exceed our interest cost on the bonds – especially at this time (2010) when the FED has the interest rate as close to zero as it can go. But the Wall Street brokers and law firms engaged in this $Billion dollar business already have all the politicians that would have the opportunity to make this change for the good of the economy "in the bag." (Senator Charles Schumer of New York has gotten so many millions from Wall St. that he no longer accepts any more "campaign contributions" personally, but sends the money over to the Democratic Party's general election campaign fund, thus buying more political influence for Wall Street.) There is no <u>quid pro quo</u>. (L. "this for that") agreement – written or spoken, but we Americans know how politics works: Politicians do nothing to hurt the source of funds that gets them elected – to hell with the economy! So there is virtually no chance that such a smart move that Perpetuals represents will ever happen. A snow ball's change in Hell!

The <u>politics-economics nexus</u> is also found in President Obama's winning election campaign when he used simultaneous stock market and housing market crashes to declare we were in a recession, to win votes from McCain who had correctly said at that time that "the (economics) fundamentals are fine." (In Chapter 4, Causes of the Recession, we provide the data that proves McCain right.)

Insider trading violates investors' reasonable expectations that securities markets are fair and orderly, which is the most important function of stock market regulators in any capitalistic economy. An "insider" is defined as an officer or director of a corporation and any shareholder that owns 10% or more of a corporation's stock. There are two kinds of insider trading. One is open and above board – reported to the SEC weekly and printed in newspapers everywhere. Their capital gains are taxed at much lower rates than what they would have to pay if the money was ordinary income. This is how and why corporate officers pay themselves huge salaries and give Uncle Sam as little as possible. Those of us, who do not have the opportunity to get paid at low capital gains rates, call this a loophole in the tax laws, but it is perfectly legal. (In Chapter 5, Cures for the Recession, we detail how raising capital gains taxes will help forestall future recessions.)

The other kind of insider trading is done by insiders like Stephen Friedman, a former Goldman-Sachs CEO and economic advisor to President George W. Bush, who bought Goldman shares while he was chairman of the NY Federal Reserve bank and also on the Goldman Board of Directors. Goldman was made into a bank by Treasury Secretary Paulson (an ex-Goldman CEO!) in October, 2008 and became a Member Bank of the Federal Reserve System. Friedman, therefore was not allowed by FED rules to be trading Goldman stock, but he did so for five months before he got a waiver from the FED rules. He made more than $3Million on shares traded in that time period. Antitrust laws prohibit interlocking directorates for just this reason, which is what this appears to be. He may not have violated the letter of the law, and had to get a back-dated waiver, but he certainly did violate the spirit of the law and serves as an example of the "bad smelling" insider trading the public abhors, because such is not a part of "fair and orderly markets" that capitalism requires and the SEC is supposed to maintain.

The situation also brings to mind what's wrong with the FED's regulations of banking: It's a Self Regulating Organization (SRO). The banks regulate the banks. The regulators are the regulated. This is a no-brainer conflict of interests. Self regulation does not work. The big fancy office building in Washington where the FED is headquartered just contains hundreds of high paid employees none of whom can make the banks do anything. They make rules, but the rules are not enforced and there is no penalty for breaking the rules. Currently (early 2010) Bank of America, Citigroup, and J.P. Morgan Chase, all Member Banks of the Federal Reserve

System each have more than the 10% of the nation's deposits in violation of banking regulations that prohibit that.

Here's a simple formula to calculate profit/share from insider trading:

π = p-c, where π is the profit/share, p is the price the shares are sold for, and c is the cost/share. Total profit is the profit/share X the number of shares.

This is not rocket science; it is just a simple "buy low, sell high" transaction, but the insiders get the option to buy at a price below the current market price so they could immediately exercise their option and make a profit based on the difference between their cost and the market price. Such deals are available only to insiders – corporate officers and executives – who get stock options as a big part of their compensation package. The options are to buy the stock at a price lower than the market price any time in the future. So, the firms granting these options are using them as an incentive for the executives to get them to do whatever it takes to make the stock go up because this then makes the stock option a way for the executives to make a lot of money that is taxed much lower than the personal income tax would be on the same amount of money.

From a local newspaper, we got the following data: a Mr. Kenneth M. Duberstein, a Director of Boeing Co. "exercised an option for 2,400 common shares at $37.94 each on Feb. 11. He sold the shares at $60.50 each."

π = p – c = $60.50 - $37.94 = $22.56 profit/share

Total profit = 2,400 shares X $22.56 = $54,144, that is taxable at ½ the personal income tax rate (or lower, depending on what rate applies to his regular personal income).

Bank of America and J.P. Morgan Chase each have a greater share of certain regional markets than allowed by Antitrust Laws.

There are other SRO's in our economic system that are also failing to regulate. The NYSE is an SRO – designated as such by the SEC, which is supposed to regulate securities markets. The NYSE regulates the NYSE. The regulated are the regulators. This is a no-brainer conflict of interests. Self regulation does not work.

The NASD is an SRO – designated as such by the SEC, which is supposed to regulate securities markets. The NASD regulates the NASD. The regulated are the regulators. This is a no-brainer conflict of interests. Self regulation does not work. Proof <u>par excellence</u>: Bernard Madoff, who was President and CEO of NASD.

NASD stands for the National Association of Securities Dealers, who are SEC registered Broker/Dealer (B/D) firms that are not members of the NYSE. Therefore, NASD firms trade in stocks that are not listed on the NYSE. This market is called the Over The Counter (OTC) market. Instead of the NYSE tape that continually reports all trades of its listed stock, the NASD runs its own Automated Quotation system called NASDAQ.

You will see in Chapter 4, Causes of the Recession, how the SRO's were prime causal factors. And you will, therefore, see in Chapter 5, Cures for the Recession, that SRO's must be replaced.

Another politics-in-economics problem goes by the expression "turf wars." This is internal politics in the government whereby different agencies have claimed jurisdiction over certain regulatory procedures and they fight against intrusion by any other agency that might try to take away some of what they consider their "turf." The management goal for any organization, including the federal government administration, is to make $1 + 1 > 2$, but turf wars make $1 + 1 < 2$. Turf wars are counter productive, but are part and parcel of the politics-economics nexus that inhibits cooperation among agencies to work together to solve economics problems.

You will see in Chapter 4, Causes of the Recession, how turf wars were a cause of the recession. And you will, therefore, see in Chapter 5, Cures for the Recession, that a "super regulator" is needed to nullify the negative effects of turf wars.

That "super regulator" will have to have the authority to eliminate all the turf wars, and do all the regulating of all financial institutions not regulated by the present system of regulation. We suggest that there is one, and only one, solution to properly regulate the financial sector: THE BANK OF THE UNITED STATES OF AMERICA.

This institution would be able to do what the FED does not and can not do: regulate banking and control the money supply. This good central bank will regulate the terms of all loans. Mortgages are loans. Credit cards are loans. Margin accounts are loans.

In macro-economics there is a concept called "the accelerator," which has a function similar to the accelerator (gas pedal) in a car – it speeds things up. What it speeds up in the economy is the increase in AGG D, and, therefore economic growth (more output) and an increase in employment. It works like this: Let's say there is an increase in government spending $(+\Delta G)$ that via the multiplier leads to an increase in National Income $(+\Delta Y)$. This increase in income leads to an increase in Consumption $(+\Delta C)$, and as businesses have to produce more they increase their productive facilities. This is an increase in "real" Investment $(+\Delta I)$. The accelerator as calculated value is the ratio of the change in Investment to the change in Consumption $(\Delta I/\Delta C)$.

The late great economist, Paul Samuelson's Ph.D. dissertation at Harvard contains a multiplier-accelerator mathematical model of the economy. (We heard that his wife, a mathematician, worked out the equations.)

The single most important economics concept for the purposes of this book – to explain the causes and cures for the 2008-09 recession – is "leverage"; specifically financial leverage. Leverage is a concept that comes from physics, whereby with a lever and a fulcrum you can multiply the mechanical advantage to move something – say lift a heavy object. In economics, leverage refers to the ratio of debt to equity. The higher the debt is as a percentage of equity, the higher the leverage. Equity is the owner(s) money; debt is borrowed (other peoples' money). Leveraging allows the business (or individual) to do more business than could be done with just the equity money. Let's take a simple case we are all familiar with from personal finance: Buying a house by taking out a loan – the mortgage. The down payment is the equity; the mortgage is the debt. If the down payment is 10%, then the debt is 90%; so, there are $9 borrowed for every $1 of equity. The leveraging is 9:1. If you went into the housing business and had $100,000, you could buy $1Million worth of houses: leveraged 9:1 (sometimes expressed as 10:1, because you have done 10 times the value of your equity).

In business, leveraging has to do with the firm's capital structure – the percent of the funds in the business coming from different sources. The two major external sources of funds in corporations are from the sale of stock and loans. Stock is the equity money; loans are debt. There is a correct (theoretically sound) ratio for any business. Too much debt is bad; so is too little. The optimum amount of debt can be established for any business by calculating what cash flow will be at the worst point in the business cycle. Debt must be "serviced" with cash – the interest must be paid to the lenders – whether it is a bank loan or from the sale of bonds. But in business – unlike homeowners' mortgages – no amortization of the principal of the loan is required for bonds, and bank loans can carry the same provision.

Leveraging is the way all kinds of businesses expand their business. The Wall Street brokers and bankers are highly leveraged. "Regular" accounts in the brokerage business are margin accounts. Margin is the down payment to buy stocks. If the margin is 50%, you need only 50 cents for every dollar spent to buy stocks; if it's 25%, you need only a quarter for every dollar spent to buy stocks. The brokerage firm lends you the difference. But the loan made to you increases the broker's leverage because the broker borrowed the money from a bank. The broker therefore, does 2, 3, or 4 times as much business because he is using other people's (the lending bank's) money. The margin requirement is set by the FED. The FED is the banks. The banks regulate the banks. The lower they keep the margin the more leverage the broker has. Therefore, a big source of the leveraged speculation that drives up stock prices in a boom-to-inevitable bust stems from the margin account – the regular way of doing business on Wall Street.

The SEC requires brokers to maintain a certain level of Net Capital (Assets minus Liabilities), and as the boom in the stock market is fueled by leveraged speculation, the brokers got the SEC to "amend" the Net Capital rule so that they could expand even faster than what the margin accounts allowed. The "amendment" was mostly just doing away with the Net Capital rule, which effectively "neutered" the SEC's regulatory force in the stock market, because the SEC had only the Net Capital rule left since it had long ago made the NYSE and NASD SRO's.

The amendment of the Net Capital rule was done at the behest of the big Wall Street brokers lead by Hank Paulson, the Goldman-Sachs CEO at that time. (Mr. Paulson's net worth currently – early 2010 – is $700 Million; pretty good for a Dartmouth English major football player!)

As we shall see in Chapter 4, Causes of the Recession, leveraged speculation for capital gains in the stock market was a prime cause of the boom-and-bust crash. So, in Chapter 5, Cures for the Recession, stopping leveraged speculation is the most important step in the process.

Leveraged speculation caused the housing market crash.

Leveraged speculation caused the commercial real estate market crash – just now (early 2010) getting into high gear.

Leveraged speculation caused bank failures – 140 in 2009, and an even greater number predicted for 2010.

Leveraged speculation caused oil prices to go to $150/barrel and gasoline to $4-$5/gallon. The margin requirements on the Commodities Futures Trading (CFT) market are only 10% or less. Hidden and secretive "energy trading units" at Goldman-Sachs and Citigroup each made $667 Million in 2008. And they are back at it today (Feb. 2010) doing better than before the bust because they now have their own bank within the holding company parent of the brokerage firm. In September, 2008, Goldman-Sachs added a bank to its firm, so now it does not have to borrow to carry out its leveraged speculation. (We find it "smelly" that it was Hank Paulson – an ex-Goldman-Sachs CEO – as Treasury Secretary put in $10Billion into the Goldman-Sachs bank in October of 2008, one month after the bank was set up on paper. $10Billion is just the amount that Goldman was owed on the insurance it bought from AIG for its "packaged mortgages" securities THAT AIG COULD NOT PAY!

Though we know it is an insult to your intelligence, we want to review the basic idea of graphing variables along axes. We don't want you to turn out like our insurance man on Cape Cod, a Dartmouth economics major, who told us he "never understood the graphs!"

The next page is a full size sheet of graph paper. In graphing values for variables, you start at the origin O, which is the middle of the graph.

Positive values for the variable on the horizontal axis are to the right of the origin, and negative values go to the left of the origin. Positive values for the variable on the vertical axis are up from the origin, and negative values are down from the origin. This means that when we are dealing with variables that only have positive values we use just the upper right quadrant of the graph. All the other three quadrants would be where negative values are plotted.

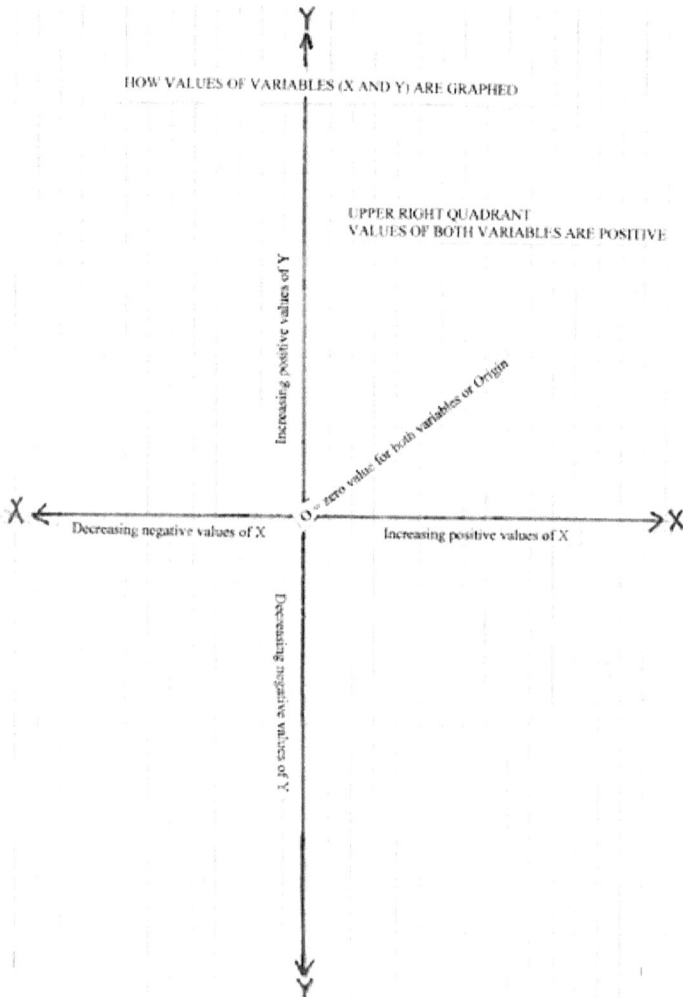

HOW VALUES OF VARIABLES (X AND Y) ARE GRAPHED

UPPER RIGHT QUADRANT
VALUES OF BOTH VARIABLES ARE POSITIVE

Increasing positive values of Y

zero value for both variables or Origin

Decreasing negative values of X

Increasing positive values of X

Decreasing negative values of Y

Let's, at this point, put concepts together to develop an understanding of how the whole macro-economy fits together. We feel confident that you now understand simple two-variable graphs; so, we will go from verbal definitions of the concepts to simple equation representations and then to graphs.

Let's start with the fundamental concept that National Income and national output, GDP, are exactly the same thing looked at from different points of view. Remember the circular flow model of the economy – Illustration 1-1 – where we concluded that "what goes around, comes around" so that conceptually you could see how the dollar amount of spending is equal to the dollar amount of output? Illustration 1-4 is another way to see the same thing in a different format – a two-variable graph with National Income, Y, on the vertical axis and national output, GDP, on the horizontal axis.

Since $Y = C + 1 + G$ and $GDP = C + 1 + G$, things equal to the same thing are equal to each other (remember that theorem from geometry?) Therefore, actual levels of Y and GDP are both somewhere on the 45 degree line coming out of the origin, which we can call the aggregate supply line for the economy, AGG S. This is sort of analogous to the supply curve in micro-economics analysis, whereby quantity supplied is a function of price – $Q_s = f(P)$. In this MACRO model, the actual quantity produced, GDP, is a function of aggregate demand, AGG D. So it is similar to supply and demand determination of an equilibrium price, but what is determined is the level of national output. The total level of spending is on the Y axis, and the total level of output is on the X axis. The more the spending, the more the output. If spending decreases, so does output.

ILLUSTRATION 1-4
INCOME/OUTPUT MODEL OF AN ECONOMY

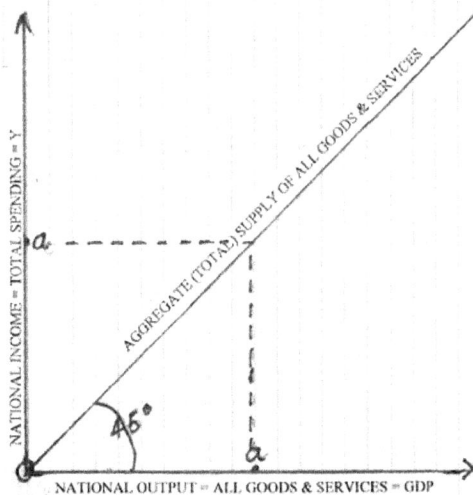

Let's add the three categories of spending to the graph, one at a time. Illustration 1-5 is the Consumption function, C. Consumption is (largely) a function of income - C = f(Y). Wealth (W), is also a determinant of consumption – more wealth = more consumption, but if we say C = f (Y & W), we have more than two variables, which is difficult to graph on a two dimensional graph. We'll let the 200 Ph.D. economists that work at the FED get all the data for changes in Y and W and "run regressions" to show the relative importance of the W factor for C. (It's not much.) Illustration 1-5 is a simple two-variable graph for the consumption function, C = f(Y). At income E, consumption and income are equal. They are equal anywhere along the 45 degree line from the origin, O, because 45 degrees is exactly the middle of a 90 degree angle, which is what the graph is. At incomes above E, where consumption is less than income, the difference is savings – S = Y – C. At income less than E, where consumption is more than income, the difference is called "dis-saving."

With this two-variable straight line function, we can write the straight line equation that describes it – C = a + bY, where a is the intercept on the C axis and b is the slope of the function -$\Delta C/\Delta Y$. The slope of the consumption function is also the marginal propensity to consume – k. Since MPC is in reality, up in the 90% range, the slope of our consumption function is not steep enough compared to reality.

ILLUSTRATION 1-5
THE CONSUMPTION FUNCTION

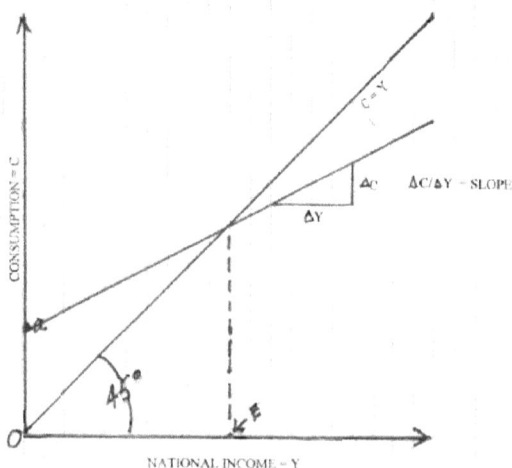

Illustration 1-6 puts the consumption function on a graph that represents ALL spending in the economy, which we call aggregate demand

AGG D – so, we have to add the other two categories of spending, I (Investment) and G (Government) to get total spending –
AGG D = C + I + G so as to determine the equilibrium level of Y and GDP. But neither business capital spending, I, nor government spending, G, are a function of either Y or GDP, so we can not use our graphs to show what they are. I ≠ f(Y or GDP), and G ≠ f(Y or GDP). (≠ means "is not.") Following the K.I.S.S. principle (Keep It Simple, Stupid!), we will just add on a fixed percentage of total Y to consumption, C, for I and for G.

We know that consumption is about 70% of our GDP at this time, which leaves 30% for Investment (I) and Government (G) spending combined. Let's just split it in half and say they are 15% each. This realistic approximation flies in the face of something we recently heard Mitt Romney, the unsuccessful candidate for the Republican Party's nomination for president in 2008, say when doing a book promo review on CNN: He said that government spending was now (2009) 30% of GDP, which is way too high for his philosophical biases that government is too big and spending too much money. He would likely call 15% too much; that's the way regressives are; but progress calls for more government spending because in the 21st century we are moving into a service economy, AND IT IS GOVERNMENT THAT PROVIDES SERVICES. We currently have 70% of the labor force in the service sector, which is normal, natural and desirable path of economic growth and development. So, it is, therefore, normal, natural and desirable that government spending gets bigger, not smaller as Romney and all regressives harp on. We want to have progress in the economy, not regress.

ILLUSTRATION 1-6
EQUILIBRIUM OUTPUT

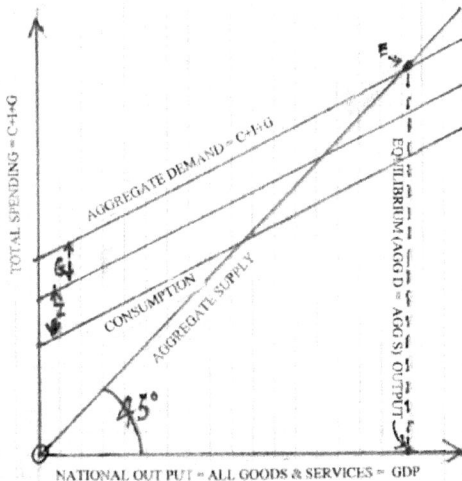

NATIONAL OUTPUT = ALL GOODS & SERVICES = GDP

CHAPTER 1 APPENDIX:
THE ABC'S OF MACRO-ECONOMICS

A. NATIONAL INCOME

1. C = Consumption expenditures = dollars spent for consumer goods
2. I = "real" Investment expenditures = dollars spent for capital goods
3. G = total expenditures by Governments: federal, state and local
4. Y = National Income = C + I + G

B. NATIONAL OUTPUT

1. C = total amount of Consumer goods produced
2. I = total amount of Investment goods produced
3. G = total amount of Government goods and services produced
4. GDP = Gross Domestic Production = C + I + G

C. TAUTOLOGIES – DEFINITIONAL IDENTITIES – <u>NOT EQUATIONS</u>

1. Y ≡ GDP ≡ NATIONAL INCOME ≡ GROSS DOMESTIC PRODUCTION
2. AGG D ≡ Aggregate Demand ≡ $C + $I + $G ≡ TOTAL SPENDING
3. S ≡ I national Savings ≡ national Investment

DEFINITIONS OF OTHER MACRO-ECONOMICS VARIABLES

1. α (alpha) = the Accelerator = $\Delta I / \Delta C$ (Δ = "change")
2. MPC = Marginal Propensity to Consume = $\Delta C / \Delta Y$
3. MPS = Marginal Propensity to Save = $\Delta S / \Delta Y$
4. MPC + MPS = 1.: MPC = 1 – MPS and MPS = 1 – MPC (.: = "therefore")
5. k = the multiplier = number that calculates the maximum theoretical ΔY from a Δ in AGG D   k = 1/MPS

CHAPTER 2:
GOVERNMENT AND DEBT

There is so much massive misunderstanding about government deficit spending, and national debt, we need to have this separate chapter on that one subject alone.

In July 2010 we heard President Obama say that failure to control the federal budget would result in debt that his children and grandchildren would not be able to pay. It was very disheartening to hear him say that because on March 11, 2010, we wrote to him explaining why this line about "passing on the burden of the debt to our children and grandchildren" is what Rahm Emanuel would call, "Bullshit." We include, at this point, a copy of that communication and President Obama's reply, which sort of indicates he read our definitive explanation that should have put an end to that stupid, conservative, regressive type thinking that both Republicans and Democrats repeat ad infinitum, especially at election times, because it is a prime example of the demagoguery practiced by all to get your vote. Also a prime example of how politics has a negative effect on the economy.

Maybe, we should start by defining some of the terminology. A "demagogue" is a person who tells someone something that is not true (but the person being told the lie thinks it is true) for the benefit of the demagogue. For example, say you are running for office – to get votes you say "the government should balance its budget, just like we all have to."

Most voters believe that, but you know that it is bad economics to require a balanced budget. Why? Because we could not have contra-cyclical fiscal policy if government spending and revenues always had to be equal, which is what a balanced budget is. To prove the validity of this point, all we have to do is look what happened to government spending in all those states that have a balanced budget law in the 2009-10 recession. When their tax revenues declined because of the recession, they had to fire many employees and cut back social programs. School teachers were let go by the thousands, police and firemen, too. And "safety net" social services for the unemployed were not available because the states had no money to fund them. THE WARRANTED CONCLUSION: A BALANCED BUDGET MAKES A RECESSION WORSE.

And it is also bad on the upside of the economic cycle – when there is full employment and economic growth – putting back into the economy the expanding tax revenues – balancing the budget causes inflation because when there is full employment the increased spending can not draw more resources into production; it can only bid up the prices – inflation. Many balanced budget advocates don't even consider this problem on the upside of the cycle. All they really want is the government to spend less so that taxes can go down. But a balanced budget is revenues and spending exactly equal, whether the revenues are low or high. We can cite this situation as another example of the fallacy of composition. What is good for the individual – low taxes and low government spending is bad for the economy when the economy needs more spending to reach full employment.

Let's call our most recent explanation about the national debt, that we communicated to President Obama – Exhibit 2-1, and the reply we got – Exhibit 2-2, and then go back to 1967 and look at our first explanation, which is in the form of a response to a Wall Street Journal editorial. The editorial and our response were picked up by Glen Mills, who at the time was the Dean of the School of Speech at Northwestern University for his book Reason in Controversy. We include the editorial as Exhibit 2-3 and our response as Exhibit 2-4. In the editorial you will see the very same arguments are made today by the same people – those who think the U.S. is going bankrupt, government spending is too high, and we are creating debt that will be a burden to our children and grandchildren.

A couple of these current nay-sayers would be Prof. David Gergen of the Harvard Kennedy School, and the renowned TV, and now NPR reporter, Ted Koppel. On a TV roundtable discussion about government spending recently, we saw Prof. Gergen mouth the word "bankruptcy" as a possible outcome from government deficit spending and increasing national debt. On Monday, August 9, 2010, Mr. Koppel said on NPR, "When all those Treasuries we sold to China come due – they want their money back – our children and grandchildren will have to pay."

Well, let's say it again – loud and clear - in case you missed it before: NOBODY EVER HAS, NOR ARE THEY NOW, NOR WILL THEY EVER HAVE TO PAY OFF THE NATIONAL DEBT.

The nation is being run on a leveraged capital structure that includes debt as a permanent part of its capital structure. ("Capital" in this sense is money, not economic real capital.) JUST LIKE ALL WELL-RUN BUSINESS DOES.

Financial leveraging in business is determining the maximum amount of debt the business can carry – pay the interest on. It then has that much more money to make money with. When the bonds or other loans to get that money come due, they just sell new bonds to pay off the old ones, BUT THE DEBT JUST GOES ON AND ON; IT IS NEVER PAID OFF PERMANENTLY.

This is the same way that the national debt is handled. When bonds come due, we just sell new ones to pay off the old ones. THE NATIONAL DEBT IS NEVER PAID OFF. There are always new investors who want to get in on the safest security in the world: U.S. Treasury obligations. Maybe, the editorial department of the Wall Street Journal riles against government debt, but the Wall Street brokers who make $Billions underwriting these new issues every week love the business. With interest rates being held as close to zero as you can get, you don't have to be a rocket scientist to figure that the underwriting costs for the national debt costs us more than the interest. And there is a way to avoid these underwriting fees: issue "perpetuals" – bonds that never come due, no maturity date. If the buyer wants his money back, he just sells the bond to someone who wants the interest. When interest rates change in the economy, the price of the bond changes to reflect the difference between the stated – coupon – rate and the market rate.

Another bogus issue inre: the national debt is that it takes an increasing percentage of the federal budget to pay the interest. Since it is the NATIONAL debt, it should be NATIONAL income that is the basis for paying the interest, not the federal budget. When that calculation is made using OMB – the federal government's Office of Budget and Management – figures, it shows that it will only take, at most, over the next decade, three tenths of one percent of the national income to pay the interest on the national debt. We submit that it is only common sense that when any entity – a person, or business, or government, or nation can carry its debt with just three tenths of one percent of its income that is not a problem. There will be no bankruptcy, no burden on our children and grandchildren, nothing to lose one moment of sleep over.

Between our communication to President Obama on this subject and the response to the Wall Street Journal editorial in 1967, we ran into the S.O.S. (Same Old Sh--) in an editorial in the Orlando Sentinel. So, being good publicly motivated economists, we undertook to explain in a reply essentially the same as we did for the Wall Street Journal editorial. We include the Orlando Sentinel editorial as Exhibit 2-5, and our reply as Exhibit 2-6. Both of these were forwarded to President Obama with our communication with him (Exhibit 2-1) because they were done prior to it. And to emphasize the important points.

The whole issue for economists is that we have to have contra-cyclical fiscal policy – deficit spending in recessions and surpluses in inflationary times – to be able to keep the economy on a full employment growth track. Only the federal government is big enough to make a difference. However, it would be better if state governments did not have balanced budget laws so they could keep people employed in downturns. And not make recessions worse as they tried to balance their budgets. PEOPLE ARE MORE IMPORTANT THAN MONEY.

States could and should run a leveraged capital structure just like the federal government AND WELL-RUN BUSINESSES. They could sell bonds to cover their deficit spending, and sell re-funding issues when they came due JUST LIKE WELL-RUN BUSINESSES DO. Or save the continuing underwriting fees and put out "Perpetuals," which the brokers would not like, but we want what's good for the people, not the brokers (even though we were SEC Registered as such for many years.).

In case we missed it earlier, it is necessary in modern 21st century economics to understand that the old contra-cyclical monetary policies – "easy money" and "tight money" do not work. On the "easy money" side, the 2009-10 recession provided inescapable final proof of the ineffectiveness of low interest rates to help the economy. And the so-called "credit crunch" was also inescapable proof that the money supply can not be increased by any government action. The "tight money" policy – for fighting inflation is also a complete failure in that the costs far outweigh the benefits. Let's use the data from 1982 to prove this point: Paul Volker, then FED CHMN. under Reagan, stopped inflationary pressures by raising interest rates to 16%, but at the cost of 10+% unemployment.

THE WARRANTED CONCLUSION IS THAT ONLY FISCAL POLICY CAN HELP THE ECONOMY.

EXHIBIT 2-1 PAGE 1

TO : PRESIDENT OBAMA, OUR FRIEND

FROM :   Dr. & Mrs. Frank DeFelice
         Rainbow Resort
         Lot 470
         700 Co. Rd. 630A
         Frostproof, FL 33843

DATE : MARCH 11, 2010

SUBJECT : 21ST CENTURY MACRO-ECONOMICS
          THEORETICALLY SOUND AND PRACTICAL

In an earlier memo, we suggested a new theory of government finance that embodies "very conservative leveraging", which can actually be done by doing nothing -- without announcing any new policy -- because that's the way government finance has been run for many years, is being run now, and should continue to be run.

Why? Because a balanced budget, which is great politics (everyone is for baseball, apple pie and a balanced budget, right?) is actually bad economics. To understand why this is so, check out our reply to the recent standard BS "balance-the-budget" editorial in the Orlando Sentinel, "Red Ink Alert" (copies of both enclosed).

We made the same argument in response to the same editorial in the Wall Street Journal in July, 1967 (43 years ago!) titled " Government and Debt"; both of which were re-printed in Glen Mills' Reason in Controversy, 2nd edition, Allyn and Bacon, when he was Dean of the School of Speech at Northwestern University.

At this point in time, we can up-date the argument using current OMB projections that show it will cost only 3% of National Income to carry our National debt. That is not a burden to anyone.

We are approaching 80 and have never been "burdened by" -- had to pay -- the National debt. Neither have our children, our grand-children nor our great grand-children. Neither will your children, your grand-children , nor their grand-children be "burdened by" -- have to pay -- it.

When John Maynard Keynes was asked about what happens in the long-run when contra-cyclical fiscal policy (deficit spending) debt comes due, he said, "In the long-run we are all dead", which is true but a bit glib of an answer to something the public INCORRECTLY perceives as a big problem. (We even saw David Gergen mouth the word "bankruptcy" on a TV talk show about government spending !)

A better explanation would be : we just keep doing what we have always done : sell re-funding issues of Treasuries as issues come due. (Just like WELL-RUN businesses do !) This shifts "the burden" to those who buy the Treasuries (the Chinese).

EXHIBIT 2-1 PAGE 2

A better solution would be to issue "Perpetuals", bonds that never come due, as they do in England.

You can keep talking "balanced budget", it's great politics, but you should tone down the rhetoric like Bill Clinton told you do with your "economic crisis" speeches (which ▓▓▓ probably was THE factor that got you elected). In both cases, you have made the problem worse than it really is. (In our book, What All Americans Need To Know About Economics (forth-coming), which will be the definitive work on the causes of the 2008-09 recession, such talk by you is cited as an important causal factor for the recession because John McCain was right when he said the economic fundamentals were fine when he said it.)

Financial leveraging in business has to do with the debt/equity ratio (D/E) on the balance sheet, but National Income accounting is not done like business accounting. Therefore, we need look only at debt-carrying capability to ascertain the risk involved.
Low risk, very conservative leveraging in personal finance is that debt can be 2 ½ times - 250% of - personal income, and in this calculation the debt has to be amortized (paid off). National debt, therefore, that _is_ only 28% of National Income and never has to be paid off is miniscule – very low risk, very safe leveraging – and really not a problem at all.

We respectfully suggest that your (un-spoken) policy about the National debt be : BENIGN NEGLECT. As the economy grows, and, therefore also National Income, what is incorrectly perceived by the public as a problem becomes less and less of one over time.

Copies: Rahm Emanuel, David Gergen, Michael Aronson, Larry Trador, Jack Massey

Post Script : Don't listen to those conservative Republican Friedmanite economists like Ben Bernanke and Larry Summers inter alios that are stuck with worn-out defunct 20th century macro-economics nonsense.

THE WHITE HOUSE

WASHINGTON

April 29, 2010

Dear Friend:

Thank you for sharing your thoughts with me. I have heard from many Americans concerned about the Federal budget deficit and government spending, and I appreciate your perspective.

I am committed to making my Administration the most open and transparent in history, and part of delivering on that promise is hearing from people like you. I take seriously your opinions, and respect your point of view on this important issue. Please know that your concerns will be on my mind in the days ahead.

Thank you again for writing. I encourage you to visit WhiteHouse.gov to learn more about my Administration or to contact me in the future.

Sincerely,

EXHIBIT 2-3   PAGE 1

EDITORIAL FOLLOWED
BY LETTER TO EDITOR

THE DREARY CYCLE[1]

WAR AND POLITICS BEING WHAT THEY ARE, THE CONGRESSIONAL JOINT Economic Committee is probably correct in figuring that the Administration is again underestimating the cost of the Vietnam war. If so, it is up to Congress to take the appropriate action.

Last year, it may be recalled, Government officials put the cost about $10 billion below the actuality—a calculation the cynics considered not unrelated to the then prospective November elections. The upshot, as the committee says, was havoc in the economy. Congress was unable to examine the advisability of a tax increase in its true light; combating inflation was left almost entirely to monetary policy and a near-crisis developed in the money markets.

Now, "the same dreary cycle of events threatens again in 1967," the Congressional group warns. More specifically, Vietnam spending in calendar 1967 may run $4 billion to $6 billion over the original estimates. The possibility adds weight to the predictions that the budget deficit in the current 1968 fiscal year may be $30 billion or more.

[1] Wall Street Journal, July 11, 1967, p. 16. Reprinted by permission of the Wall Street Journal.

[379]

Granting the difficulty of reckoning expenditures in any war, the committee members nonetheless suggest that the Administration could do a considerably better job. They urge "timely conveyance to Congress of the latest estimates," and the Administration has promised to try to bring its figures up to date later this month.

But there is much more to it than merely improving the reliability of the fiscal outlook. The prospect of ever-increasing Vietnam costs makes it imperative to reduce Federal nondefense spending. Since the Administration has no stomach for the task, it goes to Congress by default.

It's often alleged that it is all but impossible to effect significant savings; so many costs are fixed or uncontrollable. Some are, to be sure, but the budget is ripe for pruning, as President Johnson himself unintentionally underscored in a recent speech.

Pointing with unjustified pride to how much the Government is spending domestically while fighting a war in Vietnam, the President mentioned the following: The poverty program has been increased every year and is going up 25% this year. Education is $12 billion this year, three times the level three years ago. Health, a little over $12 billion, also triple what it was three years ago. A new "far-reaching" model cities program.

To call that kind of binge irresponsible is putting it mildly. Projects like the so-called war on poverty are an administrative mess as even federal officials occasionally concede. Not only that: if all the poverty spending has made any sizable dent in the problem, it must be news to the poor.

In the light of such wild and wasteful outlays, it is an insult to the taxpayer for the Administration to keep insisting on higher taxes later in the year. Plainly the budget is in terrible shape; the right way to deal with it is not to aggravate the onerous tax burden on the people but to restrain the outpourings of the executive branch.

The Republicans in Congress and some of the more level-headed Democrats are talking bravely of finding substantial savings amid the budgetary chaos, but the obstacles are formidable and the hopes appear dim.

Congress, after all, is still dominated by liberals. In addition, any politician hesitates to pare or eliminate projects in being, on the venerable if not necessarily valid theory that the more dollars go out the more votes will come in. And Congress' own piecemeal, horse-and-buggy mode of tackling the budget makes it hard to weigh one program against another, establishing reasonable priorities.

Despite all the hurdles, a condition of rapidly mounting war and non-war costs, building a towering deficit, can fairly be called critical; Congress must be importuned to rise above its frailties. For if our profligate Governmental planners are not held in check, they will set in motion a cycle of events that will be not only dreary but desperate.

EXHIBIT 2-4   PAGE 1

GOVERNMENT AND DEBT[a]

EDITOR, *The Wall Street Journal:*

The "Review and Outlook" column of the July 11 edition of your paper is another dreary exhortation that the federal budget be balanced. This seems to be a regular feature of your paper and undoubtedly has wide appeal in the business community where there is strong propensity to make a grossly inaccurate analogy between business and government budgets. The government is not like the department store in Phoenix, nor any other business, for that matter, for a number of reasons. First, it is not a profit-seeking institution. And it is not the case that it just turned out that way; it was never intended to be. Unlike any business, its debt is not externally held. In addition it has money-creating powers.

If there is room for analogy with business, it is in the area of the need for and the capacity to carry debt. Do you know of any prudently managed business that does not need debt? And as far as capacity to carry debt is concerned, the record is clear—it is increasing much faster than debt. I would suggest that any business with the same level and stability of earnings would be foolish not to carry far more debt than what the government presently carries.

There is a rule of thumb in personal financial management that an individual can safely carry a total debt of two and one-half times his annual income. And built into this safe limit is amortization of the principal. With continuous refunding an absolute certainty, a national debt that is less than half of national income should be no cause for concern for anyone, least of all the business sector where markets for government debt issues are strong and trading is always brisk.

[a] *Ibid.*, July 26, 1967, p. 14, as excerpted. Original letter used by permission of Mr. DeFelice.

EXHIBIT 2-4   PAGE 2

But there is a far worse error that such pap about a balanced budget commits. And that is the complete disregard for one of the most elementary points of modern economic theory.

In modern economic theory the level of spending is the key determinant of output, employment, and prices. Though federal spending has been *decreasing* as a percent of total spending in the economy, it remains as the only sector over which much control can be exercised. Business and consumer-spending, which constitute all the nongovernment spending, sky-rocketed last year in spite of the Fed's attempt to curtail them with tight money and the highest interest rates ever. This should serve as sufficient evidence that monetary policy alone cannot curb inflationary spending—particularly the unsustainable level of investment spending done by the business sector because buoyant optimism about profitability far outweighs the increase in interest rates and large internal sources make market shortage of funds irrelevant. In such a situation as prevailed last year the government should decrease spending or increase taxes, or do some of both to hold down the level of aggregate spending. But please note: under any of these alternative recommended policies, the budget would *not* be balanced; there would be a surplus, not a balance.

At other times—like now—the total level of spending in the economy will not be enough to keep all our resources fully employed. In this situation the government should increase its spending, decrease taxes, or some of both to raise the level of total spending. Under any of these alternative recommended policies the budget would *not* balance; there would be a deficit. So unless the level of total spending in the economy were "perfect" there should always be either a surplus or a deficit. And it would be highly unlikely that the surpluses and deficits would be equal and offsetting.

Furthermore, requiring a balanced budget would *not* be neutral in its economic effect. In a business downturn—like the present one—tax revenues automatically decline. To require a cutback in government spending at such a time would only aggravate an already bad situation. The converse holds when the economy is in an inflationary boom.

The federal budget therefore is an important tool to be used for the important economic goals of growth, full employment, and price stability. And this is not a distortion of government's rightful duties. To the contrary, such action is required by the Employment Act of 1946. It is only of secondary importance that the budget balance. This is not some

EXHIBIT 2-4   PAGE 3

economic heresy; it is the currently accepted doctrine of the science of economics. Most economists, like myself, who *last year* did advocate a tax increase did so to reduce an inflationary level of spending—not to balance the budget. Currently the correct fiscal policy is to reduce taxes and/or increase government spending to reduce unemployment and increase output—the budget be damned.

Sincerely yours,
FRANK DeFELICE, Ph. D.
University of North Carolina

Let's fast forward to February 3, 2010, which is in the 21st century, when there appeared in the Orlando Sentinel the forever resounding refrain about deficit spending and the "crushing debt burden on future generations." It is included here as Exhibit 2-5. Our response to this editorial is Exhibit 2-6. From them you can see the same rhetoric as in the July 1967 Wall Street Journal editorial and our response, which is also remarkably similar, except for the fact that the numbers are all much larger now. This is a good place to introduce DeFelice's Law of Economics Numbers: They all get larger over time. Now we talk in Trillions of dollars vs. Billions back in the last century. So, let's use some current (August 2010) numbers and do the same analysis of deficit spending and national debt as before.

The National Debt as of August 28, 2010 stood at $13.5 Trillion, but the current National Income is $15 Trillion! Debt, therefore, is less than one year's National Income. Remember that very conservative debt-to-income ratio for individuals is that debt can be 250% of income. And in the calculation for individuals, amortization – paying off the loan – is built in to the calculation. The National Income does not have to be used to pay off the National Debt – just the interest. This is so because when government debt issues – U.S. Treasury issues come due, new ones are issued and sold to pay off the old ones. Given this fact, we can modify our conclusion that nobody has ever, nor will ever have to, pay the National Debt to: WE (THE U.S.) ALWAYS HAVE AND ALWAYS WILL PAY OFF OUR DEBTS WHEN DUE. This is why U.S. Treasuries are the highest quality, lowest risk securities in the world.

Here are more current facts about the National Debt: Of the $13.5 Trillion, $9 Trillion is held by Americans. So, we largely owe it to ourselves! The balance, $4.5 Trillion is held by foreign governments, including the Chinese. When the Treasuries held by the Chinese come due – which they do all the time – we pay them back every penny right on time. Where do we get this money to pay them? From them! When their bonds become due, we sell them another batch to pay off the old ones. This is the automatic re-funding of the National Debt that goes on every week. Remember earlier, we said that the burden of the debt fell on the Chinese? To the extent that they continue to buy new issues they are assuming the "burden." But, the Chinese hold only a small percentage of U.S. Treasuries. Thousands of banks hold $Billions of Treasuries, which constitute the prime – safest, low-risk-loans in their portfolios. So, we are not relying on the Chinese to finance our National Debt; most of it is held by Americans – banks, brokers and businesses. These people realize that a debt that is less than one year's National Income is nothing to worry about. We always pay our debts in full when due, which is probably a better way to look at the situation than to say no one has to pay the National Debt; BUT BOTH STATEMENTS ARE TRUE.

Frank DeFelice, Ph.D.

Something on your mind?

What we think

The nation's red-ink alert

The federal budget is on the road to ruin, with long-term deficits that threaten the nation's economy and security. But instead of heading for an exit, Barack Obama would step on the gas.

In unveiling his proposed budget this week, the president declared, "We simply cannot continue to spend as if deficits don't have consequences." Amen. The consequences include diverting dollars from investments that would make America more prosperous and secure, forcing Uncle Sam to depend even more on China and other foreign creditors, leaving a crushing debt burden on future generations, and raising the risk of another economic meltdown.

But while the president's plan includes tax hikes and spending cuts to offset some borrowing, here's the bottom line: This year's red ink would reach $1.56 trillion, higher than last year's record $1.41 trillion. Next year's would be $1.27 trillion, meaning the federal government would still be borrowing one of every three dollars it spends.

The deficit would fall to $706 billion by 2014, but, ominously, resume rising and top $1 trillion again by 2020. And that number assumes a return to sustained economic growth. The near-term rationale for deficits — propping up the economy — would be long gone.

Focusing on the budget's impact for Florida — more bucks for Everglades restoration, fewer for NASA — misses the bigger picture. For all the lip service he pays to fiscal responsibility, Mr. Obama would not do nearly enough to bring spending in line with revenues.

The last Democrat in the White House, Bill Clinton, largely shelved his campaign plans for extra spending when he faced big deficits. Not so with Mr. Obama.

In his State of the Union speech, the president touted a spending freeze, but said it would exclude national security as well as Medicare and other entitlement programs. As a result, he would raise overall spending

The gist:
If President Obama won't heed his own warnings about the deficit spending, Congress must.

next year by 3 percent.

For example, he would pump billions more into foreign aid, research and education — such an important for federal spending when the nation is drowning in debt. The increases include $17 billion for Pell grants, roughly doubling that program for college students. The president also wants to make it an entitlement. This is the same guy who couldn't find $3 billion a year to preserve U.S. leadership in manned space exploration.

Mr. Obama would let tax cuts passed under President George W. Bush expire for families earning more than $250,000 a year for individuals earning more than $200,000. He would impose higher levies on big businesses, including banks and oil companies. Those are defensible steps, especially given the budget chasm.

But the president also would expand his middle-class tax break of $800 per couple and $400 per individual another year, at a cost of more than $60 billion. He would blow another $30 billion or so on $250 checks for each Social Security recipient, regardless of income, because they aren't in line for a cost of living increase. These are politically smart, fiscally dumb ideas.

The president would leave the real heavy lifting on cutting the budget to a bipartisan commission. Such a panel is needed, but its prospects for success will be slim if Republican leaders won't embrace it.

Members of both parties who are serious about dealing with the deficit will not exclude any part of government — even the Pentagon — from scrutiny in Congress' version of the budget. They'll reject unaffordable spending and tax cuts. They'll put Washington on the road to a more sustainable future.

TO : THE EDITORS, ORLANDO SENTINEL
    633 N. ORANGE AVENUE   EXHIBIT 2-6   PAGE 1
    ORLANDO, FLORIDA 32801

FROM :   Dr. & Mrs. Frank DeFelice
             Rainbow Resort
             Lot 470
             700 Co. Rd. 630A
             Frostproof, FL 33843

DATE : FEBRUARY 3, 2010

SUBJECT : RESPONSE TO YOUR "THE NATION'S RED-INK ALERT" (2/3/10)

The federal budget is NOT "on the road to ruin with long term deficits that threaten the nation's economy and security".
The correct discretionary fiscal policy tool – the only way to help the economy – is deficit spending. Deficit spending is NOT "diverting dollars from investments that would make America more prosperous and secure" but spending more on those investments.
We do NOT "depend on China and other foreign creditors" to fund our deficit spending. U.S. Treasuries are auctioned off to the highest bidders; so whomever will pay the most gets them. The Chinese know a good investment when they see it, and by bidding up the price they will pay, keep our interest costs low.
There is NOT a " crushing debt burden left on future generations" because automatic re-financing of the debt that goes on every week means that nobody will ever have to pay it off.
There is no "security" issue from the purchases of our debt by foreigners as you imply. What are you suggesting – that the Chinese and other "foreigners" will foreclose on the U.S.? Or will they invade us? Get serious!
No mainstream qualified economist (as we are; check our credentials) would accept your notion that deficit spending or the National debt would somehow "risk another economic meltdown". This is just pure nonsense used by you and others who are caught up in the idea that debt per se is bad.
Inre: the red ink numbers – $1.5, 1.41 and 1.27 trillion – you should apply DeFelice's Law of Absolute Numbers: Absolute Numbers Mean Absolutely Nothing. In theoretically sound economic analysis you have to look at debt simultaneously with debt carrying capacity : the National Debt and National Income. When you make this calculation you find that · National debt is only 2 8 .% of National Income. Is this good or bad? Compare that with the rule-of-thumb used for mortgage lending, which is a borrower can safely carry two and a half times his annual income. Of course the term of the loan and the interest rate have to be factored in, and mortgage payments include amortization of the principal. The National debt – NO MATTER HOW BIG AS AN ABSOLUTE NUMBER – is such a small percentage of National Income that it poses no threat to our economic system. We are NOT, therefore, "drowning in debt".

EXHIBIT 2-6 PAGE 2

Looking at specific spending and cuts you mention, you are very parochial to oppose Pell Grants but favor manned space expenditures. From the national economic point of view, increased spending for both is in order at this time.

You imply that Mr. Obama should "bring spending in line with revenues"; i.e., have a balanced budget. A balanced budget is NOT good for the economy – not now, hardly ever. Look at what happened in Florida and all the states with balanced budget laws when the recession hit. They had to raise taxes, cut spending or some of both, all of which make the recession worse. If the federal government had such a stupid law, the recession would have regressed to a full blown Depression.

A balanced budget – spending equal to revenues – is bad on the topside of the economic cycle because the tax-take revenues that increase with the economic up-swing should not be spent; they cause inflation at that point in the cycle. Correct discretionary fiscal policy at that time is to have a surplus – NOT a balanced budget.

Only in a perfect world would the level of aggregate demand be exactly what is necessary for non-inflationary full employment. We do not live in a perfect world, so we will always need to run deficits or surpluses – not a balanced budget.

Copy: Prof .David Gergen

CHAPTER 3:
MONEY AND BANKING

From a micro-economic technical point of view, "money" is anything acceptable in payment for debt. Back in the Great Depression, when people had to go to the doctor and had no money to pay for the $2 office visit. (That's right; it was $2 then!), they brought produce from their garden or a chicken to pay the doctor. The doctor accepted this as payment; therefore, a chicken was money.

We are more interested in money in the macro-economic sense of what important functions it has for the operation of the economy. The chicken-doctor situation was the transactions function of money, but for that method of transaction to work in the macro-economy it would require a "coincidence of wants" that would be a very inefficient way to carry out economic transactions. That is, the patient wanted the doctor's services and the doctor wanted the chicken. This transaction worked because there was a coincidence of wants. It's a barter transaction that only works in isolated situations; and would not work in the macro-economy. So, a monetary unit is the necessary as a medium of exchange, so that individuals do not have to look far and wide for the person who has what they want and who also wants what they have to barter – the coincidence of wants problem is avoided.

Money also performs the function of "store of value." That is, money not spent is saved to be spent later. When people do that they are storing the value represented by the money not spent presently.

"Money" in the macro-economic sense is short for the money supply, which consists of the total amount of currency in circulation and the total credit balances in commercial banks checking accounts, which are called Demand Deposits (DD). Currency in circulation, which is Federal Reserve Notes (NOT government obligations), accounts for only about 20% of the money supply; DD for 80%. And about 90% of all transactions take place using checking account (DD) money.

Since the government does not issue currency, the question arises as to what "backs" money. The short answer is: "nothing." Currency is not backed by gold or silver or anything tangible. It derives its value from its purchasing power. What can you exchange it for, and how much of it does it take to buy what you want. People only hold money as a store of value because they have faith the government will control prices – not let them rise excessively – so that the purchasing power is not lost. It's psychology in economics – as long as people think that the value will be maintained – that's what "backs" money. That is why the government is required to control inflation.

Governmental economic policies to control inflation are carried out by the FED which has done a reasonably good job at keeping inflation down. Unfortunately, those actions of the FED to keep inflation in check cause unemployment to rise. The government also has a responsibility to fight unemployment, so the FED is caught in an endless battle to keep inflation down but not to cause unemployment.

The trade off between the two was described many years ago by an economist by the name of Phillips: the Phillips curve. This is another two-variable relationship which can be explained very easily on a simple graph, which are two-dimensional.

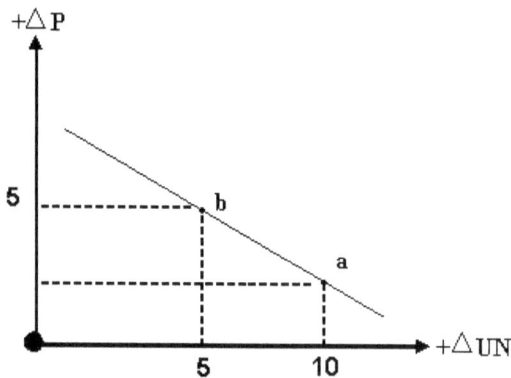

$+\Delta P$ = price level increase $+\Delta UN$ = unemployment increase

Point a = low inflation and high unemployment (early 2010 situation)

Most economists will settle for a 5% increase in the price level to get down to a 5% unemployment (point b). Currently (early 2010) we have 10% unemployment and virtually zero % inflation – not acceptable. We are better off with more inflation and less unemployment because when unemployment is high, economic growth slows down (less output), standard of living declines, and distribution of income is more inequitable. With inflation, we get more output, more economic growth, the standard of living increases and income distribution is more equitable. The inflation index (BLS's CPI) becomes an index to adjust the incomes of those hurt by inflation. For example, annual Social Security (SS) payments are increased by the percentage increase in inflation. So, the adjustment for inflation is a much easier to handle than the economic havoc wreaked by high unemployment.

There are basically just two kinds of banks: commercial banks and "thrift" institutions. The essential difference used to be that only the commercial banks had checking accounts. But several years back the "thrifts" – savings banks, savings and loan associations, and credit unions – developed a way for their customers to access their funds like commercial bank customers do – writing a check. Previously, customers at thrifts had to withdraw their funds to use them to pay for things. To compete with commercial banks' checking accounts, the thrifts developed a "product" called "Negotiable Order of Withdrawal" (NOW), which lets them function just like the checking accounts at commercial banks. All the thrifts were originally intermediaries – membership organizations whereby those who placed their savings there were providing loans for members, but that changed with the introduction of NOW's. Credit unions are non-profit institutions and can, therefore, loan at lower rates than either commercial banks or savings banks which have to make a profit to pay dividends to their owners – the shareholders.

The most important function of the commercial banks was, and still is, that their lending operations create money. We will see later in this chapter exactly how that works. If lending creates money, then when loans are repaid money is destroyed. The money supply is decreased. So, whether the money supply is increasing or decreasing depends on the ratio "of loans made to loans paid."

When thrifts were just intermediaries – moving money from one customer to another – they could not change the money supply like the commercial banks. But with NOW's, they also can change the money supply. The underlying fundamental fact that makes money supply changes come about is that all banks have a fractional reserve system – only a fraction of deposits have to be held as a reserve – called the Reserve Requirement (RR) – against the liability the bank incurs when it takes customers' deposits. Deposits in banks are a liability for banks, so that those banks who are stupid enough to brag about how big their deposits are, are just advertising how big their liabilities are. They owe the total amount of the deposits to depositors, but only have a fraction of it available. If all the depositors came at one time to get the balance in their accounts – called a "run on the bank" – no bank would have enough to satisfy all their customers' demands.

The difference between the deposit amounts and the RR is called Excess Reserves (ER), and this is what the banks have AVAILABLE to lend out. Just because it is available does not mean it will get loaned out, and when the banks do not choose to make loans, we get what is called a "credit crunch," which is just another description of a decrease in the money supply.

Some banks get their charter – their right to go into the banking business – from the federal government. We call these banks "national banks." Others get their charter from a state government. We call these "state banks." You can generally tell them apart by their name. If the word "national" is in the name, it is a federally chartered bank; if it is not, it is a state chartered bank.

All national banks must become members of the Federal Reserve System (the FED), and state banks may join if they choose, which most big banks do. If a bank is a member of the Federal Deposit Insurance Corporation (FDIC), it must become a FED Member Bank.

The FDIC insures customers accounts up to $250,000 (a temporary increase put in to bail out customers whose banks failed in the 2009-10 recession because the limit was $100,000 but many customers had more than the insured amount – dumb customers!?), which it finances by charging all members a small fee – percentage of deposits – plus it has a line of credit from the U.S. Treasury. In 2009 it paid out $Billions to the depositors in the 140 banks that failed in that year. All those banks that failed were Member Banks of the Federal Reserve System, which tells us that the FED is failing to properly regulate banking. Banks fail because they make bad loans – ones that are "non-performing" – not being paid back like the "sub-prime" mortgage loans made to people with insufficient income to make the payments, and they also engage in risky business – e.g., a "trading desk," which does nothing but speculation for short term gains in various markets. Such trading was a factor in the commodities futures market in driving up oil prices to $150/barrel and gasoline to $4-5/gallon. And these poor, bad, wrong banking practices are still going on today (early 2010) because there is no authority to stop them. Sure, they are a little more selective in mortgage lending, but they all still have trading desks and engage in all the non-banking activities that lead to the stock market and housing market crashes.

In England there is a Bank of England. In Canada there is a Bank of Canada. In France there is a Bank of France. In Japan there is a Bank of Japan. These are the central banks of those countries that regulate banking and control the money supply in those countries. The Federal Reserve System (FED) is the U.S. central bank, which is supposed to regulate banking and control the money supply as is required of all central banks. The FED does neither. 140 Member Banks of the Federal Reserve System would not have failed in 2009 if they were properly regulated. And the so-called "credit crunch" of late 2008 into 2009 and still continuing into early 2010 is evidence that the FED failed to control the money supply. "Credit crunch" is a synonym for the banks not making loans. When the banks do not make loans, the money supply decreases.

The central bank is not supposed to decrease the money supply in a recession; it is supposed to increase it. So the FED did not carry out its other central bank responsibility – control of the money supply – for the good of the economy. UNLESS AND UNTIL we have a good central bank – one that performs those two essential functions of a central bank – we will continue to have financial fiascoes that sometimes precipitate negative changes in the real economy: reduced output and high unemployment.

The reasons why the FED does not, and can not, perform the essential functions of the central bank are:

1. The Member Banks, where monetary policies are supposed to be carried out, are independent businesses, run for their own benefit regardless of what the economy needs.
2. The FED is an SRO (Self Regulating Organization) in which the regulated are the regulators. This is a no-brainer conflict of interests. Self regulation does not work.
3. Neither Ben Bernanke, the current FED Chairman, nor Barney Frank (Chairman of the House Financial Services Committee), nor Chris Dodd (Chairman of the Senate Banking Committee) can "make them (the banks) do anything," said Barney Frank after Geithner threw $Billions into the banks and started buying up their bad loans to no avail. (Maybe we should revert to prayer as Hank Paulson did in the fall of 2008, when he did not know what to do about the financial system problems and called his wife, Wendy, and asked her to pray for him.)
4. The Federal Reserve SYSTEM IS the SYSTEMIC RISK in the economy, which is ironic because there were those in government who thought the FED could be the watchdog to stop those in the financial sector from doing things that endangered the financial system. The FED is not really a risk to the financial system; it is a certainty that it will do the wrong thing because it has a fatal flaw in its make up (repeating for emphasis): private business – the Member banks of the Federal Reserve System – can not be expected to carry out public policy when it is not in their own best interests to do so. This is something that has been known from the beginning and is summed up by a cute "one liner" in all economics textbooks: "You (the FED) can not push up a balloon by a string." This is a tacit admission that the FED can not do anything to help the economy

(the balloon) up when it is down. Recent experience proves that point again.

Interest rates were lowered to near zero (!) with no measurable effect on helping the economy.

5. It is sad to say, but what is in the best interests of the banks to do is what is BAD for the economy. And is just not in the downturns of the economy, when they reduce their lending, which is the right thing for them to do in their own best interests, but when the economy is at the top of the cycle, the banks are increasing their lending, which is good for them, but bad for the economy because they are increasing the money supply which adds to the inflationary pressures at that point. At the top of the cycle we are close to full employment; therefore more spending can not put more resources to work; it can only bid up prices – cause inflation.

6. Our economy is at risk because money and banking can not be controlled for the public good. You need only to understand what the FED is to see why these problems occur. The FED consists of a Board of Directors with headquarters in Washington, 12 regional federal reserve banks (with branches), and thousands of independent commercial banks that are Member Banks of the Federal Reserve System. The Member Banks are, therefore, the FED. The FED is not some outside agency in Washington with authority over the Member Banks. The Member Banks staff the regional federal reserve banks' board of directors where regulative rules are made for each of the 12 regions (not uniform throughout the system). The banks regulate the banks. The FED is an SRO. No good. It can not be fixed. It needs to be replaced by a good central bank:

THE BANK OF THE UNITED STATES OF AMERICA, owned and operated by the people, for the people (NOT for the financial sector as is the case with the FED).

The financial sector is comprised of about 8,000 banks. This is NOT counting each bank location as a separate bank; i.e., Bank of America with thousands of locations where it has a bank is just one bank; thousands of brokerage houses; thousands of insurance companies and hundreds of other financial institutions, two national securities exchanges, and a dozen regional stock exchanges. All of these thousands of businesses added together account for only 10% (in normal times) of the U.S. economy. There are three important conclusions to draw from that fact:

1. The stock market is not the economy.
2. Monetary and fiscal policies to correct financial sector problems at the expense of the economy is a case of "the tail wagging the dog."
3. No single firm in the financial sector, regardless of its individual size is "too big to fail." Such a failure could not cause widespread problems in the real economy because by itself is insignificant relative to the size of the economy. (This is another application of DeFelice's Law of Absolute Numbers: Absolute numbers Mean Absolutely Nothing.)

Hank Paulson's repeated assertions that if he had not bailed out AIG, "unemployment would have gone to 25%" is absolute nonsense. The correct way to look at the whole situation is to point out that if the regulators – the FED and the SEC – did not allow the boom-and-bust cycle to take place, there would have been no unemployment at all. In the waning days of the Bush (43) Administration, when financial firms were starting to fail, Treasury Secretary Paulson called his wife and said, "Wendy, something has to be done; they're expecting me to do something, and I don't know what to do; pray for me." What he did was the bailouts of businesses that should have been allowed to fail. AIG is an insurance company that sold coverage to brokerage firms guaranteeing that the interest would be paid on all those packaged up sub-prime mortgage loans that brokers had on their books. Goldman-Sachs had $Billions of such securities, so when the housing market crashed and mortgages were not being paid, they stood to lose $Billions if AIG could not make good on their insurance, which they could not. AIG made a big mistake in setting the premiums for those policies, and should have paid the price for their poor (stupid?) management decisions – go out of business. We find it "smelly" that the first bailout money for AIG was $10 Billion that went directly to Goldman-Sachs in October 2008 where Paulson had been CEO prior to his Treasury Secretary stint. Citigroup got $45 Billion.

Bailouts, in general, are wrong for three reasons:

1. When a firm can not operate profitably, it is a signal from the market that either its output is too high priced (and is not selling) or not enough people want it for them to produce it profitably. It makes no difference whether the firm is producing a good or a service nor what industry it is in – which includes the financial sector. It is just sheer nonsense that any firm in any industry that fails is a threat that the entire economy could collapse. Either way, the market signal is

saying: "get out of business." That gives the economy the use of scarce resources in those firms to be used more efficiently – by lower cost producers or to produce other wanted products.

2. In the long – centuries – view of economic growth and development, structural change is of the essence; - it's what economic development is all about. Certain industries die; others replace them. All economies start out as agricultural. Nations have to feed themselves. When agricultural production gets so efficient that one farmer can produce enough food for hundreds of people, that releases labor from the agricultural sector to into manufacturing. Non-profitable farms are shut down providing more resources for manufacturing. Manufactured output replaces agricultural output – the agricultural sector declines and the manufacturing sector grows. When firms in the manufacturing sector can not be run profitably, they should be allowed to fail so that their resources can be used where they will produce something that has enough demand for it to be profitable. Profit is the signal from the market that it is something people want. Non-profitable operation of a business is a signal from the market that people do not want the product.

3. If the economy is to grow and develop, firms must be allowed to fail. GM and Chrysler, who were also bailed out with taxpayers' money, should have been allowed to fail. Signals were sent by the market telling them to do so. There is no need to maintain the production of any goods that can not be produced profitably. We do not need to keep "our automotive industry" because the third stage of economic growth and development is to move out of production of goods to the production of services. That is where we are now. 70% of the U.S. labor force is now (early 2010) in the service sector.

There is no such thing as an "investment bank." Investment banking is a function of brokerage businesses. A synonym for investment banking would be "underwriting." Underwriting is the process of preparing paperwork required to sell new issues of securities. The SEC, and state securities ("Blue Sky") laws require certain information to accompany the offer of new securities to prospective buyers. This information is contained in a little booklet called the Prospectus (Offering Circular at the state level). A Principal at the SEC registered brokerage firm that is putting the new securities on the market must sign at the bottom – underwrite – that the Prospectus contains all the SEC required information – what the firm is using the money raised for, who the officers and directors of the corporation are, a current certified financial statement plus everything the SEC thinks potential investors should know to be informed investors. (Since the SEC is a big bunch of lawyers, the Prospectus is a big bunch of legalese gobble-de-gook that nobody reads!)

Repeating for emphasis: There is no such thing as an investment bank, just investment banking, which is underwriting of new issues to be put in the market – sold (brokers are essentially salesmen) – by an SEC registered broker, whose salesmen are also SEC registered as Registered Representatives ("reps").

Broker/DEALER is the correct designation of SEC registered firms in the brokerage business because they not only "broker" – act as an agent between buyers and sellers – they also are in the securities business for themselves – buying and selling for their own account. They act as principals in that case. They "take a position" – buy for their own account – in certain issues, and sometimes become "market makers" in those issues. There are some small SEC registered Broker/Dealers (B/D's) that deal in just one firm's stock; e.g., IBM.

B/D's have to disclose the capacity in which they are dealing with customers. They can be either brokers – agent; or dealers – principal. As a broker, they buy or sell for the customer – act as his agent in the market. As a dealer, they buy or sell for the customer from (for) their own account. They choose whichever way they want to handle their buy/sell orders, but they have to inform the customer of their capacity on every transaction. Sometimes it is beneficial for both the customer and the B/D to buy for and sell from the B/D's account. Stocks are quoted in the market at bid and asked prices. If the B/D can buy it down close to the bid price, he can "mark it up" – add to what he paid – and sell it to the customer for less than what the customer would have paid if the B/D bought at the ask price and added a commission. When you think a little about the way brokers work, you can see that they have what, for the customer, is a negative incentive, because if they are working for you as agent – for a commission, which is based on the price, the higher the price, the more commission they make!

The least well understood, but one of the most important, macro-economic fundamental facts is how money is created. That's right, money is created, not printed by the government. What makes it a little difficult to understand is that you need to know a little elementary accounting. You need to know what a balance sheet is, what assets, liabilities and equity are and the standard double entry – debit and credit – method used in accounting. (There is an appendix to this chapter, Elements of Accounting, if you need to refresh your understanding of the basic concepts.)

There is a simple basic equation that helps to understand the balance sheet: $A = L + E$, where A = Assets, L = Liabilities, and E = Equity. Assets are what a firm owns; Liabilities are what a firm owes; and Equity is the difference between the two, which can be determined by simple algebra:

A – L = E. Equity is sometimes called Net Worth and in banking accounting: Net Capital.

Perhaps the best explanatory method for understanding money creation would be to explain how a bank gets started (so you would know how to do it if you decided to). First, you charter a corporation, which is done at the state level of government. In your application, you need to name your directors (usually a minimum of three) and your corporate officers (also a minimum of three), specify what line of business you are going into, how much stock you plan to issue, and file this with a small fee. A corporation raises equity money by selling stock to the public, and by directors and officers putting in their own money. Stock sold to the public must be registered with state authorities, a division of the Attorney General's office, or with the SEC if it is to be sold in inter-state commerce (across state lines), and underwritten by a licensed Broker/Dealer (B/D). "Underwriting," you will recall is what the general public calls "investment banking," a function of B/D's – NOT a bank. You have to provide potential purchasers of your stock with all the pertinent data they need to know to make an informed decision as to whether or not this stock would be a good investment for them. The underwriting function of B/D's guarantees that all the necessary information has been provided and is contained in the Offering Circular ("Prospectus" at the federal level), which must be presented to potential purchasers of all new issues of stock, which makes it the official sales document. Stockbrokers are basically salesmen, and like all salesmen like to "puff the product" – say things to make a sale – which sometimes are not true.

Let's say we want to capitalize our bank at $4 Million. (Capital requirements to start a bank are set by government authorities at the state or federal level – depending on whether you are starting a state or national bank.) We go to a big NYSE broker – say Merrill Lynch (ML) – to see if they will help us raise this money. They laugh at us because a $4 Million issue is not worth their time and efforts. The standard underwriting fee is 1% of the $4 Million = $40,000 and "blue sky" (state) laws generally limit sales commissions to 10%, which would be only (!) $400,000. They are not interested in such small deals; so, we find a small local National Association of Securities Dealers (NASD) broker that will help us. They sell all $4 Million of our stock, deducting a 1% underwriting fee and $400,000 sales commissions, and give us the proceeds: $3.56 Million. Now comes the double entry accounting: The cash is an asset; to increase an asset account, you debit it; and you must credit something on the other side of the balance sheet (or it won't balance!) – stockholders equity is the proper credit: common stock. Now that you have your required Net Capital, you need a building to do business from. Let's say we want a 6,000 SF building, which can be built @ $200/SF - $1.2 Million, but we do not want to use our capital for a building.

We are not in the real estate business; we are in the banking business and we make money by making loans, not by owning buildings. So, we get the building built, sell it to an insurance company (who have billions of premiums they have to invest so they can pay claims) and we lease it back from them. This changes nothing on our balance sheet; we still have $3.56 million we can lend out. We open the door for businesses and get customer deposits from other banks by offering "freebies" - free checks, free notary services, free money orders, maybe even toasters and microwaves - anything but interest on their checking account balances, which was found to be an underlying cause for the bank failures during the Great Depression and, therefore, outlawed. When customers make deposits, the accounting is debit cash and credit liabilities - accounts payable. Customer deposits are a liability of banks. If a (stupid, not us!) bank brags about how large their deposits are, they are just (stupidly) indicating that they have big liabilities! With customer deposits their net capital does not change because the cash coming in offsets the deposit liabilities. We call customer accounts Demand Deposits (DD), because that's what a checking account is.

Banks are not required to keep all the money in the bank to cover all DD's. We have a "fractional reserve" system. The fraction of the DD's that must be set aside is called the Required Reserve (RR), and the balance of the deposit is called the Excess Reserve (ER). The ER can be loaned out, and when the proceeds of these loans come back into the banks (ours or any bank), they are an increase in the Money supply (M) because DD's are 80% of the money supply. MONEY IS THUS CREATED BY THE BANKS MAKING LOANS. NOT BY THE GOVERNMENT PRINTING IT.

Of course, the process is reversible. When the borrowers pay off the loans by decreasing their DD's, the money supply is decreased. Whether the total money supply in the economy is increasing or decreasing depends on the ratio of "loans made to loans paid," which is a dynamic process -- changes being made over time, "24/7" as they say.

But wait, there is just a little more to it than the initial loan and initial decrease in DD's. Our bank can only increase the money supply by the amount of ER's we have, but the banking SYSTEM -- thousands of banks -- can increase the money supply by a multiple of the ER's because of the fractional reserve requirement. As the initial increase in DD gets spent it moves to other banks DD's, who in turn gain ER's that they can lend out, so that there is an expansion of the money supply that takes place similiar to the multiplier effect on National Income from a change is AGGD, but unlike the value of the multiplier, which gets bigger with a higher MPC; the expansion of the money supply is smaller, the higher the RR. As a numerical value it is the reciprocal of the RR as a percentage.

Let's say our RR is 20%, which is .20 (= 1/5), the reciprocal of which is 5 (1/.20 = 5). The theoretical limit to the expansion of the money supply throughout the entire banking system is 5X the ER. It never does reach the maximum expansion for several reasons, the most important of which is that the reserve ratio is not the same for all banks, and banks do not have to lend their ER's. Banks are independently owned private businesses whose business is making loans. Banking is a profitable business only if they make good loans -- ones that they are confident will be repaid with interest on time.

When banks do not have confidence that they will get paid back, they do not loan. This occurs during recessions, which are not good times to make good loans. The borrowers represent an unacceptable risk. This is what causes what is commonly called a "credit crunch" -- which is what happened in the 2009-10 recession. The money supply was decreased by this correct response by the banks to their goal of making profit via good loans. So, a very important conclusion to be made at this point is that banks doing what is good for them is at the same time doing what is bad for the economy. The money supply should be increased in recessions, not decreased. On the up-side of the business cycle, banks are "beating the bushes" to make loans because most all borrowers are doing well and it's, therefore, low risk to do so. But increasing the money supply at this time is bad for the economy -- when we are at full employment -- because the additional money can not generate more output, just higher prices -- inflation.

We need to bring our central bank, the FED, into this explanation of the money creation process. The FED sets the Reserve Ratio (RR) for all Member Banks of the Federal Reserve System. We are a Member Bank because one thing we did to get customers was provide insurance for their accounts via the Federal Deopsit Insurance Corporation (FDIC). When we became a member of the FDIC, we were required to become a Member Bank of the FED. We were required then by the FED to hold a specified RR as a deposit in the regional federal reserve bank. (They debit cash and credit customers' accounts just like we do.) They then "loan" this cash out, mostly by buying U.S. Treasury obligations: Bills, Notes and Bonds. Over the years the years (the FED was established in 1913), it has bought so many that its balance sheet has $Trillions worth, which gives the FED $Millions of interest paid by the Treasury. Though the FED is a privately owned (surprise!; not a government agency) banking system, it is not a for-profit business, so it, therefore, returns to the U.S. Treasury $Millions every year in excess of the small return it credits to Member Banks reserve accounts.

It also uses these $Trillions of U.S. Treasuries as a means to change interest rates. This takes place by the actions of the Federal Open Market Committee (FOMC), that operates out of the NY regional federal reserve bank, selling these bonds in the open market, which drives down the price, and, therefore, interest rates up when they want to raise interest rates. (Bond prices and the interest return are inversely related because the stated interest rate on the bond is fixed. So if you have to pay more to get a fixed dollar amount, your return [as a %)]goes down.)

When the FOMC sells bonds, they are simultaneously decreasing the money supply. Whomever buys the bonds from the fed pays by decreasing their checking account, and checking accounts – DD's – ARE MONEY. This is called the FED's "tight money" policy – less of it and higher interest rates.

When the FED wants to lower interest rates, the FOMC buys bonds in the open market, driving up the price, and, therefore, lowering interest rates. Sellers are smart to take the capital gain – from the higher price – now rather than wait for the later payment of interest. There is a time-value of money: future dollars have to be discounted to get the present value of them. When the FED is buying bonds, it is simultaneously also increasing the money supply. Payments made for the bonds are an increase in DD's – checking accounts – somewhere in the banking system. Increases in DD's is an increase in the money supply – DD's ARE MONEY. This is the FED's "easy money" policy – more of it and lower interest rates. When the FED changes interest rates (returns) on U.S. Treasuries, that shifts the entire risk-return curve up or down, depending on which way the FED is going. Remember the risk-return from Chapter 1 where T-Bills were at a very lowest rate – always the lowest of all securities – with zero risk? When that rate where the T-Bills are at zero risk – the Y-intercept – moves up or down, the whole curve moves with it, thus changing all interest rates.

Regulation of banking is by the FED. The FED is the banks. The banks regulate the banks. The regulated are the regulators. This is a no-brainer conflict of interests. Self regulation does not work. The job of the central bank in the economy is to regulate banking and control the money supply. The FED does neither. In order for our economy to work well, we need a central bank that performs those essential functions that the FED does not and can not perform because of the way the FED is set up. The Member Banks are private for-profit businesses, and doing what is good for their business is bad for the economy. This is a fatal flaw in our central bank system that must be corrected if we are to develop "a better way to do business" as President Obama correctly said is necessary for us not to repeat the 2009-10 recession.

One of the places where the FED is remiss in its regulatory responsibility is in the leveraging that takes place in banks, which takes place via the increase in DD, which are equivalent to "borrowed money" in non-bank businesses. In our bank when deposits hit $35.6 Million, leveraging is 10 : 1 - $10 of other peoples' money for every dollar of ours. That's how all businesses expand – with other peoples' money – (and their profits from operations if they do not pay them out to the owners of the business – the stockholders). No leverage, no expansion. So, no leverage is poor management, but too much leverage is bad because there is risk that when business is bad, liabilities can not be met. In the 2009-10 recession some banks were leveraged as high as 30 : 1, and when their loan assets went bad – people did not pay their mortgages – the liablities exceeded total asset values, they became bankrupt. FDIC came in, closed them down (sold them to other banks with adequate capital), paid off any depositors who wanted their money – up to $250,000. 140 of such failures of Member Banks of the Federal Reserve System took place in 2009 and it is predicted that an even greater number will take place in 2010. Improperly controlled leverage and bad loans are doing them in. Both of these problems would not occur if we had a good central bank, because a good central bank regulates banks' capital structure – leveraging – and sets low-risk standards for all loans, which includes mortgages, credit cards, and margin account loans.

APPENDIX TO CHAPTER 3:
ELEMENTS OF ACCOUNTING

There are two basic accounting statements that together explain the financial situation of any business: the Balance Sheet and the Income Statement. And banks, of course, are businesses.

The Balance Sheet is a picture of a business at a point in time. It lists the asset values and the claims against those assets by either creditors of the business or by the owners. Creditors claims are called liabilities and owners' claims are called equity or net worth. There is a basic identity in accounting that says the total value of all assets must necessarily equal the total value of liabilities and equity. The Balance Sheet can be looked at as a statement showing what a business has as earning assets and on the other side how it financed those assets. Any business can have no more assets than what it has financed, either by borrowed money or by the owners' investment in the business. This is why assets must equal liabilities plus equity and why it is called a Balance Sheet.

Traditionally, assets are listed on the left side of a Balance Sheet, and liabilities and equity on the right side. Additions to assets are called debits by accountants, and additions to liabilities or equity are called credits. This is to allow double entry accounting to operate. That is, in accounting, any transaction requires two changes on the Balance Sheet. If, for example, a business buys some inventory on credit from a supplier, the asset "inventory" is debited, and the liability "accounts payable" is credited. Total debits and credits must, therefore, always be equal just the same as both sides of the Balance Sheet must be equal. When assets are reduced, they are credited, and when liabilities are reduced they are debited. Actually, there would be an intermediate transaction to record in this case. When inventory was sold, cash would be credited. But still the reduction of assets would exactly equal the reduction of liabilities and the Balance Sheet would still balance.

Both sides of the Balance Sheet must be equal in total, but no single item is necessarily offset by some single item on the other side. In the example above it made no difference if it was cash or inventory that was reduced when the account payable was reduced. Either way, total assets remained equal to total liabilities and equity.

Valuation of assets, except for cash, is rather in-exact in accounting statements. Generally, they are listed at cost on the Balance Sheet. Market value or earning capacity may be quite different.

Assets are generally subdivided into at least two categories: current assets and fixed assets. Current assets consist of cash, inventory, accounts receivable, and any marketable securities (stocks or bonds of other companies, or government bonds) that a business may own. Fixed assets are such things as equipment, buildings, and machinery. In addition, there may be intangible assets such as goodwill, patents, and copyrights.

Liabilities, likewise, are subdivided into current liabilities and long term liabilities. Here, the division is basically on the basis of when the obligation is due. If it is due within a year from the date of the Balance Sheet, it is a current liability. If it is not due within one year, it is a long term liability.

It is important to note at this point that the leveraging that takes place in banks is mostly a current liability because the source of funds is from the customer checking account deposits, that are DEMAND DEPOSITS, which means that they must be paid by banks immediately when customers want their money. Since banks hold only a fractional reserve for customer accounts, leveraging is very risky in banking. If all customers were to demand immediate return of the money in their checking accounts, no bank could do that. When that happens, which is called a 'run' on the bank, if the bank can not sell its assets for enough to pay its liabilities – the demand deposits – it is bankrupt and has to go out of business.

The equity accounts are indication of ownership and will differ by type of business. In a corporation, the owners' interest is shown by the stock outstanding. There may be both preferred and common stock. In addition, any profits of the business that are not paid out to the stockholders are ownership interest in the business and show up in the equity account "retained earnings." Proprietorships – individually owned businesses – and partnerships' equity accounts differ only in that the owner's name appears as the provider of capital and recipient of earnings.

The Income Statement, unlike the Balance Sheet is not a picture of a business at a point in time. It is a statement showing what has happened in a business over a period of time, usually a year. It is not necessary to understand the Income Statement to understand what goes on in the banks in the money creation process because all the accounts involved in that process are Balance Sheet accounts.

CHAPTER 4:
CAUSES OF THE RECESSION

There were three boom-and-bust cycles – called "bubbles" – that took place more or less simultaneously for a few years prior to the bust of the financial bubble that burst with the stock market crash in 2008. There was a bubble that was called the housing market bubble, but it was much broader than just housing and included commercial real estate development as well. A third bubble, not widely acknowledged, was in the commodities futures market where oil went to $150/barrel and gasoline to $4-$5/gallon.

The high price of oil and gasoline had the effect of lowering the consumption part of aggregate demand, because when the price of "other goods" – gasoline in this case – goes up demand is decreased by the amount of the additional spending required for gasoline. And there is unanimity of professional opinion that the decrease in consumption spending was the correct explanation for the recession. But that still leaves us with the necessity to explain how the financial sector problems, including the stock market crash and the housing bubble contributed to the recession. And we also need to explain how the bubbles were created.

All three bubbles have a single fundamental cause: highly leveraged speculation for short-term capital gains. In the housing market leveraging was almost infinite – meaning that no money was required to buy a house. (Remember? leveraging is the debt to equity ratio in a financial transaction.) No money down = no equity = infinite leveraging. (Any number divided by zero = infinity.)

In the stock market, a "regular" account is a margin account; so, virtually all of stock market sales are leveraged. The margin is the down-payment. When it is 25%, leveraging is 4:1, at 20%, it is 5:1; at 10%, 10:1. You get it: Leveraging in the stock market is the reciprocal of the margin requirement percentage. The balance of the purchase price comes from loans from the banks, who also leveraged, some as high as 30:1 before the crash.

In the commodities futures market, margins are down to 10% and lower. 10% would be 10:1, which means if you go into that market with $1 Million dollars, you can buy $10 Million of securities. Securities there are contracts to buy or sell commodities at a guaranteed price at some future date. One million dollars is the minimum for an individual to get into a so-called "hedge fund" (that really do not do hedging at all!). Therefore, a hedge fund with 1,000 owners putting in $1 Million each has $1 Billion, which leveraged at 10:1 gives them the opportunity to buy $10 Billion of futures contracts. That's enough buying power to drive up the price. When they have driven it up enough to cover the interest on the loan and the brokers commission plus a little more they sell…the percentage of profit can be real small, but on sales of $10 Billion the total amount of dollars is large. On Wall Street this is called "pump and dump." And it is done not only by hedge funds, but by brokerage firms for their own account and even by banks for their own account.

Cycles happen all the time in the business sector of the economy. The stock market goes up; the stock market goes down. This, by itself can not cause a recession because the stock market is just one RELATIVELY small part of the financial sector, and the entire financial sector – thousands of banks, thousands of brokerage firms, thousands of insurance companies and thousands of other financial institutions all added together – constitute only 10% of the economy in normal (pre-bubble) times.

Just to understand how unimportant any one firm in the financial sector is to the economy, let's take the case of one of the biggest firms in the financial sector: Bank of America, and note that it has thousands of branch banks all over the country (world?) but is just one bank of thousands and its failure could not, would not, affect the economy in any appreciable way. AIG is just one insurance company among thousands, and though it is big by itself, RELATIVE to the economy it is insignificant; and it would not, could not, affect the economy appreciably if it failed.

All that is needed to prove this is to apply DeFelice's Law of Absolute Numbers: Absolute numbers mean absolutely nothing. The absolute numbers we are referring to are the dollar values of Bank of America and AIG or any other quantitative measure of their size you want to use. You have to compare that number to the size of the U.S. economy to get the RELATIVE UN-IMPORTANCE of any single firm no matter how large by itself. Let's say that AIG is a $50 Billion firm. The U.S. economy is (in late 2010) a $15 Trillion economy. $50 Billion is three tenths of one percent (.003) of the U.S. economy, and therefore RELATIVELY UN-IMPORTANT. Bank of America and other financial conglomerates are bigger than AIG, but still not big enough individually to make any difference to the economy if they fail. We have hereby proved with some very simple quantitative analysis that there is no such thing as a firm "too big to fail." From this fundamental factor, it is a warranted conclusion that the financial sector fiasco did not and could not cause the recession.

Failures of the FED and the SEC are what allowed the highly leveraged speculation to take place. The FED is our central bank, and the single most important function of all central banks is to regulate banking. The central bank has to specify the terms of all loans. Mortgages are loans. Credit cards are loans. Margin accounts are loans. The purpose of all loans must be in the banking regulations. That is, there must be an economic value for the loan. We see no economic value for stock purchases to be financed by the banks. It is good for an individual speculator to speculate with borrowed funds, but what is good for the individual speculator is not necessarily good for the economy. (This is the fallacy of composition.) In fact, stock market speculation is what causes the boom-and-bust cycles – the "bubbles" that inevitably burst because the prices of securities get bid up to levels that make no economic sense. Corporations are being priced at way beyond what their real economic value is. Speculators start selling off their holdings, and when these large sell orders reach the market they can only be done at ever decreasing prices – the bubble has burst; a bubble caused by leveraged speculation from margin accounts and low interest rates; both of which are not controlled by the FED for the good of the ECONOMY. The stock market is not the economy.

The Federal Reserve Banking System – the FED – is NOT (surprise!) a government agency. It is privately owned by the member banks of the system and is operated by the banks for the banks benefit. The boards of directors of all the regional FED banks (12) and the board of directors in the Washington headquarters all have a minority of non-bankers on them, but the bankers dominate what policies the FED will pursue. So, the bankers regulate the bankers! This is a clear conflict of interests, because the FED is a quasi-public agency that is supposed to regulate banking for the public good. And what is good for banking is not what is good for the economy. In fact, what the banks do that is good for them is, in many cases, bad for the economy. Details of this were explained in Chapter 3, Money and Banking and in Chapter 1 when we were explaining monetary policy. But is very worthwhile to state at this point that contra-cyclical monetary policy as practiced by the FED does not work. It does not do what they think it will do. It does not increase business investment spending or consumption spending by lowering interest rates. And it can only curb inflation by rising interest rates to the point that unemployment goes over 10% and the economy slows down. By keeping the margin requirements and interest rates low, it helps the stock market speculators to create bubbles, which are bad for the economy.

Low interest rates are also a prime factor in the housing bubble. So, the FED was deficient in its duty to do what is good for the economy. But the terms of the mortgage loans, which should also be controlled by the FED and were NOT, are likely a bigger factor in the housing bubble then the low interest rate. After all, if you can speculate in the housing market with no money of your own, the interest rate makes little difference, at least over the short term, which is the time horizon for speculators. They only had to hold these speculations 2 years to claim a tax exemption for the capital gains. A couple claiming that they sold their residence could get $200,000 gain tax free, AND DO IT REPEATEDLY! We should, therefore cite the IRS as a causal factor in the housing bubble. But Congress writes the tax code, so chalk this one up to Congress.

There were several "products" developed by the brokerage industry that were instrumental in running up stock prices. Leveraged Buy Outs – LBO's – are a mechanism whereby one firm buys out another with someone else's money. Doing business with someone else's money is what leveraging is all about. The "someone else" could be either banks making loans or brokerage firms selling securities to investors or some of each. When it is someone else's money, the interest rates are low, and you only are doing the buy-out for the purpose of pumping up the value of the resulting firm enough to sell out in a couple of years for a big capital gain – taxed MUCH LOWER than income tax, the higher the leverage, the better. This is just another "pump and dump" operation.

The general public wanted to get in on this short term trading for capital gains, so the mutual funds part of the securities industry developed a mechanism called Exchange Traded Funds – ETF's. A mutual fund by definition is a long term investment strategy and they are not traded on exchanges. The Investment Company Act applies to all mutual funds sold to the public, and it is required that they be registered with the SEC.

The SEC should never have registered a mutual fund for short-term trading; it is an inappropriate use of that investment vehicle. Selling stock to the public requires SEC registration from which a Prospectus is generated that has to be presented to any potential buyer of the security. The rules require that the management fees for mutual fund managers be "reasonable," which in practice is down around 1-2%. Before you conclude that mutual fund managers do not make much money, multiply $Billion by 1%. Even a small fund, with, say $100 Million X 1% ain't peanuts.

If stock is not sold to the public, the SEC has no say in the offering terms nor in the compensation of the managers. This is the loophole that allows hedge funds to pay their managers 30% of the gains they make in their short-term "pump and dump" highly leveraged speculation. And this is another failure of the SEC leading up to the stock market crash. The word "public" in their concern about the sale of new securities should be amended to include private sales as well. If it is in the Law, which it is, then the makers of the Law – Congress – are responsible for this loophole that allows a mutual fund, which is what hedge funds are, to do whatever they please, and that turns out to be harmful to the economy.

Another failure of Congress, a cause for the recession, is the repeal of the Glass-Steagall Act, which was put in place in the Great Depression to separate bankers and brokers because it was found to be bad business for the economy. There were many bank failures then, with millions of people losing everything because the banks financial well being was too closely tied to the stock market. The stock market crash of 1929 destroyed hundreds of banks. Depositors lost everything; there was not FDIC at that time to guarantee bank deposits. We can still see the looks of glee on all the bankers and brokers surrounding President Clinton when he signed the Bill that Congress passed to allow the banks and brokers to get back together. The one-bank holding company became the dominant form of organization in the financial industry. Big banks added brokerage firms – for example, Bank of America added Merrill Lynch. At the height of the financial fiasco, Treasury Secretary Geithner advised firms to buy a bank or start one, which is what Goldman Sachs did in September 2008. And in October 2008 the Treasury put $10 Billion into Goldman, which is the amount AIG owed Goldman on the insurance Goldman took out for the mortgage backed securities – called CDO's – that were starting to fail. AIG could not make good on the insurance, but with friend Geithner at the U.S. Treasury their problem was solved by becoming a bank.

There are other Collateralized Debt Obligations – CDO's – beyond the mortgage backed ones. Hotshot salesmen in $1,000 Armani suits for the brokerage firms went around the world looking for any income stream that they could sell to investors. They sold bonds – that's the Debt and Obligation that goes with bonds – with the revenue stream as the Collateral. Selling new securities is the investment banking FUNCTION OF THE BROKERAGE FIRMS. (There is no such thing as an investment bank.) And investment banking is the big money maker for brokerage firms: underwriting fees, which entail little more than writing your name on a piece of paper, are at 1-2%. Think that is not much? Multiply 1-2% times a $Billion.

Then there are sales commissions for selling the new issues that are 10% for stocks (but less for bonds). 10% X $Billion is $100 Million! And many Billions of dollars of new securities are sold every year. That's "production" that the big banks like Bank of America were excited to get into their firm, but when B of A was forced to take in Merrill Lynch and found out what bad shape they were in, they balked and got the Treasury to throw in $Billions, which is ironic because when the financial sector bailout started and all the mega bank CEO's were called to Washington, B of A did not want or need a bailout, but were forced to take $Billions so that the public would not know which banks were in trouble and which were not. This cover-up by the Treasury – run by a banker! – was to avoid a run on those big banks that would have gone down from a run because their assets did not have enough value to cover their liabilities. That's bankruptcy. That's how leveraging in banks, which is done with demand deposits, can put them out of business when they make risky loans. Risky loans should not be allowed by the banking regulators, but the banking regulators are the bankers themselves! The FED is an SRO – Self Regulating Organization – which is a conflict of interests. The regulated can not be the regulators! Does not make sense. Self regulation does not work. Holding all those worthless mortgage backed securities is what did them in, and is further evidence of why brokers and bankers should be separated, NOT PUT TOGETHER AS GEITHNER HAS DONE. Because Wachovia had brokerage operations right in its holding company, they were put out of business by all those bad mortgage-backed and other CDO's generated by the brokers. More evidence of why bankers and brokers should be separate as they were under Glass-Steagall, which was repealed by a law that President Clinton endorsed. (Could Chelsea Clinton's job AS A HEDGE FUND MANAGER be tied to this? Some people, not us, would argue that her multi-million dollar income [not salary; 30% of capital gains is what they get – much lower taxes than income tax] – was "bought and paid for" by this wonderful opportunity for the banks and brokers to get back together to make their robbery and pillage bigger and better than ever.)

Congress makes the laws; so, to the extent that the repeal of Glass-Steagall is a cause of the financial fiasco that precipitated the recession, Congressional failure is a factor in causing the recession. And these huge banks and brokerages, that were made much bigger by Geithner to the point that both the banking industry and the brokerage industry are now oligopolies is an indication of the failure of the Anti-Trust Division to promote competition by stopping all mergers and consolidation that result in restraining trade. The bigger the firms are in any industry, the fewer there are; and the fewer there are, the less competition there is. The oligopolies now in existence in the banking and brokerage industries are just like oligopolies in all other industries: they are able to set prices, bypassing markets, which is the only fair way that prices should be determined in capitalism.

The SEC is supposed to maintain "fair and orderly markets" for securities. Markets are not fair when big oligopolies can move prices by themselves, as they can, and are doing. This is a failure of the SEC that has dire consequences for the future operation of our capitalistic system. Capitalism needs a stock market for two purposes: capital formation and liquidity.

Capital formation is the process by which money is converted to real economic capital – productive facilities such as manufacturing plants –

(remember from Chapter 1: In economics capital is NOT money!). Investment banking and capital formation are one and the same. Money is converted to real economic capital when brokerage firms sell NEW issues of stock or bonds to provide the money necessary for businesses to be built, grow and develop. Economic growth and development is dependent on this transition of money to real capital to take place. The reason why we capitalized "new" issues of stock is that there is a misconception that capital formation takes place on the NYSE. It does not; new issues come to market OTC – Over the Counter – which means not on exchanges. Stock exchanges like the NYSE for example are a place where people holding shares they own, that are listed on the exchange, go to find a buyer. They then sell and buy shares of some other firm. An exchange takes place, but no new capital is added to the economy. The stock market is not the economy. NYSE stands for New York Stock EXCHANGE.

The liquidity part of the SEC's job has to do with maintaining fair and orderly markets for the securities that investors get for putting their money into the stocks or bonds sold by corporations through brokers to start or expand their businesses. If investors did not think that they could get a fair price for their stock or bonds when they wanted to sell, they would not buy them to begin with. That's what liquidity is all about: the ability to convert these assets – stocks and bonds – quickly and easily into cash. But the right price is the issue. The right price, a fair price, is determined in the market by the forces of supply and demand. A fair market is a competitive one; one where there are no buyers or sellers big enough by themselves individually to affect the price by just their own actions. That's the kind of market that the SEC is supposed to maintain, BUT IT DOES NOT. Huge brokerage firms like Goldman-Sachs, Citigroup and JP Morgan Chase can, and do, affect market prices when they buy or sell $Billions of securities all day long every day. Currently, Goldman-Sachs accounts for as much as 25% of all trades on the NYSE. Fair markets also require that all buyers and sellers have the same information about the market at the same time. In economics, we call this requirement "perfect information." This condition of fair markets is NOT the case, since only the big brokers located in New York with super-fast computers can get all the pertinent data before all other buyers and sellers. These super-fast computers and location in New York are very expensive thus creating an "entry barrier" for other buyers or sellers to get into the market. "Free" entry into the markets is a requirement for them to be fair – competitive – and to eliminate excess profits. Since the brokers regulate the brokers, these requirements would lower their profits; so they will never happen. SEC regulates for the good of the brokers, not FOR THE GOOD OF THE ECONOMY.

Other deficiencies of the SEC, or more precisely the basic reason why securities markets are not fair and orderly is that the SEC declared the

NYSE to be a Self Regulating Organization – SRO, WHICH MEANS THE REGULATED ARE THE REGULATORS! This is a no-brainer conflict of interests. Fair and orderly markets for securities are needed for our capitalistic economic system to work right, not for the good of the brokerage industry. There are many securities not listed on exchanges. These are traded – bought and sold – by firms that are not member firms of the NYSE. They are OTC brokers and are organized as the National Association of Securities Dealers – the NASD. In place of the ticker tape that reports all NYSE transactions, the NASD has an Automated (computerized) Quotations system called NASDAQ. The SEC has further abrogated its responsibility to maintain fair and orderly markets by also designating the NASD an SRO. The example par excellence that self regulation does not work in the NASD is simply to note that the biggest swindler of all time, Bernard Madoff, was the President of the NASD!

The only control the SEC had over the brokerage industry was the net capital requirements. But that control was "neutered" in the early days of the most recent financial bubble when the big brokerage firms lead by Paulson from Goldman-Sachs went to the SEC and got capital requirements lowered so that they could leverage more to make more money. "Neutering" means that the SEC has virtually no control over the brokerage industry. The warranted conclusion is that the SEC is just a nice cushy position for old political party hacks who have lost their elected positions, but want to hang around Washington to hang around with their old friends. The first Chairman of the SEC was none other than Joseph Kennedy, whom we knew as Ambassador Kennedy, because he was a former Ambassador to Great Britain, another political appointment! Like most politicians, those at the SEC are lawyers whose combined knowledge of economics would not fill a thimble.

To this point, we have detailed how the boom-and-bust cycles, "bubbles" – the stock market, housing and commodities futures were all caused by highly leveraged speculation for short-term capital gains via a number of "vehicles": LBO's, ETF's, CDO's, margin accounts, and last but not least – hedge funds. This highly undesirable activity was aided and abetted by institutional failures of: the SEC, the FED, the Anti-Trust Division of the Justice Department, and last, but not least, Congress. These cycles are not per se a recession.

The recession was created in part by the mass media incorrectly reporting that the stock market and housing market crashes actually were the recession, whereas the actual recession did not start until some time later when the general public interpreted these market crashes as a recession. When the mindset of the public grew very concerned about the negative news in those two markets they began to reduce spending. When spending goes down, output goes down. When output declines for two successive quarters, a recession has begun. (This is the traditional definition of a recession.) We reject the National Bureau of Economic Research's (NBER) new definition that a recession starts at the peak of the upswing of the economy. They look not only at output, but other variables as well. And when they did that they got a mixed message! Some variables said it was a recession at that point, and some said it was not. So, the economists that do research for NBER (it is NOT a government agency) got together via a conference telephone call and voted to disregard the variables saying it was not a recession, thereby declaring a recession started at the top of the business cycle. This is not a science. We call it B.S.; nonsensical and stupidity par excellence. When output declines two quarters in a row, we start to get increasing unemployment. That's when you know that we are really in a recession. There are many times when there is a slight dip in the output of the economy for one quarter, but these are just aberrations that we go through without much increase in unemployment, and, therefore, they do little real damage. It's when unemployment gets pushed up by falling output that we have a real recession. The most important factor causing the recession was psychological in nature: people thought there was a recession and acted on that – cut down on spending – and that caused the recession. (Remember Chapter 1: "the effect of expectations?") This is not the whole story, however.

While this decline in aggregate demand was starting, there was another factor that was driving the negative mindset that came out of the 2008 presidential campaigns and goes by the name of demagoguery. A demagogue is a person who tells another person something that may not be true but the demagogue thinks the person might think it to be true – for the demagogue's benefit. Politicians are prime examples of demagogues. They all tell their constituents – for the purpose of getting their vote – what the constituents want to hear. 99% of all voters think a deficit in the federal budget is bad. It is, therefore, good politics to be against deficits, but we know, and many politicians do too, that the deficit of the federal government AT THIS TIME is the only way to fix the economy. Sometimes a surplus is required to help the economy. So, that means that a balanced budget: no deficit nor surplus is only good when the economy is perfect, but we do not live in a perfect world. Therefore a balanced budget is bad economics, but politicians pander to the voters' ignorance of this to get their votes. They all – regardless of party, race, creed or religion – think a balanced budget is what their voters want them to be for. So, even if they know it is not good economics, they still espouse it to get elected. All the states that have balanced budget laws have done something that makes recessions worse. They have to cut spending, when they should be increasing it to help offset the decline in aggregate demand coming from the consumption and business sectors.

In spite of the NBER's dating the start of the recession at the PEAK of economic activity December, 2007, the economy grew in the first two quarters of 2008. That's when presidential politicking for the November elections got going hot and heavy. In the course of the debates between Obama and McCain, McCain said that the fundamentals of the economy were "sound" even though both the stock market and housing markets had crashed. He was right. Two successive quarters of economic growth, unemployment was not yet a problem, and even though output declined slightly in the third quarter, and it was positive for the year are facts that indicate that the fundamentals were OK. Obama leaped on this CORRECT McCain assessment of the economy like ugly on the ape, because everyone – the electorate – all "knew" that the stock market and housing market woes were a recession. They were all wrong, but politicians feed on telling people – especially the electorate – what they want to hear. They are all demagogues, even Obama. He harped so much about being in the worst recession since the Great Depression (that we lived through, and remember very well) that millions of Americans believed him and started "hunkering down" waiting for the storm to pass. The economics of "hunkering down" is to increase saving – for the rainy days sure to come.

Increased savings means decreased consumption, and in an economy where consumption is 70% of aggregate demand, it does not take much of a decline in consumption to have a big effect on output and employment. The multiplier (remember it from Chapter 1?) works in a negative way also, making the final effect on the economy several times the initial decrease in consumption.

By repeatedly raising the specter of another Great Depression, there is no question that Obama used the financial sector fiasco and housing market bust to win votes in the November election. "If the President-to-be says we are in a recession, we must be," millions of Americans reasoned. And when they acted on that incorrect analysis by Obama they did cause the actual recession – with reduced output and high unemployment – to take place. It's a good example of the effect of expectations, and also of how political demagoguery hurts the economy. The only real question in all of this is did Obama really know that we were not in anything even close to the Great Depression. And if so was he just using McCain's faux pas to get elected? Whichever, we have to conclude that all those "worst recession since the Great Depression" speeches were, in fact, a prime cause of the recession. He almost single-handedly transformed a run-of-the-mill stock market downturn into a recession. But he, like all politicians remembered why George H. W. Bush did not get re-elected: "It's the economy, stupid!" which can also be correctly cited as the principal cause of his party's failure in the 2010 mid-term elections.

If all Americans took the time to check whether it was McCain that was right or Obama, we might not have had the recession, because McCain was right. Similar misunderstandings about important economics factors such as deficit spending, the National debt, and a balanced budget by most Americans hinder the recovery process. The question that remains in all of this is: Do the elected officials – any or all of them – understand the real economic importance of these factors; and, if so, do they just use the public's ignorance to get elected, or are they just as ignorant of the real facts as the general public? But these are political questions. We are economists, and know that good economics is often bad politics and good politics is often bad economics. But like "cycles are endemic in capitalism," we reject this also as inevitable.

CHAPTER 5:
CURES FOR THE RECESSION

In the short-term, what was needed was an increase in Aggregate Demand to offset the decline in Consumption spending. Only the federal government has the capability to make this happen. It has the fiscal policy tools of tax reductions or increased spending, or some of each. But before any of these policies are undertaken, we need to determine how much short Aggregate Demand is from the amount when unemployment was at an acceptable level (5% or so).

You can rough estimate it, as we did, using a sheet of graph paper and the methodology employed in Chapter 1 in Illustration 1-6 – Equilibrium Output with a couple of modifications. You do not have to have the three lines that added together $(C + I + G)$ determine Aggregate Demand, just the top line, which is Aggregate Demand. And you can simulate reality by using the graph squares as a scale.

Illustration 5-1 is what economists see when there is a decrease in Aggregate Demand, and by putting this on a scale model you can read off the results. One square for $2 Trillion makes it difficult to read what any part of a square actually is, but economics is an in-exact science; we just want to get the right direction of movement of the important variables.

On Illustration 5-1, we have labeled the pre-recession Aggregate Demand curve AGG D_O. The subscript O is to indicate that it is the Original (pre-recession) AGG D. The new AGG D, after the decline, is labeled AGG D_n. The subscript n is to indicate it is the new AGG D. We have the AGG S line on as before at 45 degrees from the Origin, which makes it equi-distant from both axes, because that is where the level of output will be determined. (Remember? Output and spending are different measures of the same thing.) The Original AGG D determined the output at E_O, and when we read down to the output axis, we can also read employment because they move roughly equivalent with each other. At E_O we had "full" employment which we indicate on the graph as N_F. Actually it was at about 5% unemployment, which we consider an acceptable level of unemployment.

Now look at what happens to output and employment when AGG D shifts down – shown as - Δ on the graph – which is how we show a decrease in AGG D. AGG D now intersects AGG S at E_n, and when we read off the output and employment axis, both output and employment have decreased, which means that unemployment has increased. The percentage decline in output and the percentage decline in employment run roughly approximate; so, we go from 5% unemployment to about 10%, which is indicated on the graph N_n.

ILLUSTRATION 5-1
DECREASED AGGREGATE DEMAND

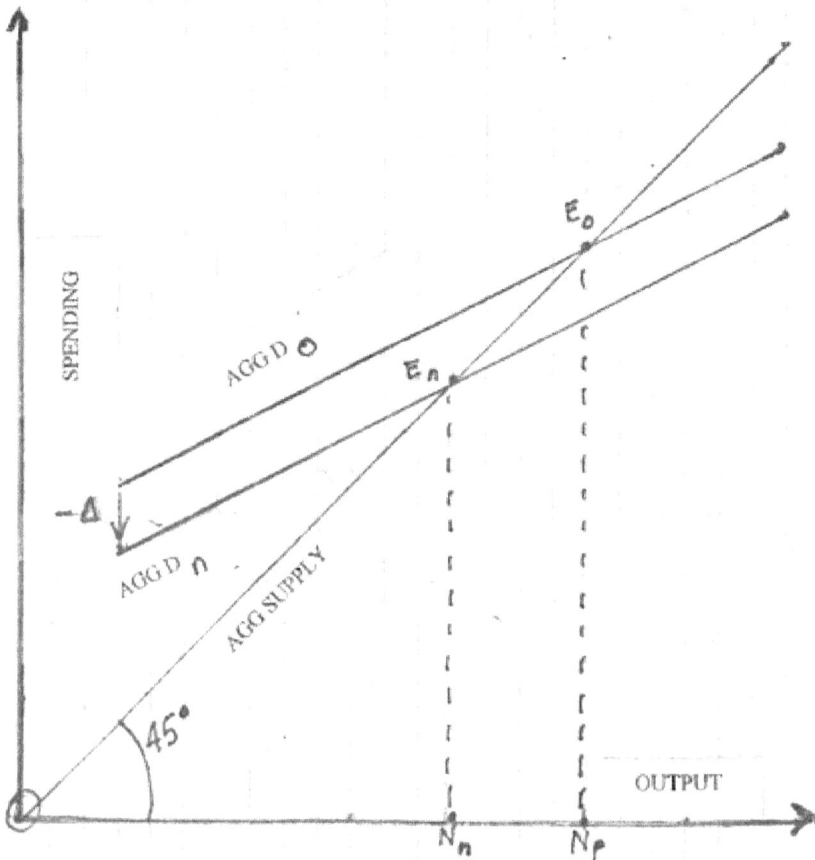

The slope of AGG D on our graph is the slope of the Consumption function, which we set at 1:2; that is for every change of income of 2, consumption changes by 1, which you can read right off the graph (output and income are one and the same, remember?). Therefore, for a change of income of 4, consumption changes by 2. (Remember? The slope of a function is the ratio of the "rise" to the "run.") But "rise" is going up the slope, but when there is a decrease in AGG D, we are going down the slope. In other words, the marginal propensity to consume (MPC) works both ways – for an increase in income and for a decrease in income. That means that the multiplier, k, works both ways also. So the decrease in output and employment is a multiple of the decrease in AGG D. We can read this multiplier effect right off the graph. (That's why we used an easy-to-read MPC of ½.) From the graph, you see the decline of AGG D is 2 squares (2 squares = $4 Trillion), and from the output-income-employment axis you can see the change (decrease) is 4 squares ($8 Trillion).

This analysis and results can also be determined by applying the concepts and simple formulas you learned in Chapter 1. The basic formula is: $\Delta Y = k \, (\Delta AGG \, D)$, where $k = 1/MPS$, and $MPS = 1 - MPC$. Let's start with this last formula and determine MPS. We assumed MPC as ½ (so as to have easy-to-see numbers to manipulate). Therefore, $MPS = 1 - ½ = ½$, and $k = 1/.5 = 2$. Putting this value for k into the basic formula to determine ΔY; we have $\Delta Y = 2 \, (2) = 4$, which is exactly what we read off the graph. For a decrease of 2 in AGG D, there is a decrease of 4 on the output-income-employment axis. Or you can just substitute GDP (the basic output measure) in the formula and say: $\Delta GDP = k \, (\Delta AGG \, D)$. And remember that output and employment move in the same direction (even if not 100% proportionally).

What we conclude from this is that we can quantify what happens to output and therefore employment when there is a decrease in AGG D either by a scaled graph or by formula. You should also note that the multiplier works both ways – that is – it multiplies the effect of changes in AGG D in both directions up AND DOWN.

Now we should make our simplified analysis of the problem more realistic by making several changes. First, you should note that the MPC in the real world is up in the 90+% range. Let's use 90%, so as to make calculations easier to understand. What happens to the multiplier with a change of the MPC from 50% (= ½) to 90%? The multiplier, k, is the reciprocal of the MPS. When the MPC is 9/10, the MPS is 1/10. (Money not spent, is saved, by definition.) The reciprocal of 1/10 is 10/1 = 10 = k = the multiplier. Now, for a change in AGG D of any amount, the change in output will be ten times the change in AGG D. That would be the result if we were calculating the result of an infinite geometric progression and nothing else changed during that time period. Neither of these two factors are realistic, which is just another way to say that comparative-static analysis is far removed from reality, which is just another way to say only dynamic analysis – where we take into account changes of other variables over time – is used. One change taking place in a recession is that saving goes up, which lowers the multiplier effect. Another change further reducing aggregate demand is the decrease in business capital spending, which we can symbolize by - ΔI. And from this fact, we can create another concept similar to the accelerator, $\Delta I/\Delta C$, called the "decelerator." Named as such because the effect is to further slow down the economy ("negative acceleration" would by an oxymoron). Another category of business spending that decreases with a decrease in aggregate demand is inventory. A profitable level of inventory in business is tied to the level of sales. When sales go down, inventory must be decreased to keep it at the most profitable level.

And change in the third category of spending, government (G), also takes place over time as taxes from business and individuals decrease from lower profits and lower income because 32 states have balanced budget laws and are required to reduce spending as revenues decline. This makes aggregate demand decline still further, the recession worse and unemployment higher. Balanced budgets at the state and local government levels are bad for the economy. So, too, is a balanced budget at the federal government level. We do not like to "chew our spaghetti twice" but...recently (late 2010) the din from the so-called "fiscal responsibility" crowd has grown so loud that President Obama appointed a commission to report to him on ways to reduce the deficit in the federal budget so, we felt it necessary to repeat much of what we pointed out in Chapter 2, Government and Debt, to Mr. Erskine Bowles and the commission President Obama appointed. To wit: There is an implicit, underlying, and INCORRECT assumption that a balanced budget per se is a good thing to do. It is NOT. It is bad economics. A balanced budget requires deficit reduction, and deficit spending is the only "tool" to get us out of the recession and back to full-employment non-inflationary economic growth. Therefore, reducing government spending and/or increasing taxes to balance the budget is bad for the economy at this time.

Social Security (SS) is a part of this necessary government deficit spending. It is bad economics to raise SS taxes and/or reduce benefits at this time. In the long run, only one simple adjustment is necessary for SS to go on as promised: NO CAP ON TAXABLE EARNINGS. This makes this form of taxation much fairer than the regressive way it is being done now, whereby people below the cap pay a higher percentage of their income than the rich folks. Let the Wall Street fat cats pay SS taxes on every dollar made in the zero-sum games they play in the securities markets. We will have to raise capital gains taxes to the income tax levels, closing the loophole they presently use to minimize taxes.

Dynamic analysis – taking changes over time into account – makes the amount of the deficit spending required much larger than the initial decrease in consumption spending. The multiplier gets bigger as saving goes up, and the other sectors of the economy – business and government – decrease their spending. Deficit spending is what is called "stimulus" by non-economists. And it makes a world of difference where and how the deficit spending takes place. It also changes the amount of the deficit spending depending on where and how it is applied. The multiplier effect applies mostly only to the consumption sector of the economy. It works like this: we cut taxes for consumers; they have more money to spend, which makes an increase in income and spending as it goes around to many "pockets" of consumers.

The stimulus as passed by the Congress had over 50% of the total amount going for tax reductions for business. Lowering business taxes creates a deficit but businesses do not spend the extra income in a recession because the demand for their output has declined. It was real poor economic analysis to think that if businesses had more money they would hire more people thereby reducing unemployment. (Reducing business taxes was a ploy to get Republicans on board to get a stimulus bill passed, but it was a waste of taxpayers' money, a boon for business, and stands as prime example of how politics has a negative effect on trying to do what is right for the economy.) The whole "job creation" idea was wrong. What was needed is WORK creation. That is done by government spending for building up the social part of the economy's capital structure – the so-called "infrastructure" – highways, bridges, dams, etc. There was a supplemental bill passed by Congress for infrastructure. It was for $50 Billion, which seems like a lot until you apply DeFelice's Law of Absolute Numbers: Absolute Numbers Mean Absolutely Nothing. $50 Billion RELATIVE TO A National Income of $15 Trillion is just three tenths of one percent (.003). Too late and too little! That $50 Billion is very similar to "pork barrel" or "earmarks" done by Congress to let the folks back home see something being done for them so as to win their votes for re-election.

The stimulus could have been done for a smaller deficit if the entire amount was spent by the government for all the "pork barrel" and "earmarks" that Congress people wanted.

Given the decreases in aggregate demand ensuing the initial decline in consumer spending and the very poor application of the stimulus funds, the amount of stimulus provided was only about one-third of what was necessary.

The cure for recessions in the long term centers around institutional reform. The SEC has completely neutered itself by declaring the NYSE and the NASD Self Regulating Organizations (SRO's) and by reducing the net capital requirement for brokers to almost non-existent levels. It can be made over into a government agency required by law to perform the essential functions of a stock market in capitalism: capital formation and fair and orderly markets for securities stemming from capital formation.

The FED, on the other hand, can not be reformed and must be replaced by a good central bank. A good central bank regulates banking and controls the money supply. The FED can not and does not do either of these important functions hardly at all because of a fatal flaw in the make up of the Federal Reserve System whereby private businesses – the member banks – are not able to perform public policy functions of the financial sector because doing so is not in their best interests as profit-seeking institutions. WE NEED A BANK OF THE UNITED STATES OF AMERICA owned and operated by the people, for the people.

A little of what Mr. Nixon called "specificity" is needed at this point inre: to what a good central bank will do that the FED does not do. Regulation of banking requires that all loans at all banks for all purposes be regulated by the central bank for the good of the economy not for the good of the bankers. Mortgages, margin accounts and credit cards are all loans. The terms and security (risk) of all should be specified and enforced by the central bank. For example, mortgages should require a down-payment of at least 20% of the appraised value of the property. And an income test that shows the borrowers' capability to amortize the loan. We see no credible reason – in terms of what is good for the economy – for loans to be made for people to buy stocks. In fact, stopping margin accounts is stopping one of the prime causes of stock market booms and busts that can and do lead to real economic problems of decreased growth and unemployment – as was the case in the 2009-10 recession. More constrained mortgage lending will also reduce the likelihood of a boom and bust in the housing market...similar reasoning applies to credit cards. The requirements for this type of loan should also be specified by a good central bank. Personal finance was leveraged by easy credit card loans; so, should also, therefore, be curtailed as a reduction in leveraged speculation capability. LBO's – Leveraged Buy Outs – of one business by another – were also financed by banks in some cases. Such loans were aiding the borrower in leveraged speculation that drove up the stock market to its inevitable crash. Banks were not only loaning the commodities market speculators 10 times the amount of their equity, but were also speculating for their own account. BANKS SHOULD NOT HAVE TRADING DESKS. But stopping that would have little effect now because of the way banks and brokers are in bed together in the one-bank holding company configurations which were encouraged by Geithner – for example Bank of America has Merrill Lynch within it, Goldman-Sachs started its own bank with $10 Billion from Geithner, JP Morgan Chase has Bear Stearns within it, et cetera.

Bankers and brokers so closely connected was a prime cause for the bank failures of the early 1930's after the stock market crash of 1929, and is also a cause of the bank failures of the 2009-10 recession. With banks holding stocks in their assets portfolios, or loans to buy them – when the stock market crashes, their net capital disappears, and their liabilities – demand deposits – quickly are far in excess of their ability to meet them, which makes them bankrupt. In the Great Depression we did two things to stop this from happening again. FDIC was formed so that depositors would not lose all their money when banks failed as was the case in the 1930's. And the Glass-Steagall Act was passed to keep banks and brokers apart. The repeal of Glass-Steagall is a prime cause of the leveraged speculation stemming from the huge bank/broker firms that grew up after its complete repeal under the Clinton Administration. So, the long-term cure for recessions requires the re-institution of a law separating banks and brokers. These mega bank-brokerages are so big they violate anti-trust laws as well as current banking regulation limiting size of any one bank to no more than 10% of all deposits. These two industries – banking and brokerage – are now oligopolies and like all oligopolies have the power to set prices and do so. Firms need to be made smaller so that competition will determine prices.

The other major function of a central bank – control of the money supply – which the FED can not do (Barney Frank said early on, "You can't make them [the commercial banks] do anything.") What the economy needed done was for them to increase the money supply, which is done by them making loans. Recently (December 2010) we heard Mr. David Wessel, the economics editor of the Wall Street Journal, say on NPR that the "FED PRINTED $600 Billions" after an announcement by the FED that they bought $600 Billion of Treasury securities. Buying securities is NOT printing money. Ben Bernanke, FED Chairman, went on TV to explain that buying bonds does NOT mean there is any more money in circulation, and that the purpose of the $600 Billion purchase was to drive down interest rates. When bond prices go up, which they do when some entity buys that much, interest rates fall. We noted earlier that Wessel is not an economist and does not understand how money is created, but he writes on economics subjects for the WSJ and NPR considers him an expert, so they unwittingly spread his stupidity to the general population. This undermines the case for the necessity of a central bank that can control the money supply.

Early in the recession there was some talk of replacing the FED, but when it reached Geithener's ears he said that if we did "we probably would come up with the same thing as we presently have." In other words, "why bother." So, just some tweaking of the current system was all that was done. Some of what a good central bank is supposed to do; i.e., control credit card loans, was broken off from the FED and a new agency was set up to oversee this part of what is in reality just another form of loans.

There are already so many "alphabet soup" agencies involved in the regulation of the financial sector that there are "turf wars" to the extent that regulators and regulations are often in conflict with one another. Before the new credit card agency, we had the FDIC, the FED, the SEC, the CFTC, the Treasury Dept., and the Comptroller of the Currency. A new good central bank would take over practically all of what these agencies do. It would be the "Super-Regulator" that would eliminate the "turf wars" by taking over the functions of most of the "alphabet soup" agencies. And a Bank of the United States of America would make loans – increasing the money supply – in those times when the commercial banks following their profit motivations did not want to do so.

This good central bank is the only way to stop highly leveraged speculation that leads to boom and bust cycles, and will control the money supply for the good of the economy – increasing it when it needs to be increased and decreasing it when it needs to be decreased. It will be able to adjust interest rates in the same way the FED does – by buying or selling Treasuries.

A new good central bank is the sine qua non condition for affecting a long-term cure for the financial fiascoes that too often precipitate problems in the real economy.

Our critics say that it is easy for us to advise such an institutional change, but "how could it be done?" they ask. Really quite easily: just nationalize the two top tiers of the FED – the Washington headquarters and the regional banks. That cuts loose the thousands of member banks that do what they want to do anyway regardless of what the national economy needs.

We know that "nationalization" is a loaded word and smacks of socialism, but we predict it would go over with hardly a wrinkle because most Americans think the FED is already a part of the federal government. We should then put someone in charge of our Central Bank who knows how to regulate banking. One name comes quickly to mind: Sheila Bair, who has presided over 305 bank failures in the last three years. These would all be Member Banks of the Federal Reserve System, and stands as evidence par excellence that the FED does not do a good job of bank regulation. All these banks failed because they were not stopped from doing things that well-run banks should not do – like, for example, running a "trading desk."

The institutional changes that are necessary for the long-term cure for recessions require enabling legislation. It is not difficult to see that the financial sector would really get its back up if the necessary changes were discussed as proposed legislation. They would do what they always do when changes would hurt their pocketbook. Firms such as Goldman-Sachs that make $100 Million/DAY, pay lobbyists $Millions to go to Washington to tell the legislators what it is OK to change and what should not be changed. They call this "lending our expertise" because they know that the legislators generally do not know the difference between a bank and investment banking. This is exactly how the new so-called "financial sector regulations" came about; and will, therefore, be nothing to stop the highly leveraged speculation that drove up stock prices to the inevitable crash. Worse than that fact is the fact that the regulated are the regulators. There has been no change in how regulations are to be enforced. The NYSE is still the regulator for the NYSE; the NASD regulates the NASD; and, don't forget, the Commodities Futures Market – regulated by a commission, which is made up from the market participants – self regulation again! Oil prices and therefore gasoline prices are just about now (late 2010) where they were before the recession; and why wouldn't they be? Nothing has been done to stop the highly leveraged speculation that allows firms like Goldman-Sachs to make close to $Billion annually "trading" in the CFTC "regulated" market. The $Billions made there make Goldman employees rich, but does nothing good for the economy – actually hurts the economy because all "the little people" – the American populous that reside everywhere except Wall Street have to pay more for gasoline: a zero-sum game – their $Billions of gains are all Americans' loss. We've got to stop this. What is traded on the CFT market are securities; should be regulated by the SEC as such; as should the CFT market, which is also an Exchange. The "E" in SEC is for securities Exchanges.

The whole idea of a "commission" as a regulator should be re-thought. It seems that when government does not know what to do to solve a problem, they appoint a commission. This is how the SEC came about – the government did not know how to prevent another stock market crash like the 1929 one. Then who do they get to run the commission? Insiders! – people who are in the brokerage business, lawyers and old party hacks who have been defeated. Currently the SEC is a bunch of lawyers who dwell on bringing civil suits to try to recover the funds robbed by Wall Street racketeers in one scheme after another. It is not an independent agency; it is political. The make up of the commission has to reflect which political party is in power, and has a majority of members from that party!

We need financial economists running the SEC – economists who understand that the proper role for a stock market is in capitalism (repeating) – to facilitate capital formation and to ensure fair and orderly markets for securities stemming from capital formation. This is miles distant from what the SEC presently does; they have allowed via designation of the NYSE and NASD as SRO's, the establishment of a betting arcade. It is common parlance in the brokerage business to call purchases of stock "a bet" on the issuer of the stock. Economists know what fair and orderly markets are, and the conditions required.

TO : PRESIDENT OBAMA, OUR FRIEND

FROM : **Dr. & Mrs. Frank DeFelice**
672 Windridge
Linville, NC
Mail: 2152 Land Harbor
Newland, NC 28657

DATE DRAFTED : JUNE 30, 2010

SUBJECT : FINANCIAL SECTOR REFORM ? NO :
LA PLUS CHANGE, LE MEME CHOSE.
"DEJA VU, ALL OVER AGAIN", L. BERRA.
WHAT WE LEARN FROM HISTORY IS THAT
WE DO NOT LEARN FROM HISTORY.

What's been done to date to cure the causes of the 08-09 recession is equivalent to a band-aid on a patient needing major surgery.

The major surgery required are institutional changes (nothing worth doing is easy!) :
1. The SEC does not properly perform the important functions of a stock market in capitalism : capital formation and liquidity. It has relinquished its responsibility to those whom it is supposed to regulate. It has defined the NYSE and the NASD as SRO'S – Self Regulating Organizations. The regulated are the regulators. Slf regulation does not work. Unless and until you make the necessary changes in the SEC, we will continue to have financial fiascoes that can and do lead to recessions in the real economy whereby millions of people are hurt, while the Wall St. crowd, including Larry Summers, go on with their multi-million dollar incomes derived from market manipulation via highly leveraged speculation for short-term capital gains.
2. The FED is what Rahm Emanuel (and maybe Joe Biden) should describe as N.F.G. – Not Very Good . It is essentially an SRO whereby the bankers regulate the bankers. It does not, and can not, do the essential job of a central bank : regulate banking and control the money supply. About 300 Member Banks of the Federal Reserve System have failed this time around, which is prima facie evidence of bank regulation failure. And the so-called "credit crunch" is nothing more than the failure of the FED to control the money supply for the good of the economy. The FED can not make banks lend. No lending – the money supply decreases – bad for the economy in a recession.

The financial reform package recently passed by Congress will fail to solve financial sector problems because the interpretation and application of the rules is to be made by the regulators, which in the case of the NYSE, NASD, AND THE FED are the regulated.

In summary, there are two sine qua non requirements to avoid recessions of this type over the long term :

1. Institutional reform of the SEC, and
2. A good central bank.

And the permanent cure for these recessions is public education and understanding of 15 fundamental facts of macro-economics (see enclosed list), which should be taught in the public schools, that Arne Duncan could have required in the Race to the Top money because those grants required more science in the curriculum. ECONOMICS IS A SCIENCE.

Copies : Rahm Emanuel, Joe Biden, Ben Bernanke, Larry Summers, Arne Duncan

Post Script :

"Killing an ant with a howitzer " (or whatever) Boehner said ! Au contraire, mon ami. You are trying to kill and 800 lb. gorilla with ant spray.

Here's the test for financial sector reform : Does it stop highly leveraged speculation? If not, there will continue to be boom and bust cycles.

Frank DeFelice, Ph.D.

CHAPTER 6:
CONCLUSIONS

"A better way to do business post-bubble," as President Obama challenged us to find is possible. Required is the stop of HIGHLY LEVERAGED SPECULATION FOR SHORT TERM CAPITAL GAINS, the seminal cause of the financial sector problems that precipitated the recession, which did NOT begin at what the NBER says was the peak of economic activity – December 2007. The economy grew in the first two quarters of 2008, declined in the third and fourth quarters, but rose for the year. If it rose for the first two quarters of 2008, how can December 2007 be the peak?! Therefore, the recession began in late 2008, or early 2009, but definitely not in December 2007. Neither the stock market crash nor the housing sector decline constitute a recession. The stock market is not the economy.

Institutional reform is a <u>sine qua non</u> requirement for "a better way to do business."

The stock market's necessary role in capitalism – to aid in capital formation and to maintain fair and orderly markets for the issues stemming from capital formation is not being done satisfactorily by the SEC.

The essential functions of the central bank – control of the money supply and regulation of banking – are not being done satisfactorily by the FED.

The SEC can be "repaired"; the FED can not. ("You can not push a balloon up by a string.") The FED's fatal flaw is that it is a quasi-government institution, like Fannie Mae and Freddie Mac. And is absolutely clear that this type of public policy management does not work. The profit interests supercede the public policy needs.

Unless and until we can establish a central bank that can perform the essential functions of the central bank FOR THE ECONOMY, we will continue to have financial sector problems – as we have had repeatedly for over 200 years! – that often lead to real economic problems: unemployment and decline in output.

Since the entire financial sector – thousands of banks, thousands of brokers, thousands of insurance companies plus thousands of other financial institutions constitute only 10% of the economy (in normal times), there is no such thing as "too big to fail." This myth prevails largely because bankers and brokers are the people Obama has chosen to do economic analysis and repair of the economy damaged by bankers and brokers!

Business failure is normal, expected, AND DESIRABLE so that the economy can more efficiently allocate resources, grow, and develop. Therefore, GM and Chrysler should have been allowed to fail.

There is no such thing as "our jobs." It is normal, natural AND DESIRABLE that the manufacturing sector decline so as to free up resources for movement to the service sector, the third phase of economic growth and development, which we are currently entering. 70% of employment currently (early 2010) is in the service sector.

This movement of the economy into the service sector is also why it is GOOD for government to grow. Services are largely supplied by government agencies.

21st century macro-economics EXCLUDES the following 20th century ideas as defunct: markets know best, Friedmanite economics, Self Regulating Organizations – NYSE, NASD, and the FED – prices determined by supply and demand, and balanced government budgets.

21st century macro-economics INCLUDES enhanced regulation by the SEC, enforcement of Antitrust Laws, a good central bank, reinstatement of required separation of banks and brokers, modern Keynesian economics, primacy of contra-cyclical fiscal policies, very conservatively leveraged government finance, higher capital gains taxes, and general public understanding of the difference between political demagoguery and theoretically sound economics, and that the price of oil and stocks are manipulated by oligopolistic brokerages via "pump and dump" methods.

Because there is a "better way to do business post-bubble" (Obama), cycles are NOT endemic in capitalism. However, the so-called financial sector reforms done in the 2010 legislation passed by Congress and signed into Law by President Obama do NOT reform the financial sector to any extent whatsoever. The test is: Do the reforms stop highly leveraged speculation for short term capital gains? They do not, and it is not surprising when you know how the specifics came about. The folks from Wall Street sent their emissaries to Congress and told the Congress what changes would be OK by them and what changes would not. Congress does not want to kill the golden goose that supplies all of them with millions of dollars for campaign funds and even provides them with cushy jobs – for example Chelsea Clinton as a hedge fund manager, Larry Summers as a managing director of a hedge fund at $5 million/year, Bill Bradley as a hedge fund manager, and on and on and on.

It is sad to conclude that what we learn from history is that we do not learn from history. That is no more forcefully demonstrated than by the fact that Glass-Steagall which was a solution to the bad-for-the-economy arrangement of banks and brokers together back in the Great Depression was repealed and banks and brokers were not only allowed to get together, but actually such arrangements were promoted by Treasury Secretary Geithner. Geithner, the man Obama chose to lead the recover from the recession, has actually made things worse. The oligopolies in the brokerage and banking industries have led to unprecedented opportunities for those industries to engage in price fixing for their own benefit, and are currently (late 2009) starting the next bubble in the stock market and commodities futures markets. We would wager that Goldman-Sachs, that has a secretive energy trading unit that made $667 Million in 2008 did better in 2009 because they now have their own bank so that they can leverage without borrowing from a bank, and margin requirements on the commodities futures exchange have remained very low – down around 10%. Here's a "pregnant" question for those of you really interested to find out if the so-called financial reforms have done any good: How much did Goldman-Sachs make from its secretive energy trading unit in 2009? We bet it's more than 2008. Did Mr. Hall, who headed that unit in 2008, and complained he got only $100 Million, which is 15% whereas hedge fund managers get 30%, quit and start a hedge fund as he threatened or did Goldman-Sachs decide to pay him more than 15%, which is what they claim they have to do to keep such "highly talented producers" from quitting? Think the basic data to answer this question can be gleaned from SEC filings, or you could ask Jesse Ventura on his Conspiracy Theory TV show to ask Goldman executives directly.

When the American public, more specifically the electorate, is persuaded about the veracity of the following fifteen facts – and institutional changes are made – we will have a chance to avoid these recessions that have plagued us for over two hundred years:

1. The stock market is not the economy.

2. The entire financial sector is only 10% of the economy.

3. No firm is "too big to fail."

4. Business failure is good for the economy.

5. Monetary policy does not work.

6. NYSE is a Self-Regulating Organization (SRO).

7. NASD is an SRO.

8. The FED is an SRO and a quasi-public institution like Fannie Mae and Freddie Mac, all of which are failed management models.

9. Self regulation does not work.

10. Only fiscal policy can improve the economy.

11. The national debt cost is miniscule.

12. Nobody ever has to pay off the national debt.

13. Political demagoguery hurts the economy.

14. The FED is fatally flawed and must be replaced.

15. Money creation.

APPENDIX INTRODUCTION

This Appendix contains 80 pages (as of September 23, 2011) of communications, mostly between us and Barrack Obama and his Administration, along with ten responses from The White House over President Obama's signature.

But it starts with a copy of an (unpublished) piece we wrote for the Journal of Political Economy (JPE) in February 2009 that condemns the Obama presidential campaign for using the stock market and housing sector problems vs. John McCain because doing so was a prime cause of the recession. (Maybe, because JPE is published by the University of Chicago where Obama was a faculty member, they did not want to "hurt" one of their own by publishing proof of his demagoguery?)

Later in February 2009, we wrote to the Wall Street Journal (WSJ) as input into a symposium they convened, detailing the FED and SEC failures (that did not get corrected in the 2010 so-called "financial sector reforms.")

On March 5, 2009, we fed more input for the WSJ symposium in Washington, D.C., in which we explain the cause of high oil and gasoline prices, that is currently (early 2011) again causing high oil and gasoline prices. (It is NOT a supply and demand phenomenon.)

Also, in March 2009, you can see from an (unpublished) piece we wrote for The Journal of Finance that we believed that "cycles are endemic in capitalism." In 2011, we no longer believe that to be the case. That was "received doctrine," but we think it is a "cop-out" because nobody has taken on the task of clearly defining the causes of such aberrations so that the corrective actions to stop them could be undertaken. But we did.

On the other hand, we still (early 2011) believe that the FED is not capable of performing the important essential tasks for a central bank, and must, therefore, be replaced. The functions and deficiencies were first spelled out in the February 26, 2009 communication to the WSJ, and are repeated throughout the book several times because this is the most important institutional change that must be made to have a chance to stop recessions.

More on those two subjects was submitted to The Journal of Finance on March 15, 2009, that they chose not to publish.

Our first response from President Obama, dated July 16, 2009, is a response to our July 8, 2009 communication to him (both included), followed by our further response to him dated July 28, 2009 that he responded to on August 10, 2009.

Our July 22, 2009 letter and President Obama's August 21, 2009 response are next.

On July 30, 2009, we wrote to the WSJ because another Mr. Hall, in addition to the one at Goldman-Sachs – was featured on the front page of the

July 25-29, 2009 <u>WSJ</u>, who was also paid $100 Million for $667 Million trading profits he made for Citigroup. We could not accept this as coincidence, but the WSJ did not reply.

On August 5, 2009, we again made the case for a new central bank and we made hand-written notes on all the copies sent to Obama's Administration people – Rahm Emanuel, the Council of Economic Advisors (CEA), Ben Bernanke and also on the copies to Barney Frank and Senator Baucus because they were working up the financial sector reforms bill. And we did consider The White House August 10, 2009 letter as a response to it until we noticed it was a repetition of an earlier response!

Our August 11, 2009 letter to the President is classic statement of what is wrong with a balanced budget and what is wrong with the often heard lament that "we are passing on a debt burden to our children and grandchildren."

On August 18, 2009, our letter to Mary Schapiro, the SEC Chairperson, castigates the SEC for not doing what the Law requires it to do: provide fair and orderly markets for corporate securities.

Next is the August 21, 2009 letter from President Obama and our response.

An August 25, 2009 letter to U.S. Attorney General Eric Holder details the deficiencies of the anti-trust people in the Justice Department at enforcing anti-trust laws. We should also add at this point, that it was not only the Garn-St. Germain Act that allowed mega bank-brokerage firms to get bigger, but also the Gramm-Leach-Biley Law signed by President Clinton.

There are several communications between us and the Department of Education in an attempt to get them to require those public school systems applying for the $Billions available under "Race to the Top" grants to add a course in their curricula on economics. Adding science was a requirement to get the money. Economics is a science, but none of the Education Department people that responded to us understood that fact. They think economics education has to do with students' personal finance. And they repeatedly incorrectly said that they could not have any say in what the curriculum should be in public schools making a "turf" problem where none actually existed.

Our "Accountability Test" for Ben Bernanke was sent out several times starting on December 19, 2009. Over time, the number of failed banks increased from 125 to 305 through 2010.

Our February 19, 2011 memo to John Boehner, which should stand as the classic and theoretically sound answers to the "government and debt" and "entitlements" problems, and our March 15, 2011 attempt to educate the public about the cause of high gasoline prices and what they can do about it, are the best.

We have since added two more communications: On September 2, 2011, we advised the new Chairman of the Council of Economic Advisors (CEA), Dr. Alan Krueger, on HOW TO FIX THE ECONOMY and on September 23, 2011, we advised Senator Bernie Sanders on HOW TO STOP THE GASOLINE PRICE RIP-OFF.

Next is our ninth letter from President Obama dated March 6, 2012 and our reply, and last, but definitely not least, is our tenth letter from the President and our response.

Frank DeFelice, Ph.D.

Submitted to the Journal of Political Economy   February 20, 2009

2008-09 ECONOMIC MALAISE: NON-ECONOMIC CAUSES

FRANK DEFELICE, PH.D.*

THESIS: POLITICAL-PSYCHOLOGICAL FACTORS CAUSED THE ECONOMY, IN WHICH "THE FUNDAMENTALS WERE SOUND", AS JOHN MCCAIN SAID DURING THE CAMPAIGN, TO BECOME UNSOUND.

GIVEN THAT ECONOMIC THEORY HAS A HIGH POLITICAL PHILOSPHY ELASTICITY, THERE IS STILL ROOM TO LAY BLAME FOR THE DOWNTURN ON OBAMA'S "MAKING HAY" WITH MCCAIN'S STATEMENT BY POINTING OUT THE STOCKMARKET-FINANCIAL SECTOR FIASCO, WHICH BOTH OCCURED PRIOR TO THE CHANGE IN THE REAL ECONOMIC FUNDAMENTALS: EMPLOYMENT AND PRODUCTION.

WE COULD WRITE AN EQUATION WHERE THE ECONOMY IS THE DEPENDENT VARIABLE AND POLITICAL AND PSYCHOLOGICAL FACTORS (SOMEHOW QUANTIFIED) ARE AMONG THE INDEPENDENT VARIABLES. BUT, THAT OF COURSE, WOULD BE COMPARATIVE STATIC APPROACH WITH AN INCORRECT IMPLICIT CETERIS PARIBUS ASSUMPTION. AND EVEN THOUGH WE KNOW THE REAL WORLD IS MUTATIS MUTANDIS, WE DON'T KNOW THE TIME FRAME OF THE CHANGES: I.E., THE LAGS BETWEEN CAUSE AND EFFECT.

WE DON'T WANT TO BE GUILTY OF POST HOC ERGO PROPTERHOC BUT WE DO KNOW THAT IF ONE POLITICAL-PSYCHOLOGOCIAL FACTOR THAT CAN CAUSE ECONOMIC CHANGE OCCURS BEFORE THE CHANGE, IT IS REASONABLE TO ASSUME CAUSE AND EFFECT.

WE ARE NOW IN THE "EFFECT OF EXPECTATIONS" BALLPARK. WE KNOW THAT IF ENOUGH PEOPLE BELIEVE SOME ECONOMIC EVENT WILL OCCUR AND THEY ACT BASED ON THAT BELIEF, IT WILL HAPPEN.

REWIND BACK TO THE MCCAIN-OBAMA CAMPAIGN DEBATES. WHEN MCCAIN SAID "THE FUNDAMENTALS OF THE ECONOMY ARE SOUND", OBAMA JUMPED ON THAT LIKE UGLY ON THE APE, BECAUSE ALL POLITICIANS REMEMBER WHY GEORGE BUSH (41) LOST: "IT'S THE ECONOMY, STUPID!"

BY USING MCCAIN STATEMENT ALONG WITH THE STOCKMARKET AND HOUSING NEGATIVE NEWS, OBAMA CONVINCED MILLIONS OF AMERICANS THAT THE ECONOMY WAS BAD, WHICH IT WAS NOT AT THAT TIME. AND THAT IS EASY TO PROVE QUANTITATIVELY. UNEMPLOYMENT WAS NOT HIGH, GDP HAD NOT DECLINED TWO SUCCESSIVE QUARTERS - THE DEFINITION OF A RECESSION - AND THE DECLINE IN WEALTH EFFECT FROM BOTH STOCK AND HOUSING VALUE DECLINES WAS NOT ENOUGH PER SE TO CAUSE A RECESSION.

BUT WITH THE MEDIA - ALL OF THEM: LIBERAL OR CONSERVATIVE AND ESPECIALLY THE OBAMA CAMPAIGN PUSHING THE BAD NEWS, PEOPLE DID START TO REDUCE CONSUMPTION ON A BROAD SCALE. THUS: A RECESSION WAS CREATED: THE EFFECT OF EXPECTATIONS: THE POLITICAL-PSYCHOLOGICAL CAUSE.

So, what do we conclude from this essay?

1. All's fair in love, war and politics?

2. The end justifies the means; i.e., if you don't get elected, you don't get to do any good? (No Doctor of Philosophy can accept that premise.)

3. The system is flawed: You have to be unethical and immoral to get a position to do some good. (This assumes Obama knew he was fear-mongering to get elected; did he know?

4. Mass media should be controlled so as not to do things contrary to national interests?

5. All of the above?

6. None of the above?

Frank DeFelice, Ph.D.

TO: WALL STREET JOURNAL
DATE: FEBRUARY 26, 2009
SUBJECT: YOUR MARCH 23 - 24 SYMPOSIUM

IF THEY DO NOT CONCLUDE THAT A U.S. OWNED AND OPERATED CENTRAL BANK
SHOULD REPLACE THE FED, THEN THE DEFICIENCIES OF THE FED: *FAILURE*
TO: 1. CONTROL THE MONEY SUPPLY, 2. STOP LEVERAGED SPECULATION
IN THE STOCKMARKET,, AND 3. ENFORCE PROPER CREDIT STANDARDS IN THE
HOUSING MARKET WILL AGAIN CAUSE THE SAME PROBLEMS WE NOW HAVE.
AFTER ALL, THE FED IS A QUASI-GOVERNMENT INSTITUTION LIKE FANNIE
MAE AND FREDDIE MAC THAT EVERYONE AGREES DID NOT DO THE PUBLIC
POLICY PART OF ITS JOB. TAKE OVER OF THE FEDERAL RESERVE BANKS IS
NECESSARY. THEY WILL BE OUR CENTRAL BANK, OWNED AND OPERATED BY
THE PEOPLE FOR THE PEOPLE INSTEAD OF FOR THE BENEFIT OF THE FINANCIAL
SECTOR BUSINESSES.
STOPPING LEVERAGED SPECULATION THAT CAUSES STOCKMARKET BOOMS WILL
BE A REAL DAMPER ON PONZI AND OTHER FRAUDULENT SCHEMES AS WELL AS
ON THE SO-CALLED HEDGE FUNDS THAT ARE NOTHING MORE THAN LEVERGED
SPECULATION VEHICLES BECAUSE THEY ARE ALL BUILT ON UNSUSTAINABLE
RATES OF PRICE APPRECIATION.
OUR CENTRAL BANK WILL CREATE MONEY;I.E., LEND WHEN THE ECONOMY
NEEDS IT, NOT JUST WHEN IT IS PROFITABLE TO DO SO AS IS THE CASE
NOW. THUS, THE "CREDIT CRUNCH" PROBLEM IS SOLVED FOR GOOD.
LEVERAGED SPECULATION IN THE HOUSING MARKET WILL BE STOPPED BY
SETTING PROPER CREDIT STANDARDS.

THE PRESENT MODUS OPERANDI OF THE SEC WHEREBY THEY SET UP AS THE
SUPREME COURT OF THE SECURITES INDUSTRIES AND DELEGATE REGULATION
TO THE REGULATED DOES NOT AND WILL NOT WORK. YOU CAN'T HAVE THE
FOX GUARDING THE CHICKEN COOP! AN EXAMPLE PAR EXCELLENCE OF HOW
SELF-REGULATION DOES NOT WORK: MADOFF. THE NASD IS REGULATED
BY MEMBERS OF THE NASD. MADOFF HEADED THE NASD. FINRA IS JUST
 NEW WINE IN THE SAME OLD BOTTLE.

FRANK DEFELICE, PH.D. MAINSTREAM INDEPENDENT BY-THE-PEOPLE
                       FOR-THE-PEOPLE ECONOMIST

108

TO: - Gov WEB SITE

FROM:

Dr. & Mrs. Frank DeFelice
Rainbow Resort
Lot 470
700 Co. Rd. 630A
Frostproof, FL 33843

Dr. & Mrs. Frank DeFelice
222 Paradise Peninsula
DeFelice Villa
Lake Norman, NC
Mail: Mooresville, NC 28117

PHONES: 863 635 7558   704 664 2316   CELL: 704 763 9125

EMAIL: DEFELICE.FRANK@YAHOO.COM

SUBJECT: MORE INPUT FOR MARCH 23-24 WASHINGTON SYMPOSIUM

DATE: MARCH 15, 2009

LEVERAGED SPECULATION IN THE COMMODITIES FUTURES MARKET CAUSED THE HIGH PRICE OF OIL AND, THEREFORE GASOLINE. THE LEVERAGING WAS NOT ONLY FINANCED BY THE BANKS; THEY ALSO SPECULATED THEMSELVES!

A PROPERLY OPERATING CENTRAL BANK WOULD NOT ALLOW EITHER TRADERS OR BANKS TO DO LEVERAGED SPECULATION. THIS IS ANOTHER FAILURE OF THE FED TO PERFORM FUNCTIONS REQUIRED FOR THE GOOD OF THE ECONOMY.

IT'S ALSO ANOTHER EXAMPLE OF THE FAILURE OF SELF-REGULATION SUCH AS OCCURRED IN THE SECURITES INDUSTRY.

LEVERAGED SPECULATION IN THE "BUY OUT", MERGERS, AND CONSOLIDATIONS ACTIVITES AT THE BIG BROKERAGE HOUSES WAS ALSO A BIG FACTOR IN THE STOKMARKET BUBBLE AND CRASH.

BANKS AND BROKERS SHOULD NOT BE ALLOWED TO PROVIDE THE FUNDS FOR THAT KIND OF SPECULATION EITHER, BECAUSE IT IS BAD FOR THE REAL ECONOMY. IT'S ANOTHER FAILURE OF THE FED AND THE SEC SELF-REGULATION, WHICH IS THE WAY THE SEC WORKS. SELF_REGULATION DOES NOT WORK.

IRS WITH LOW CAPITAL GAINS TAXES PROVIDES INCENTIVE FOR SPECULATION. THE NECESSARY CORRECTION HERE IS OBVIOUS.

JUSTICE DEPARTMENT'S ANTI-TRUST PEOPLE SHOULD NOT ALLOW MERGERS AND CONSOLIDATIONS AND BUYOUTS THAT REDUCE COMPETITION. SOME CEO,S ADMIT PUBLICALLY THAT BUY OUTS ARE FOR THE PURPOSE OF REDUCING COMPETION! THE BIGGER FIRMS GET, THE FEWER THERE ARE IN ANY INDUSTRY. THE FEWER THE FIRMS, THE LESS THE COMPETITION. ALL MARKETS REQUIRE COMPETITION TO WORK FOR THE BEBEFIT OF THE ECONOMY.

ACCOUNTING RULES TREATING DEBT AS A TAX-DEDUCTIBLE EXPENSE IS ALSO AN ISSUE IN STOPPING LEVERAGED SPECULATION.

DR. DEFELICE: EARNED A BA MAGNA CUM LAUDE FROM HONORS COLLEGE AT MICHIGAN STATE UNIVERSITY; AND MBA AND PH.J. IN ECONOMICS AT THE UNIVERSITY OF NORTH CAROLINA-CHAPEL HILL; HELD NDEA, FORD AND NSF FELLOWSHIPS; DID POST-DOCTORAL WORK AT DUKE IN ECONOMETRICS. COLORADO IN COMPUTER SCIENCE, AND UNDER THE LATE GREAT HENRY LATANE;

PUBLISHED ARTICLES IN <u>THE JOURNAL OF FINANCE</u>, <u>THE ECONOMICS JOURNAL</u> AND THE WALL STREET JOURNAL, AND OTHERS; AUTHORED <u>A PRIMER ON BUSINESS FINANCE</u> WAS AN SEC REGISTERED BROKER/DEALER, INVESTMENT ADVISOR, AND NASD REGISTERED PRINCIPAL.

WHAT NEEDS TO BE DONE FOR A LONG TERM SOLUTION TO OUR CURRENT MALAISE IS <u>STOP LEVERAGED SPECULATION</u>. WHEREEVER IT OCCURS: IN THE STOCK MARKET, THE HOUSING MARKET, AND THE LEVERAGED BUY OUT MARKET. WHEN THE BUBBLE BUSTS ON ANY OR ALL OF THESE MARKETS, THE UN-INFORMED MEDIA AND POLITICIANS RUNNING FOR OFFICE CONVINCE THE PUBLIC WE ARE IN A RECESSION BEFORE WE ARE! BUT THE "EFFECT OF EXPECTATIONS" TAKES HOLD. SAVINGS GO UP AND THEREFORE CONSUMPTION GOES DOWN. THE MARGINAL PROPENSITY TO CONSUME MULTIPLIER WORKS BACKWARDS TOO! SO, WE DO GET A RECESSION BASED ON "POLITICS AND PSYCHOLOGY.

AN APT DESCRIPTION OF THIS WHOLE CHAIN OF CAUSATION THAT HAS TAKEN PLACE IS: "THE TAIL WAGGING THE DOG". AFTER ALL, THE ENTIRE FINANCIAL SECTOR IS ONLY 10% OF GDP IN NORMAL TIMES (I.E., PRE-BUBBLE). NO SINGLE FIRM IN THAT SMALL SECTOR IS "TOO BIG TO FAIL". JUST AS MCCAIN WAS RIGHT DURING THE CAMPAIGN WHEN HE SAID, "THE FUNDAMENTALS OF THE ECONOMY ARE STRONG"; HE IS RIGHT NOW SAYING THAT BANKRUPT BANKS AN BROKERS SHOULD BE ALLOWED TO FAIL. DARWINIAN PRINCIPLES APPLY TO THE GROWTH AND DEVELOPMENT OF ECONOMIES JUST LIKE TO SPECIES: SURVIVAL OF THE FITTEST.

THE PERMANENT SOLUTION IS TO ERADICATE ECONOMIC ILLITERACY IN THE GENERAL POPULATION. HAVE TRIED TO DO SO FOR OVER FOUR DECADES WITH VERY LIMITED SUCCESS, WITH THE ADULT POPULATION. ONLY IF WE START WITH THE KIDS IN HIGH SCHOOL IS THERE ANY CHANCE TO GET THE PUBLIC ON THE SAME PAGE AS ECONOMISTS. AM WRITING A BOOK FOR USE AT THE HIGH SCHOOL LEVEL AS MY PART IN THIS ABSOLUTELY ESSENTIAL PROCESS. TELL THE OBAMA PEOPLE THAT THEIR THRUST INTO EDUCATION SHOULD JUST BE THROWING MONEY AT THE PROBLEM OR BUILDING NICER SCHOOLS (THOUGH THIS SPENDING, AS IS ALL SPENDING - EVEN FOR EARMARKS IS STIMULUS). ANY SCHOOL DISTRICT THAT WANTS MONEY (VIRTUALLY ALL!) MUST AGREE TO HAVE A REQUIRED COURSE IN BASIC ECONOMICS UNDERSTANDING AS A REQUIREMENT FOR GRADUATION. N.B. PASS THIS ON TO ARNE DUNCAN, SECRETARY OF EDUCATION.

KEEP ME IN MIND FOR THE NOBEL WHEN THIS ALL COMES TO FRUITION.

PLEASE AND THANK YOU.

Frank DeFelice, Ph.D.

P.S. Am old enough to remember the Great Depression. Hope it's not that what we learn from history is that we do not learn from history.

Submitted for publication to JPE circa March '09

CAUSES AND CURES FOR THE 2008-9 U.S.ECONOMIC MALAISE

Frank DeFeltce, Ph.D.*

From my credentials*, you can bet the farm I know what the causes and cures - short term, long term and PERMANENT are for the current economic malaise.

My kids always urged me to give short answers to economic questions which is quite difficult because the economy is a complex dynamic social structure. ("Dynamic" here is in the scientific meaning: constantly changing over time. In Latin we'd say *Mutatis mutandis*. Too much economic analysis is on a comparative static basis, in which an implicit and incorrect ceteris paribus assumption is made. For example, a U.S. Senator said during the record high oil prices, "All you have to do is increse supply and the price will go down". It's that simple". Not really, Senator)

Back to the requiremnt for a short answer as to the cause of the current economic malaise: LEVERAGED SPECULATION. This is the basic cause of both recent boom-and-bust cycles in the finance and housing sectors. Before explaining how and why this occured, let's consider another short AND RELEVANT answer developed over the years for all those who ask when told you are an economist, "What is the economy going to do?" Here's my five-word one sentence answer that is right 100% of the time: CYCLES ARE ENDEMIC IN CAPITALISM. Differnt cycles have differing causes and cures. Actually "cures" is too strong a description of what can be done. Amelioration is all we can shoot for. We can not make how the economy works "perfect"; only better. Therefore, we ameliorate the boom-and-bust cycles by reducing the capability for people to do what causes them.

As Mr. Nixon used to say, "Some specificity, please".
1. Eliminate margin accounts in the brokerage business. There is no legitimate economic reason why leveraged purchases of securites is necessary or desirable.FOR THE GOOD OF THE ECONOMY. This, of course, begs the question: "What is the role of the stockmarket in a capitalistic economy?". The NYSE is, after all, only a place where exchanges take place. Tradin' one security for another is what it is all about. THERE IS NO EFFECT ON THE REAL ECONOMY for the billions of shares traded every day save a marginal increase in consumpteon from incresed wealth when prices go up. And when prices decline, a decrese in consumption based on a decrease in wealth! This by itself would not slow the economy down much, but when it happens simultaneously in the housing sector, and when a politician uses these endemic occurences to sell himself as the savior of the system that he says is on the brink of disater, . when it was not, then widespread declines in consumption and capital spending do cause the becline in the real economy. It's a well known phenomenon in economics known as the "effect of expectations"

2. Repeal the "one bank holding Co." rule: i.e., repeal the repeal of the Glass-Steagall Act of 1933, which was enacted for good cause, when all except conservative right-wing nuts saw no problem w/banks and brokers in bed together. Going back to Glass-Steagall will eliminate the availability of low interest loans from one side of the business: banks to another side of the same business: brokers. But we have to be careful of overkill. Capitalism does need a mechanism for firms to raise capital. And a market for those securities sold to raise money for firms when the stockholder wants out. Regulated Broker/Deaers can provide both of these necessary functions, but LEVERAGED BUYING IS NOT NECESSARY. And the NYSE does not raise capital. There is nothing in U.S. law requiring public support for the NYSE, brokers or bankers. But there is a law requiring the government to do what's necessary for price stability. And leverased speculation does the opposite of stability; it creates volatility.

3. Eliminate leveraged speculation in the housing sector. The unholy broker-banker alliance is at work here too. The mortgage loans are "securitized" so that both the bank and the broker are making money on the housing boom. Highly leveraged, infinitely actually: NO MONEY DOWN! speculation took place in the housing sector.

4. Raise capital gains taxes to above income tax rates. This will lengthen the time period speculators will have to hold their speculative asset purchases. It's just a figment of imagination going back to Reganomics supply side, trickle-down thinking that thinks incorrectly that lowering capital gains taxes will help the economy.

5. Do away with the IRS' $500,000 tax free profit for capital gains on homes owned by couples for only two years. It's just an incentive that fuels the housing sector boom with its inevitable bust.

How to accomplish 1. - 5.:
Establish a BANK OF THE UNITED STATES.
Why a BANK OF THE UNITED STATES?
Because there is a fatal flaw in the make-up of the Federal Reserve System that discourages it from performing essential functions:
1. CONTROL OF THE MONEY SUPPLY,
2. PRICE STABILITY:
    A. IN THE STOCK MARKET, AND
    B. IN THE HOUSING SECTOR.
3. SETTING CREDIT STANDARDS.

What is the fatal flaw?
Thousands of commercial banks, that are PRIVATELY OWNED BUSINESSES are relied upon to carry out PUBLIC MONETARY POLICY. In the current situation, doing what is best for the banks is bad for the economy. When negative news about the stockmarket causes a decline in spending throughout the economy, the banks decline making loans because they fear defaults, which is rational FOR THEM. However, FOR THE ECONOMY they are reducing the money supply (THIS IS THE "CREDIT CRUNCH") at exactly the wrong time to the detriment of the economy. So, what's good for the member banks of the FED is bad for the economy = the fatal flaw of the FED that must be fixed for a long term solution to the current economic malaise.

A U.S. CENTRAL BANK WOULD NOT WORK THE WAY THE FED DOES . IT HAS NO STOCKHOLDERS AND IS NOT PROFIT MOTIVATED. IT WILL DO WHAT'S GOOD FOR THE ECONOMY. A U.S. CENTRAL BANK WOULD ACHIEVE PRICE STABILITY BY LIMITING LEVERAGED SPECULATION. IT COULD SET MARGIN REQUIREMENTS HIGH OR ELIMINATE THEM IF NECESSARY. IT COULD SET DOWN PAYMENTS HIGH FOR MORTGAGES AND ENFORCE INCOME STANDARDS FOR BORROWERS. IT COULD PROVIDE EMERGENCY CAPITAL LOANS AND LIQUIDITY WHEN NECESSARY. IT WOULD HELP THE TREASURY RAISE MONEY AT RATES GOOD FOR THE TREASURY. AS IT IS NOW, ON THE TOP SIDE OF THE CYCLE WHEN THE CORRECT MONETARY IS HIGH INTEREST RATES TO FIGHT INFLATION, THE TREASURY HAS TO FINANCE THE GOVERNMENT DEBT AT HIGH INTEREST RATES. A U.S. CENTRAL BANK COULD AMELIORATE THIS CURRENT CONFLICT BETWEEN THE FED AND THE TREASURY.

SUMMARIZING:
1. THE SHORT TERM CURE FOR THE ECONOMY IS QUITE SIMPLE: INCREASE AGGREGATE DEMAND TO THE FULL EMPLOYMENT LEVEL.
2. THE LONG TERM CURE: A U.S. CENTRAL BANK.
3. AND THE PERMANENT CURE: ERASE ECONOMIC ILLITERACY.
   SPECIFICITY?
THE STOCKMARKET IS NOT THE ECONOMY.
WALL STREET IS NOT THE ECONOMY.
NYSE IsNOT THE ECONOMY.
A BALANCED BUDGET WOULD BE BAD FOR THE ECONOMY.
THERE IS NO SUCH THING AS AN INVESTMENT BANK.
THERE IS NO SUCH THING AS A BUSINESS TOO BIG TO FAIL.
LONG TERM ECONOMIC GROWTH REQUIRES CHANGE. SOME INDUSTRIES DIE SO OTHERS CAN BE BORN. BAILOUTS ARE BAD.
THERE IS NO SUCH THING AS "OUR JOBS".
ECONOMICS IS A SCIENCE.
ECON ECONOMIC ANALYSIS REQUIRES MUCH MORE THAN ANECDOTAL DATA.

* DR. DEFELICE EARNED AN MBA AND PH.D. AT UNC-CHAPEL HILL;
IS AACSB TERMINALLY QUALIFIED IN BOTH ECONOMICS AND FINANCE;
HELD A DEA, FORD, AND NSF FELLOWSHIPS;
DID POST-DOC WORK AT DUKE (ECONOMETRICS), COLORADO (COMPUTER SCIENCE),
        AND UNDER THE LATE GREAT HENRY LATANE;
PUBLISHED IN THE JOURNAL OF FINANCE, THE ECONOMICS JOURNAL , WALL
        STREET JOURNAL AND OTHERS;
AUTHORED A PRIMER ON BUSINESS FINANCE
WAS AN SEC REGISTERED BROKER/DEALER, INVESTMENT ADVISOR, AND
        AN NASD REGISTERED PRINCIPAL.

3A MAGNA CUM LAUDE HONORS COLLEGE MICHIGAN STATE UNIVERSITY

TO : PRESIDENT OBAMA

FROM :

Dr. & Mrs. Frank DeFelice
672 Windridge
Linville, NC
Mail: 2152 Land Harbor
Newland, NC 28657

DATE : JULY 8, 2009

SUBJECT : FINANCIAL GIANTS <u>SHOULD BE</u> TRIMMED
"THE OBAMA ADMINISTRATION DOESN'T WANT SO MANY AROUND ANYMORE".
BUT GEITHNER IS MAKING MORE OF THEM AND BIGGER!

1. Goldman-Sachs became bigger when Geithner and Paulson (ex-Goldman CEO!) told them to become a one-bank holding company last September, which they did and they gave them $10 Billion.

2. Geithner forced Bank of America to take Billions of the bailout money EVEN THOUGH BANK OF AMERICA DID NOT WANT NOR NEED THE MONEY! That make them much bigger.

3. Geithner forced BofA to buy Merrill Lynch, which created a huge financial behemoth.

4. Geithner put Billions into Citigroup, making it bigger.

Putting the FED in charge of these "systemically significant" companies would be ludicrous if it wasn't downright stupid.

The systemically risky companies are the member banks of the Federal Reserve System. Their profit motivation forces them to decrease the money supply (CAUSING A "CREDIT CRUNCH") exactly at the time the money supply should be increased: AS HAPPENED IN THIS RECESSION, IN THE GREAT DEPRESSION, AND WILL CONTINUE TO HAPPEN <u>AD INFINITUM</u> UNTIL OUR CENTRAL BANK NO LONGER RELIES ON PROFIT-SEEKING INSTITUTINS TO CARRY OUT PUBLIC POLICY.

These huge financial institutions would never have come about except for the Garn-St. Germain Act of 1982 that repealed these kind of conglomerates not allowed under Glass— Steagall, which was necessary New Deal regulations of banks.

Congress does not want the FED to supervise our financial system. The FED has proven in many cases it can not do the job.

We can get rid of these financial sector fiascos permanently by doing two things:
1. Repeal Garn-St. Germain, and
2. Nationalize the Federal Reserve REGIONAL banks as our:
BANK OF THE UNITED STATES OF AMERICA.
Let the member banks go off on their own as regulated banks under the control of the Bank of the U.S.; which then becomes our Super Regulator of the entire financial sector. More alphabet soup agencies is NOT the answer.

Ask Geithner to prove to the American people that Goldman-Sachs, Bank of America, Citigroup etc. have to be so big. They should be made SMALLER;i.e., broken up by the anti-trust people in Justice because they tend to lessen competition.

The Treasury Secretary and the FED regulating the financial sector is the fox in the chicken coop.

Copies: Diana Farrell, Deputy Director, White House National Economic Council
         Jim Kuhnhenn, Associated Press; Rahm Emanuel; Ben Bernanke,FED Chmn.
         Council of Economic Advisors
         Any and All Mass Media

Frank DeFelice, Ph.D.

July 16, 2009

Dear Friend:

Thank you for your views on my Administration's work to fix our economy. Our Nation's current recession has been caused by irresponsibility and poor decision-making that stretched from Wall Street to Washington to Main Street. It started with the housing market, where bets were made on risky loans wrongly marked with safe ratings. As property values declined and loans went into default, investors panicked. Banks stopped lending, businesses began to struggle and lay off workers, who then struggled with their own bills.

I understand that some people think we should let banks fail, while others support taking them over. I believe we need aggressive action to get credit flowing again. Credit sustains our economy; it allows families to pay for college education and small businesses to expand and hire workers. Without the flow of credit, we risk years of sluggish growth, low job creation, and anemic investment.

My Administration has taken bold action to help banks start lending again. We are pairing government resources with private investment to clear away bad loans and securities that prevent banks from lending—the so-called "toxic assets." We are also restructuring the auto industry so that America can preserve jobs and lead the world in building the next generation of clean cars. We are implementing regulatory reforms in the financial sector and increasing accountability in Washington to prevent another disaster. Each change protects the well-being of American workers and taxpayers above all. For more information, visit: www.whitehouse.gov/issues/economy.

I will continue to do everything in my power to get our economy back on track. American families deserve nothing less. Thank you again for writing.

Sincerely,

116

THE WHITE HOUSE
WASHINGTON, DC 20500

ZEEH4711 8Z

SOUTHERN MD 207

Dr. Frank DeFelice
222 Paradise Peninsula
Mooresville, NC 20117

TO: PRESIDENT OBAMA

FROM:

DATE: July 22, 2009

Dr. & Mrs. Frank DeFelice
672 Windridge
Linville, NC
Mail: 2152 Land Harbor
Newland, NC 28657

SUBJECT: "WE NEED A BETTER WAY TO DO BUSINESS POST-BUBBLE".
    "GOLDMAN REVENUE UP; SO IS *COMPENSATION*
    SO IS GASOLINE AND THE CPI!
    "THERE YOU GO AGAIN", REAGAN

Guy Moszkowski, a ML analyst, predicted Goldman's earnings on July 9 @ $3.90/sh. On July 13, WSJ predicted $3.48.
On July 14, Goldman announced net income of $3.44 Billion, which is $4.93/share, and it came from "all time highs from short term trading and underwriting".

"Short term trading" is better explained as leveraged speculation for short term capital gains. And we know that Goldman is the biggest short term trader in both the NYSE and in the oil futures market. Driving up prices in those markets is what they do for their benefit to the detriment of the real economy. THE STOCK MARKET IS NOT THE ECONOMY.

When Paulson, the ex-Goldman CEO!, and Geithner told Goldman in Sep 2008, who was then a Broker/Dealer, to become a one-bank holding company, they did so and got $10 Billion of our money in October. This was needed only to capitalize their commercial bank. The bank gives them unlimited funds to fuel the leveraged speculation done by the Broker/dealer part of the firm. Since they do not have to pay loan interst to themselves for the marginal funds, their profits from leveraged speculation have increased dramatically to 65% higher than the same quarter last year.

Last year they made $667 million from oil futures trading alone, and the mgr of the energy trading unit, Mr. Hall, got ONLY $100 million for his "production" He complained that if Geithner did not let up on bonus caps, he'd quit Goldman and start a hedge fund, which is just another leveraged speculation vehicle, because they pay 30% on such "production" to guys like Hall;and he, therefore, would have got $200 million operating as a hedge fund.

Goldman repaid the $10 Billion so now they have increased pay by 33% ON AVERAGE. Hall will have to get a 100% increase to stay with Goldman. This not a better way to do business; it's worse.

It's a warranted conclusion that you are NOT doing things that are GOING TO cause bubbles again; you have done things that HAVE ALREADY STARTED bubbles again! "Déjà vu all over again", Yogi Berra. Or as the French say: la plus change. le meme chose. What we learn from history is that we don't learn from history, Dr. DeFelice

Here's the empirical evidence: the consumer price index (CPI) rose .7% last month. That's an annual rate of 8.4%. That's the worse monthly increase for many years, (and during a recession!) AND IT IS ALMOST ENTIRELY DUE TO THE HIGHEST MONTHLY INCREASE in gasoline prices in the last five years.

The gasoline price rise is caused by the "trading gains" – LEVERAGED SPECULATION – by Goldman inter alios. Goldman made as much profit in the first quarter this year as the entire year of 2008! If the hidden energy trading unit made $667 million, Mr. Hall's bonus FOR THE FIRST QUARTER WILL BE $200 MILLION! Goldman paid back the $10 Billion Paulson gave them, so the Treasury can no longer cap bonuses. BUT THE FED CAN. Goldman is now a commercial bank and federal regulators can see where those profits are coming from and control those activites that are detrimental to the economy: BUBBLES! How? The Fed sets margin requirements. If there is no margin, there are no margin loans. With no margin loans there is no leveragedspeculation driving up oil prices and starting another stock market bubble. It's really quite simple: KISS!

Bank supervision is the central banks' No. 1 responsibility around the world. Our central bank, the FED is not, will not, and can not do its essential job.

The stock market is no longer a competitive industry, it has been made into an oligopoly whereby a few large firms dominate in both the buy and sell sides of the market. That's what trading is all about. And when one firm is so big that it accounts for 24% of the trading that is no longer free market competition but the case where a few ("olig" means few in Greek) buyers determine price. Geithner is a big part of the cause of this problem, but Congress and the anti-trust people can put a stop to it:

Congress should repeal Garn-St.Germain, which allows the one-bank holding conglomerates like BofA – ML and Goldman Sachs that Geithner created so that no more can be created.

And the anti-trust people should break up . . . BofA and Goldman because it is clear they lessen competition due to their sheer size and high percentage of the market. Starting with the Regan de-regulation policy, anti-trust actions to preserve and maintain real economic competition have been largely non-existent, This would be a good step towards "a better way of doing business post-bubble".

Copies : Rahm Emanuel, Sen. Sherrod Brown, Sen. Robert Menendez, Anti-Trust Div. SEC, Catherine Dodge- Blumberg News, Scott Patterson – WSJ, Any and All Mass Media

TO : PRESIDENT OBAMA, OUR FRIEND

FROM :

**Dr. & Mrs. Frank DeFelice
672 Windridge
Linville, NC
Mail: 2152 Land Harbor
Newland NC 28657**

DATE : July 28, 2009

SUBJECT : REPLY TO YOURS OF JULY 16, 2009 (copy enclosed)

From your response, we can see that none of the carefully considered highly qualified analysis pinpointing the causes and cures for the current recession that we have communicated to many in your Administration (Rahm Emanuel, Council of Economic Advisors, Treasury Secretary Geithner, the SEC, and FED Chairman Ben Bernanke) Have reached your desk. So, we will go back to square one.
not

You and your campaign for the Presidency are in part responsible for the recession. This is because when the housing bubble burst at the same time the stock market crashed, you used that data to declare a "crisis' in the economy, whereas the real important data about the economy did show at that time that McCain was right when he said, "the fundamentals of the economy are sound". (So, he lost the election for the same reason George H.W. Bush did: "It's the economy, stupid!".)

It was good politics of you to do what you did, but it was bad for the economy. There's a lot of psychology in economics. What happened in this instance is well known in economics as "the effect of expectations". (Did your personal economics professor Larry Summers explain that to you?) When people believed your incorrect assessment that the economy was in trouble AND ACTED UPON THAT BELIEF, then that caused the negative economic effects to occur. People fear recessions and increase savings to be prepared. When savings go up, consumption goes down. Our economy is consumption driven. When consumption goes down, businesses decrease production. Decreased production means unemployment. Unemployment means further reduction in consumption. Also business spending for "real" investment – plant & equipment – declines. The multiplier effect (what Danny Kaye called "to pocket to pocket to pocket") Applied to these decreases in aggregate demand magnifies the downward pressure.

Another cause of the recession was the widespread concern generated mostly by vested interests that the stock market crash was further evidence that the economy was in recession. We have said many times and will continue to say 'til the end : THE STOCK MRKET IS NOT THE ECONOMY. (There is a relatively small negative effect from a decrease in wealth on consumption.) But if the public thinks that the stock market crash is truly a "bad economy" fact and ACTS UPON THAT MISTAKEN BELIEF, that further feeds the decrease in aggregate demand.

There's another bubble that negatively effected the economy at the same time of the housing bubble bust and the stock market crash : the oil (and gasoline) commodities market bubble. The cause of that bubble was the highly leveraged speculation (margins< 10%!) done by so-called "energy trading units" which are hidden and/or secretive operations of big Wall St. Broker/Dealer firms, e.g. Goldman Sachs and Citigroup. Both of those firms had a Mr. Hall heading up that part of their businesses and both firms made an identical $667 million (according to WSJ) last year from their highly leveraged trading in oil futures. Their trading is simply buy and sell, buy and sell, oil futures contracts over and over all day every day.They determine the price of oil (and therefore gasoline) by bidding it up; supply and demand do not determine the price of oil. Both Mr. Halls were paid over $100 million last year, while all three sectors of the real economy :Consumers, Business and Government suffered with high energy costs.

Leveraged buy-outs (LBO'S) orchestrated by Wall St. Brokers were a part of the cause of the stock market crash. So too were "hedge funds", which are not really involved in hedging, but rather in highly leveraged speculation for short term capital gains.

Banks also were highly leveraged, and therefore very vulnerable to a downturn. They even speculated in such things as oil futures contracts themselves in addition to providing the financing for brokers to do so.

It is very clear that the fundamental economic cause of all these bubbles is HIGHLY LEVERAGED SPECULATION FOR SHORT TERM CAPITAL GAINS. You don't want bubbles; stop the highly leveraged speculation. Can't stop all speculation , but you can stop the leveraging to curtail it . Amelioration is the goal; nothing is ever perfect.

"Leveraging per se is not wrong or bad. Too little is wrong; too much is bad. Therefore, there is an optimum amount. In corporate finance it is the right debt-equity ratio for that business. Banks are businesses. Therefore, their debt/equity ratios, their leveraging, should be regulated by our central bank, "the FED". Failure of the FED in this matter is another cause of the recession.

In housing there was virtually no down payment for people to buy a house. The mortgage brokers and realtors get their fees and commissions up front, and this was all that buyers put in, which meant that people buying half million dollar houses with a few thousand dollars were leveraged at 100 to 1 or more in many cases.

Highly leveraged speculation for short term capital gains (THIS IS NOT "INVESTMENT") was what drove up prices to the inevitable bust in housing, the stock market, the oil futures market, and now the commercial real estate market is going bust. The housing market boom and bust was facilitated by low capital gains tax rates and IRS rules that exempt up to $500,000 of gain from taxation, another causal factor for the recession.

And as far as "too big to fail" goes, we have seen no rationale to support that assertion; and argue, to the contrary, that no such institution exists in the U.S. economy. We base our argument on the fact that the entire financial sector –all the banks, all the brokers, all the insurance companies inter alios combined constitute only 10% of the economy in ordinary times (pre-bubble). The failure of one firm,e.g. AIG will not take down the U.S. Economy,and Geithner would know this if he were an economist or paid more attention in economics classes at Dartmouth. (Maybe not; we had an insurance man on Cape Cod who majored in economics at Dartmouth and confided to us that he never understood the graphs!) Bear Sterns and Lehman are gone; no problem. Millions of Americans are disgusted with the AIG and other bailouts. This is a real political problem for your "brilliant political strategist", Mr. Emanuel,to solve. Not us. We stick to our last: economics.

Bailouts were wrong for the auto industry, too. The underlying philosophy of capitalism (we are Doctors of Philosophy!) is derived from Darwin's Origin of Species and the idea of survival of the fittest. In economics if a firm can not make a profit ti is supposed to die. If you do not allow this process to take place (you are messing with mother nature?) You stifle growth and development and resources are mis-allocated to where the people do not want them to be.

In the long view of economic growth and development, there is a natural progression from agriculture to manufacturing to service. We are in the third stage of the process. Over 70% of our labor force presently is employed in the service sector of our economy. It's only natural, normal and desirable that manufacturing-including the auto industry – decline.

More alphabet soup agencies in the financial sector is not the solution there. The SEC is no good because it delegated its regulatory authority to the regulated' The NYSE regulates the NYSE. The NASD regulates the NASAD. Self regulation does not work – example par excellence : Mr. Madoff. The SEC Commissioners just sit up on their dais like Supreme Court Justices waiting for some poor soul who's not in the old boy loop and has to appeal their harassment of him for their interpretation of whose ox has been gored, or such other weighty decisions as to whether or not more "whereases" should be included in prospectuses. They are just a bunch of lawyer,who think they know something about finance. (They are just really political hacks, remnants of our spoils system that goes back to Joe Kennedy and likely further.)
Here, an example of their incompetence: We recently sent for a prospectus that advertised they tell the investor what the risk is. Economics is a quantitative science; risk can be calculated Bet the SEC people don't know how to do it; so it is not done and provided to investors as it should be.

To prevent "another disaster" as you put it, you need to stop highly leveraged speculation. Here's the question all youf"in the box" thinkers need to tackle : Why, in terms of what is good for the economy, do we have margin accounts? Stop them and you curtail the negative effects of leverage in the stock and commodities markets.

Currently 75% of NYSE trading is for short term capital gains, with Goldman Sachs accounting for 24%! This is indicative of a failure by the anti-trust people in the Justice Department to enforce anti-trust laws that prohibit such market domination. With big "players" like Goldman
Sachs (WHICH GEITHNER MADE BIGGER!) a competitive market gets destroyed. What we now have is an oligopoly whereby a few large firms control prices. Real economic competition requires a relatively large number of firms so that no one buyer or seller can influence price. That condition is not met on the NYSE nor in many other markets. Mergers and consolidations have gone forward unabated from the Reagan years abetted greatly by the Garn-St. Germain Act of 1982, which should be repealed FOR THE GOOD OF THE ECONOMY.

The so-called "credit crunch" was not a cause of the bubbles. Just the opposite: the bubbles were caused by the financial institutions that fueled the highly leveraged speculation for short term capital gains. The banks themselves were too highly leveraged, and they did too much lending, created too much credit, increasing the money supply too fast. So, the FED failed to correctly control the money supply on both sides of the cycle – on the way up they created too much money , and on the downside they failed to create enough. Banks stopped lending because they did not find borrowers who were credit worthy. Geithner incorrectly thought they lacked adequate excess reserves and forced them to take billions even though some did not need nor want the money; e.g., Bank of America. We now know that pouring billions into the banks did not make them lend; i.e., create money. Neither will buying up all their bad loans (toxic assets). Not having bad loans on their books is not an incentive to lend.

There's an implicit (maybe explicit!) and incorrect assumption made by Geithner to the effect "the banks got us into this mess so they will get us out". He incorrectly assumes that you have to fix the financial sector to fix the economy. This cause and effect is backwards. When the economy is fixed, the financial sector will be fixed because banks will find credit worthy borrowers. He thinks money is the life blood of the economy; probably most bankers do. But economists know better; money is just a numerairé. And in the current malaise it was poison.

We have asked Christina Romer and other economists to explain to you why "You can't push a balloon up by a string". This exposes the fatal flaw of the FED whereby they (it?) Decrease the money supply when it needs to be increased. It's well documented that the FED made that mistake in the Great Depression (which we remember!) . And the credit crunch is further evidence of its failure in this recession.

We DO let banks fail – dozens every year –but the FDIC can not figure out these huge comglomerates that go by the name of "one-bank holding companies". She (Sheila Bair) is not the only one that can not untangle them. Lawyers are billing us $950/hour trying to sort out Lehman Bros. bankrkuptcy! Geithner created two new big ones: You guessed it: Goldman Sachs and Bank of America. Repeal of Garn-St. Germain would stop this.

The FED can not be fixed to deal with "systemic problems" in the financial sector because THE FED IS THE SYSTEMIC PROBLEM. Aside from the fact that it does not properly supervise banking — good central banks set the terms of ALL loans made by banks – mortgages and margin accounts are loans – so are credit cards, the FED can not, ahs not, and never will be able to increase the money supply in downturns. (You can "not push a balloon up by a string". (Ask Christina Romer to explain this to you and to Tim Geithner.) Unless an until we establish a good central bank – one that supervises banking properly and controls the money supply for the good of the economy – we will continue to have credit crunches or financial crises or whatever you want to call them – periodically as we have had for over 200 years.

WE DESPARATELY NEED A BANK OF THE UNITED STATES OF AMERICA (like the Bank of : England, Canada, Japan, Euro. etc.) that is owned and operated by the people of America for the people of America. This will be quite easy to do actually: Nationalize the regional Federal Reserve banks. Will not the political problem of "socialism" because most Americans think the FED is already a government agency.

We also need to repeal Gam-St. Germain that allows banks to be gobbled up in huge holding company conglomerates like Goldman and Bank of America – both created by Geithner — and Citigroup.
Anti-trust action is called for vs. Goldman, Bank of America, Citigroup and others who have tended to monopolize trading on the NYSE and commodities markets.

The stimulus is the right cure for the short term. IF the government spending is enough to offset the decreases in consumer and business spending, which it is not to this point. Dragging it out over two years makes no sense to us. If it were all put in today it would probably take two years for the full effect!

A good central bank is the cure for the longer term.

And for the permanent cure, no less than the eradication of economic illiteracy in the populus is required. This is a tall order, but we are working on it. Better to shed some light than to curse the darkness. To that end we are writing WHAT ALL AMERICANS NEED TO KNOW ABOUT ECONOMICS; sub-title Causes and Cures of the 2008-'09 U.S. Recession. Being written for the High School level . With the hope and help of Arne Duncan to get a required course in all U.S. school systems. When they come and ask for money they know they have to meet certain requirements: curriculum reform to include Fundamental Economics.

Copies: Rahm Emanuel, Council of Economic Advisors, Treasury Secretary Geithner, SEC, FED, FDIC, Education Secretary Arne Duncan

TO : EDITOR, WALL STREET JOURNAL
FROM : **Dr. & Mrs. Frank DeFelice**
672 Windridge
Linville, NC
Mail: 2152 Land Harbor
Newland, NC 28657

DATE : July 30, 2009
SUBJECT : TWO MR. HALL's, TWO "HIDDEN SECRETIVE" ENERGY TRADING
UNITS, BOTH "PRODUCED" $667 MILLION, BOTH HALLS WERE
PAID $100 MILLION !?

In the July 25-26, 2009 edition, front page , we learned that Mr. A. Hall with Citigroup
did the above. Back awhile you told us that a Mr. Hall at Goldman did exactly the
same!?
We do not believe in coincidences. We do believe reporters fudge facts.
Or do you have a good explanation for this exactly identical data?

LL STREET JOURNAL.

SATURDAY/SUNDAY, JULY 25 - 26, 2009

WEEKEND EDITION

★★★★ $2.00

WSJ.com

Citi in $100 Million Pay Clash

BY MICHAEL SICONOLFI
AND AARON LUCCHETTI

A top Citigroup Inc. trader is pressing the financial giant to honor a 2008 pay package that could total $100 million, setting the stage for a potential showdown between Citi and the government's new pay czar.

The trader, Andrew J. Hall, heads Citigroup's energy-trading unit, Phibro LLC—a secretive operation, run from the site of a former Connecticut dairy farm, that occasionally accounts for a disproportionate chunk of Citigroup income.

Mr. Hall's pay package puts Citigroup in a tight spot. Rip-

ping up the contract could trigger Mr. Hall's departure and a potentially messy legal fight. But making any large payouts, even if they're based on previously agreed contracts, could subject Citigroup to political

■ Citigroup's three new directors bring Bethany connections......B3

and investor fallout.

Earlier this year, American International Group Inc.'s bonus payments of $165 million to some executives caused an outcry, given the insurer's U.S.-government bailout. Citigroup has

received some $45 billion in bailout money.

It will be an early test for Kenneth Feinberg, the Treasury Department's pay czar, who was appointed last month to a new position with the power to help set pay for top executives and highly paid employees at seven firms receiving the most government financial aid. Banks and others have a mid-August deadline for submitting pay requests to Mr. Feinberg.

"Companies will need to convince Mr. Feinberg that they have struck the right balance to discourage excessive risk-taking.

Please turn to page A6

Star trader Andrew Hall could set up a showdown with U.S. pay czar.

Reprinted by permission of the Wall Street Journal.

Frank DeFelice, Ph.D.

TO : PRESIDENT OBAMA, OUR FRIEND

FROM :
**Dr. & Mrs. Frank DeFelice
672 Windridge
Linville, NC
Mail: 2152 Land Harbor
Newland, NC 28657**

DATE : AUGUST 5, 2009

SUBJECT : " WE NEED A BETTER WAY TO DO BUSINESS POST-BUBBLE".
THE CASE FOR A NEW CENTRAL BANK FOR THE U.S.
WHY THE FED WILL ALWAYS FAIL TO DO THE JOB

The job of the central bank is to supervise banking and control the money supply.
The FED does neither of these very well. In fact, the FED decreases the money supply
when it should be increased (causing the "credit crunch") and increases it when it should
be curtailed, fueling the highly leveraged speculation for short term capital gains that led
to the cyclical boom and bust in the stock market, commodities market, housing market
and the commercial real estate market.

The failure of the FED to properly supervise the banks is evidenced by the fact that
lending practices by the banks are not standardized at a low risk level, and loans should
not be made for the purpose of short term speculation.

Making loans and controlling the money supply are two sides of the same coin. When
loans are made, the money supply increases. When loans are paid off, the money supply
decreased. Therefore, the change in the money supply is determined by the ratio of loans
made to loans paid. People in important places do not understand this simple fact.

For example, Mr. David Wessel, the economics editor for the Wall Street Journal, in a
promo interview about his book IN FED WE TRUST, On NPR on August 4, 2009 was
asked the question: "Can't the FED with just a keystroke (on the computer) create
money?" His immediate AND INCORRECT response was "YES"!

The reason the FED can not control changes in the money supply FOR THE GOOD OF
THE ECONOMY is that bank loans are made by private for-profit businesses (the
member banks of the Federal Reserve System, virtually all commercial banks in the U.S.)
For their benefit, regardless of the effect on the economy.

In fact, the normal business operation of the thousands of banks that ARE the FED runs
contrary to what's best for the economy. When the economy is on the upside of the
cycle, banks are anxious to make as many loans as they can because it is profitable to do
so. But increasing the money supply too much caused the speculative boom in prices of
stocks, housing, commodities (read "oil and gasoline") etc. to a point of inevitable bust.

The banks themselves get highly leveraged and even get into the boom markets for their own account. They saw Goldman Sachs and Citigroup making $667 million in the oil futures market, so started trading for themselves in addition to financing the broker/dealers. It's a warranted conclusion that the banks are in business to make money, not support the economy.

When the inevitable bust comes, they decrease lending, and therefore the money supply because they don't like the look of the economy and fear non-payment.
And because all the banks are so highly leveraged, they won't even lend to other banks. They are in business to make money, not support the economy.

In other word, the banks ARE the FED. The banks supervise the banks. Self-regulation does not work. The SEC delegates regulation of the NYSE to the NYSE. The SEC delegates regulation of the NASD to the NASD. Self regulation does not work. Example par excellence: Madoff.

Good supervision of banking necessitates that the terms of all loans be controlled. Mortgages, margin accounts and credit cards are loans. With proper AND ENFORCED standards for just these three areas of loans, the '08-'09 recession could have been avoided because the highly leveraged speculation for short term capital gains was financed by the banks making loans that should not have been made.

The FED can with highly undesirable consequences, fight inflation by raising interest rates and decreasing the excess reserves and thereby the money supply. An example of the "highly undesirable consequences" would be the Reagan-Volker tight money policies that raised interest rates on low risk loans to 16% and unemployment to over 10%.

But when it comes to helping the economy out of a recession, the FED is virtually powerless. Interest rates have gone to zero – no effect. Geithner forced $Billions into banks' capital – no effect. Geithner is buying up banks' bad loans ("toxic assets"). There will no effect on the real economic problems of high unemployment and negative change in GDP from any or all of these approaches by a banker (not an economist), who harbors such idiocy as "money is the lifeblood of the economy" and "the banks got us into this mess; the banks will get us out". No way Jose!

After the infusion of $ Billions, Barney Frank said, "You can't make them (the banks) do anything". Right on! This exposes the fatal flaw of the Federal Reserve System, which can not be repaired or improved upon by some more alphabet soup agencies. Such an approach makes things worse because it increase the overlapping jurisdictions problem. This well-known deficiency of the FED is explained in all principles of economics textbooks as : "You can't push a balloon up by a string". The "balloon" is the economy. The "pusher" is the FED. The FED can pull down on the string, but not push up!

The only way to get rid of this inability of the FED to perform its role for the good of the economy is to replace the FED with a good central bank that will carry out monetary policy for the good of the economy – not for the profit of the member banks.

Such a bank would be very easy to create : nationalize the 12 regional Federal Reserve banks. No pllitical problems of "socialism" will arise because most Americans think the FED is already a government agency. This will be THE BANK OF THE UNITED STATES OF AMERICA, owned and operated by the people for the people. It willset the terms for all bank loans: mortgages, margin accounts and credit cards included and it will implement tight money policies to halt speculative booms and increase the money supply in downturns, WHICH THE FED CAN NOT DO.

POST SCRIPTS

The Bank of the U.S. will be the SUPER REGULATOR of the financial sector that there is near unanimity is necessary.

There is also near unanimity that quasi-public institutions like Fannie Mae, Freddie Mac AND THE FED do not work. They run amok leveraging on the upside of cycles exacerbating a bad situation because they know they will be bailed out on the downside. Capitalism works better when the underlying philosophy includes the dictum: Live by leverage; die by leverage. Leveraging should be a TWO-EDGED sword.

Millions of Americans are disgusted with the new business "model" that says: "Leverage like hell on the upside of the bubble and when it busts, file bankruptcy or get a government bailout".

Our basic economic goal of price stability is just as important, if not more so, for financial "products" as it is for consumer goods because volatility of prices of financial "products" defines the cause of boom and bust cycles that precipitate downturns in the important economic variables: employment and growth.

If you will establish a new good central bank, not only will it create immortality for you in history, you will also become a serious contender for the Nobel Prize in economics because you will have provided the long run solution to these recurring financial "crises" that have precipitated downturns in the real economy for over 200 years in the U.S.

Copies: Rahm Emanuel, Council of Economic Advisors, FED Chairman Bernanke, Rep. Barney Frank, Senator Baucus, The Journal of Finance

Aug. 5, '09

Such a bank would be very easy to create : nationalize the 12 regional Federal Reserve banks. No political problems of "socialism" will arise because most Americans think the FED is already a government agency. This will be THE BANK OF THE UNITED STATES OF AMERICA, owned and operated by the people for the people. It will set the terms for all bank loans: mortgages, margin accounts and credit cards included and it will implement tight money policies to halt speculative booms and increase the money supply in downturns, WHICH THE FED CAN NOT DO.

POST SCRIPTS

The Bank of the U.S. will be the SUPER REGULATOR of the financial sector that there is near unanimity is necessary

There is also near unanimity that quasi-public institutions like Fannie Mae, Freddie Mac AND THE FED do not work. They run amok leveraging on the upside of cycles exacerbating a bad situation because they know they will be bailed out on the downside. Capitalism works better when the underlying philosophy includes the dictum: Live by leverage; die by leverage. Leveraging should be a TWO-EDGED sword.

Millions of Americans are disgusted with the new business "model" that says: "Leverage like hell on the upside of the bubble and when it busts, file bankruptcy or get a government bailout".

Our basic economic goal of price stability is just as important, if not more so, for financial "products" as it is for consumer goods because volatility of prices of financial "products" defines the cause of boom and bust cycles that precipitate downturns in the important economic variables; employment and growth.

If you will establish a new good central bank, not only will it create immortality for you in history, you will also become a serious contender for the Nobel Prize in economics because you will have provided the long run solution to these recurring financial "crises" that have precipitated downturns in the real economy for over 200 years in the U.S.

Copies: Rahm Emanuel, Council of Economic Advisors, FED Chairman Bernanke, Rep. Barney Frank, Senator Baucus, The Journal of Finance.

Hey Barney: Your immortality in history is assured if you est. THE BANK of THE U.S.

The FED can not be fixed. And to make it the watchdog for "systemic risk" is ridiculous. The Federal Reserve System IS the systemic risk.

Bernanke, Greenspan, Larry Summers and all those Friedmanites are riding a dead horse. Markets do NOT know better than regulators. Greenspan had to admit "I was wrong". So too are Bernanke, Geithner, Larry Summers and all of their ilk. We mainstream economists resent their stupidity.   Good luck.
Dr. Frank

129

AUG 5 '09

Such a bank would be very easy to create : nationalize the 12 regional Federal Reserve banks. No political problems of "socialism" will arise because most Americans think the FED is already a government agency. This will be THE BANK OF THE UNITED STATES OF AMERICA, owned and operated by the people for the people . It will set the terms for all bank loans: mortgages, margin accounts and credit cards included and it will implement tight money policies to halt speculative booms and increase the money supply in downturns, WHICH THE FED CAN NOT DO.

POST SCRIPTS

The Bank of the U.S. will be the SUPER REGULATOR of the financial sector that there is near unanimity is necessary.

There is also near unanimity that quasi-public institutions like Fannie Mae, Freddie Mac AND THE FED do not work. They run amok leveraging on the upside of cycles exacerbating a bad situation because they know they will be bailed out on the downside. Capitalism works better when the underlying philosophy includes the dictum: Live by leverage; die by leverage. Leveraging should be a TWO-EDGED sword.

Millions of Americans are disgusted with the new business "model" that says: "Leverage like hell on the upside of the bubble and when it busts, file bankruptcy or get a government bailout".

Our basic economic goal of price stability is just as important, if not more so, for financial "products" as it is for consumer goods because volatility of prices of financial "products" defines the cause of boom and bust cycles that precipitate downturns in the important economic variables: employment and growth.

If you will establish a new good central bank, not only will it create immorality for you in history, you will also become a serious contender for the Nobel Prize in economics because you will have provided the long run solution to these recurring financial "crises" that have precipitated downturns in the real economy for over 200 years in the U.S.

Copies: Rahm Emanuel, Council of Economic Advisors, FED Chairman Bernanke, Rep. Barney Frank, Senator Baucus, The Journal of Finance

Hey Rahm - know you're not an economist.
But this solution is just common sense
and it creates no political problems.
Do it for the good of the good ol' USA.
Best Regards.
Dr. Frank

AUG 5, '09

Such a bank would be very easy to create: nationalize the 12 regional Federal Reserve banks. No political problems of "socialism" will arise because most Americans think the FED is already a government agency. This will be THE BANK OF THE UNITED STATES OF AMERICA, owned and operated by the people for the people. It will set the terms for all bank loans: mortgages, margin accounts and credit cards included and it will implement tight money policies to halt speculative booms and increase the money supply in downturns, WHICH THE FED CAN NOT DO.

POST SCRIPTS

The Bank of the U.S. will be the SUPER REGULATOR of the financial sector that there is near unanimity is necessary.

There is also near unanimity that quasi-public institutions like Fannie Mae, Freddie Mac AND THE FED do not work. They run amok leveraging on the upside of cycles exacerbating a bad situation because they know they will be bailed out on the downside. Capitalism works better when the underlying philosophy includes the dictum: Live by leverage; die by leverage. Leveraging should be a TWO-EDGED sword.

Millions of Americans are disgusted with the new business "model" that says: "Leverage like hell on the upside of the bubble and when it busts, file bankruptcy or get a government bailout".

Our basic economic goal of price stability is just as important, if not more so, for financial "products" as it is for consumer goods because volatility of prices of financial "products" defines the cause of boom and bust cycles that precipitate downturns in the important economic variables: employment and growth.

If you will establish a new good central bank, not only will it create immortality for you in history, you will also become a serious contender for the Nobel Prize in economics because you will have provided the long run solution to these recurring financial "crises" that have precipitated downturns in the real economy for over 200 years in the U.S.

Copies: Rahm Emanuel, Council of Economic Advisors, FED Chairman Bernanke, Rep. Barney Frank, Senator Baucus, The Journal of Finance.

The Fed Can not be the watchdog for "systemic risk" the Federal Reserve System IS the systemic risk.
The long run solution to these recurring financial "crises" is to have a good central bank that can do the job. The FED can not and it can not be fixed. It must be replaced.
Your immortality in history is assured if you can get it done FOR THE GOOD of the Economy and the American people. Screw Wall St.

131

AUG 5 09 .

7,0

Such a bank would be very easy to create: nationalize the 12 regional Federal Reserve banks. No political problems of "socialism" will arise because most Americans think the FED is already a government agency. This will be THE BANK OF THE UNITED STATES OF AMERICA, owned and operated by the people for the people. It will set the terms for all bank loans: mortgages, margin accounts and credit cards included and it will implement tight money policies to halt speculative booms and increase the money supply in downtimes, WHICH THE FED CAN NOT DO.

POST SCRIPTS

The Bank of the U.S. will be the SUPER REGULATOR of the financial sector that there is near unanimity is necessary.

There is also near unanimity that quasi-public institutions like Fannie Mae, Freddie Mac AND THE FED do not work. They run amok leveraging on the upside of cycles exacerbating a bad situation because they know they will be bailed out on the downside. Capitalism works better when the underlying philosophy includes the dictum: Live by leverage; die by leverage. Leveraging should be a TWO-EDGED sword.

Millions of Americans are disgusted with the new business "model" that says: "Leverage like hell on the upside of the bubble and when it busts, file bankruptcy or get a government bailout".

Our basic economic goal of price stability is just as important, if not more so, for financial "products" as it is for consumer goods because volatility of prices of financial "products" defines the cause of boom and bust cycles that precipitate downturns in the important economic variables: employment and growth.

If you will establish a new good central bank, not only will it create immortality for you in history, you will also become a serious contender for the Nobel Prize in economics because you will have provided the long run solution to these recurring financial "crises" that have precipitated downturns in the real economy for over 200 years in the U.S.

Copies: Rahm Emanuel, Council of Economic Advisors, FED Chairman Bernanke, Rep. Barney Frank, Senator Baucus, The Journal of Finance.

Hey Ben: You broke your promise to Milton Friedman that the Fed would never again make the Great Depression mistake of reducing the money supply. Did the same in this recession! But it's something important FOR THE ECONOMY that the FED CAN NOT do. Cut out with it. do what's right. Create a new good central bank. That can do the necessary work of a central bank: the FED Can never do the job. AND YOU KNOW IT. Market do NOT know best. Greenspan admitted, "I was wrong". You Friedmanites would do the county a great service to get the hell out of the way of mainstream economics.

Aug. 5, '09

Such a bank would be very easy to create : nationalize the 12 regional Federal Reserve banks. No plitical problems of "socialism" will arise because most Americans think the FED is already a government agency. This will be THE BANK OF THE UNITED STATES OF AMERICA, owned and operated by the people for the people. It willset the terms for all bank loans: mortgages, margin accounts and credit cards included and it will implement tight money policies to halt speculative booms and increase the money supply in downturns, WHICH THE FED CAN NOT DO.

POST SCRIPTS

The Bank of the U.S. will be the SUPER REGULATOR of the financial sector that there is near unanimity is necessary.

There is also near unanimity that quasi-public institutions like Fannie Mae, Freddie Mac AND THE FED do not work. They run amok leveraging on the upside of cycles exacerbating a bad situation because they know they will be bailed out on the downside. Capitalism works better when the underlying philosophy includes the dictum: Live by leverage; die by leverage. Leveraging should be a TWO-EDGED sword.

Millions of Americans are disgusted with the new business "model" that says: "Leverage like hell on the upside of the bubble and when it busts, file bankruptcy or get a government bailout".

Our basic economic goal of price stability is just as important, if not more so, for financial "products" as it is for consumer goods because volatility of prices of financial "products" defines the cause of boom and bust cycles that precipitate downturns in the important economic variables: employment and growth.

If you will establish a new good central bank, not only will it create immortality for you in history, you will also become a serious contender for the Nobel Prize in economics because you will have provided the long run solution to these recurring financial "crises" that have precipitated downturns in the real economy for over 200 years in the U.S.

Copies: Rahm Emanuel, Council of Economic Advisors, FED Chairman Bernanke, Rep. Barney Frank, Senator Baucus, The Journal of Finance.

Hey Christina : Pls tell us that you are not a friedmanite. Regardless, you know that the FED reduced the money supply INCORRECTLY in the Great Depression and in the current recession.
That total flaw in the FED SYSTEM is the "systemic risk" for the economy. The Fed : can not be the Systemic risk watchdog.
A new good central bank is the only long-run solution to this problem.
Do it as a good American citizen ; for the good of all Americans for all time.   you know we're right.
J.P. , Ph.D.

Frank DeFelice, Ph.D.

THE WHITE HOUSE

WASHINGTON

August 10, 2009

Dear Friend:

Thank you for taking the time to share your views. I appreciate hearing from you and value your input.

My Administration is working to address the serious challenges our Nation faces. Some say we are moving forward on too many issues too quickly, but given our unprecedented circumstances, swift, deliberate action is needed. I am committed to taking immediate steps that generate job creation and economic recovery, and I am determined to make investments that lay a new foundation for real and lasting progress.

To build this new foundation, I have called for health care reform—this year—that reduces costs, protects health care choices, and assures quality, affordable care for all Americans. I am committed to building a clean energy economy that creates millions of jobs, helps to achieve energy independence, and reduces pollution as we tackle the effects of global warming. To prepare our children to thrive in the global economy, we must guarantee every child a complete and competitive education. We need to secure our homeland against threats by preventing terrorist attacks and planning for and responding soundly to emergencies. We also have an obligation to rein in our budget deficit by cutting wasteful spending and ineffective programs. We can do all this, and change the way business is done in Washington, by building the most open, transparent, and accountable government in our history.

Ultimately, the only way to solve the problems of our time is to involve all Americans in shaping the policies that affect our lives. Thank you again for writing. I encourage you to explore www.WhiteHouse.gov, which is regularly updated and more interactive than ever before.

Sincerely,

THE WHITE HOUSE
WASHINGTON, DC 20500

SOUTHERN MD 207
17 AUG 2005 PM 2 L

Dr. and Mrs. Frank Q. Felice
2152 Frank Harbor
Newland, NC 28657

28657+7528

TO : PRESIDENT OBAMA, OUR FRIEND

FROM : **Dr. & Mrs. Frank DeFelice**
672 Windridge
Linville, NC
Mail: 2152 Land Harbor
Newland NC 28657

DATE : AUGUST 11, 2009

SUBJECT : A NEW THEORY OF GOVERNMENT FINANCE :
REPLY TO OLD DUMB CONSERVATIVE IDEAS
VERY CONSERVATIVE LEVERAGING FOR GOV'T FINANCE

There is a cultural bias in America vs. debt. It goes way back to the Founding Fathers, "A penny saved is a penny earned". "Neither a lender nor a borrower be". And we did have debtor prisons for folks who borrowed and could not repay their loans.

We've come a long way from that in personal and business finance, but government finance is mired in the muck of "our children and grand children will be burdened with the government debt".

Personal finance is dominated by mega leveraging to the point of ignoring debt-carrying capacity. Conservative personal leveraging used to be that individuals could safely carry 2 ½ times their income; and that included amortization of the loan. That went out the window in the housing market boom when unsustainable rises in values allowed repetitive re-financing of all personal debt via mortgage re-financing. But many individuals who lived by leveraging, died by leveraging.

Something very similar has happened in business finance, where many businesses failed to obey the debt-carrying capacity rule : only to the level where at the perigee of the cycle it could be carried; i.e., "serviced" – the interest paid. The principal could be, and is, handled by repetitive refunding issues.

And this is how the federal government handles debt : continual refunding issues : "Treasuries" come due; sell more to pay off the old ones plus whatever amount is needed to cover current deficit spending. This CAN just go on ad infinitum because there is no shortage of buyers for U.S. debt. They are the lowest risk securities in the world.

It's really stupid and expensive (BUT GOOD BUSINESS FOR THE BROKER/DEALERS LIKE GOLDMAN) to engage in this perpetual re-financing. The U.S. (like England!) should issue "Perpetuals"; i.e., bonds with no maturity dates. We,d never have to pay back the borrowed money just the interest.
Bond holders who wanted their principal would just sell the bond to a buyer who wanted the interest. Bond values change to reflect changes in the general interest rate. If it's higher than the coupon rate, the price goes down and vice versa.

Debt-carrying capacity strategy of business finance should be applied to government finance. This combined with "Perpetuals" will put to rest the ever increasing conservative crescendo who continually sing the "we are burdening our children and grand children with terrible debt that will decrease their standard of living" song. "PERPETUALS"; I.E., BONDS THAT HAVE NO MATURIY DATE NEVER HAVE TO BE PAID. THEREFORE, NO BURDEN IS PASSED ON!!!

Post scripts:
For this to work at the state government level, balanced budget laws would have to be repealed, which they should be anyway because they work against federal stimulus spending (see enclosed clipping inre: North Carolina).

What's the limit to this approach? If debt-carrying capacity for personal finance is conservative at 2 ½ times income (including amortization). Then government finance with no amortization would be ultra conservative at 2 ½ times income, which raises the question of what income figure to use. If it's national debt, it would be logical to use national income (but conservatives would never buy that). So consider government income, which is determined simply by subtracting consumer and business income form national income. Either way we are very very conservative currently and have a long way to go before facing the kind of problems businesses and consumers are currently facing (because they are way over the line; i.e. too highly leveraged).

Copies: Rahm Emanuel, Christina Romer (CEA), Barney Frank, Senator Max Baucus

Frank DeFelice, Ph.D.

Charlotte Observer

WEDNESDAY • AUGUST 5, 2009 • 75¢ • @charlotteobserv

N.C. BUDGET

$990 MILLION IN NEW TAXES

Here's what is wrong with a balanced budget : Have to cut spending and raise taxes in a recession, which makes a recession worse!

| PUBLIC EDUCATION | NATURAL RESOURCES | JUSTICE & PUBLIC SAFETY |

OBSERVER FILE PHOTOS

$225 MILLION will be cut from grades 4 through 12. Local officials will decide where to trim.

$50 MILLION to be cut from the Clean Water Management Trust Fund each year for two years.

$30.7 MILLION to be saved over the next two years by closing seven small prisons.

Reprinted by Permission of The Charlotte Observer

TO : MARY SCHAPIRO, SEC CHAIRPERSON
Dr. & Mrs. Frank DeFelice
FROM :   672 Windridge
Linville, NC
DATE : 8-18-09 Mail: 2152 Land Harbor
Newland NC 28657
SUBJECT : "WE NEED A BETTER WAY TO DO BUSINESS POST-BUBBLE"
GEITHNER HAS MADE IT WORSE
THE SEC HAS DONE NOTHING

To make things better, you first have to delineate what was wrong; then correct your mistakes.

The single most important cause of the stock market, housing, commercial real estate and oil/gasoline bubbles was HIGHLY LEVERAGED SPECULATION FOR SHORT TERM CAPITAL GAINS.

All "regular" accounts at brokerage firms are margin accounts. This means that virtually all transactions for securites are leveraged. Currently 75% of all NYSE transactions are for short term capital gains. A new bubble has already been started by the same means that caused the just past bubble with its inevitable bust, which precipitated the decline in the real economy: lower output and high unemployment.

Boom and bust cycles in the stock market are bad for the economy. Leveraged speculation fuels the boom. For the good of the economy, there should not be margin accounts. Market volatility is bad. Good markets require stability.

The over-riding objective for the SEC should be to do what is good for the economy. To do that you need to understand the role of a stock market in capitalism. It is quite simple:
1. Provide a mechanism for capital formation to take place, and
2. Provide a fair and orderly market for owners of corporate securities to sell to buyers; i.e. , provide liquidity.

Because you are basically a bunch of lawyers, you do a good work in the capital formation part of your job. "Due diligence is what this is all about and lawyers do make sure offerings of new securities contain all the necessary legalese.

But, maybe because you are lawyers – not economists – you do a terrible job in the second part of your job: maintaining orderly and fair markets.
Securities markets used to be the closest thing to what economists recognize as perfectly competitive markets. This is the case where buyers and sellers are all relative to the market size, small, so that no individual buyer or seller can by his actions effect price. The stock market has evolved to where that is no longer true.

Goldman-Sachs currently accounts for 25% of all short term trading on the NYSE. This is not competition. This is the opportunity for a few big firms to dominate the market.

In economics this is called an oligopoly ("olig" is Greek for few, "poly" is Greek for seller). Most , American industries are oligopolies in which a few big firms set prices, which is a definition of non-competition. In competitive markets price is determined by supply and demand in the market (bid and asked in the stock market).

The bigger the firms are in an industry, the fewer there are. The fewer there are, the less the competition. Geithner made bigger and therefore fewer broker/dealers. Goldman-Sachs became   bigger and a one-bank holding company and Bank of America likewise. This lessens competition and is bad for the economy.

We need to get the anti-trust lawyers in Justice to break up these huge conglomerates.

And the people in Congress to repeal Garn-St. Germain that allows them to form.

Supply and demand do not determine oil, and therefore, gasoline prices. Highly leveraged speculators like Goldman and Citigroup do.

Last year, a "hidden" energy trading unit at Goldman made $667 million in oil futures contracts. So did Citigroup. (Hard to believe it was exactly the same in both cases! Data from the Wall St. Journal.) John Henry made so much that he bought the Boston Red Sox "with pocket change".

Two Mr. Hall's – one at Goldman, one at Citigroup got paid $100 million each for their efforts and complained that they were underpaid by $100 million! But Geithner had put caps on bonuses when he gave Goldman $10 Billion; so, Goldman repaid the $10 Billion ; so, Hall can stay at Goldman instead of starting a hedge fund where he would have got $200 Million for his "work". Hedge funds pay 30%!

The Hall at Citigroup can't get out from under Geithner's bonus cap because Citigroup can not repay the $45 Billion they got. But Geithner has figured out a way to get around this. He has appointed a man to deal with problems like Mr. Hall's, and the man is an old friend of Hall's! Citigroup will "argue" that since the Hall at Goldman is getting $200 million, we have to pay our Mr. Hall the same or he will quit and start a hedge fund. Or Citigroup will "argue" we have to pay competitive bonuses to keep these "talented" producers. Hall at Citigroup also operates form a "secretive" location: an old farmhouse in Connecticut. What they are doing is only immoral, not illegal, so we can't stop them. But we can cut their leveraging down. We recommend no margin trading at all on the CFTC. Currently it's only 10% and less! And broker/dealers and banks should not be allowed at all on the CFTC; Their businesses are in no way affected by future commodity prices. The whole thing is just a legalized highly leveraged price rigged rip-off of the American public. Gasoline prices would not keep bubbling up if they were determined by supply and demand instead of the new Robber Barrons operating out of secretive locations – and old farm house in Connecticut! - the bastards!

Hedge funds are really just another highly leveraged speculative trading device that causes the undesirable boom and bust cycles on the stock market and they should be regulated like all other funds. Because they are not public offerings they exploit your inability to regulate them like publicly offered funds. The people in Congress asked you what they can do to help you. Tell them to amend the law to include private funds of all types, which would include "private equity funds".

LBO's also cause the boom and bust cycles. The leveraging is done with securities as well as bank loans from their own bank in case like Goldman , Citigroup and Bank of America – now that Geithner has made them into (too big to fail?) financial conglomerates. The FED is supposed to supervise all banks - even those inside the big conglomerates. Sheila Bair and the FDIC are dumbfounded by the tangled web they have become. But she's not the only one that can't figure them out. An army of lawyers at $950/hour! have been trying for 9 months to sort out Lehman Brothers! It might take 9 years!

The President wants you to fix these mistakes so there will be "a better way to do business post-bubble".

The public does not know the difference between investment and speculation. The SEC mission should not include the protection of speculators. They are making bets in America's biggest legal gambling operation, not helping the economy.

The public does not know the difference between financial investment and real economic investment. Real economic investment is capital formation. Financial investment requires only some "product" where the principal is safe and a regular payment for the use of the investor's money is made.

Stocks that do not p ay dividends do not qualify as a financial investment. Such stocks are mere speculation for capital gains.

Can't blame the SEC for not knowing these things: you are mostly lawyers, political appointments; and until you get some smart Ph.D. financial economists on board AND LISTEN TO THEM, there's not much hope that you will do your part to make "a better way to do business" AS THE PRESIDENT WANTS.

POST SCRIPT

There is near unanimity among ex-insiders like us that self-regulation does not, has not, and never will work. Lumping the NYSE and NASD into FINRA is just pouring old wine into a new bottle. It does not solve the problem. It's still and SRO financed by the regulated. When the regulated are the regulators this is an obvious common sense conflict of interests (whether or not it passes lawyers test as such).

However, since you regularly work with the FED (or are supposed to), Treasury, and CFTC (Executive Order 12631), maybe, just maybe, you could make some of the necessary changes required to stop bubbles. You have to stop leveraged speculation.

Start with the CFTC : Stop margin trading and limit participants to those with a legitimate business interest in commodities futures prices.

The real stumbling block here is that Geithner runs this commission and his strong connections with Goldman, who made $667 Million last year with its "hidden energy trading unit". But the overwhelming benefit to the entire U.S. economy from stable energy prices far outweighs Geithner's buddy-buddy relationships with Goldman, Citigroup and other Robber Barons.

Do you recognize that the FED is an SRO? It's bankers regulating bankers : NO GOOD. The general public does not know this either. We are writing a book : WHAT ALL AMERICANS NEED TO KNOW ABOUT ECONOMICS Sub-title : The Causes and Cures of the 2008-09 U. S. Recession for the general public and high school students. It's purpose is the Herculean task of eliminating economic illiteracy (or at least greatly reducing it) in the populus.

We're trying to get Arne Duncan to require all school systems who come to Uncle Sam for money (virtually all) to put in a required course : FUNDAMENTALS OF ECONOMICS. Since the SEC has an education goal you should sponsor us in this work that can and will lead to the end of the boom and bust cycles that have plagued the U.S. for over 200 years.

Copies: President Obama, Rahm Emanuel, Arne Duncan, Council of Economic
                                                                        Advisors

THE WHITE HOUSE
WASHINGTON

August 21, 2009

Dear Friend:

Thank you for expressing your thoughts on corporate responsibility and oversight. A handful of irresponsible corporations bear a great deal of responsibility for our economic crisis. I share the frustration of many Americans about their actions and the era of profound recklessness that spanned from executive suites to the seats of power in Washington.

My Administration values the entrepreneurial dynamism and innovation of American business that have defined this country since its founding. But this economic crisis has made clear that we cannot allow corporate excesses and abusive practices to undermine our economy. We must end the outrageous bonuses, risky transactions, and gross mismanagement that have hurt American workers and families, leading many to lose their jobs or life savings.

Fostering an environment that promotes corporate responsibility will allow businesses to prosper while protecting consumers. Markets work best when there is transparency, accountability, and fair, well-enforced rules. To achieve this, we will enhance oversight of large financial institutions to prevent systemic failure and fraud and to curb exorbitant executive pay. We will also create a new Consumer Financial Protection Agency with the sole responsibility of protecting ordinary consumers. It will oversee consumer products, including mortgage lending, credit cards, and student loans. This framework will help end the culture of narrow self-interest and short-term gain, and promote a new era of corporate responsibility and stewardship. Join me online to read more about my efforts at: www.whitehouse.gov/issues/economy and www.FinancialStability.gov.

Thank you again for writing.

Sincerely,

143

THE WHITE HOUSE
WASHINGTON, DC 20500

SOUTHERN MD 207
21 AUG 2009 PM 4 T

Dr. and Mrs. Frank De Felice
2153 Sand Harbor
Newland, North Carolina 28657

28657+7928

TO : PRESIDENT OBAMA, OUR FRIEND

FROM :
>Dr. & Mrs. Frank DeFelice
>222 Paradise Peninsula
>DeFelice Villa
>Lake Norman, NC
>Mail: Mooresville, NC 28117

DATE : August 2?, 2009

SUBJECT : RESPONSE TO YOURS OF AUGUST 21, 2009

" Outrageous bonuses" follow outrageous highly leveraged speculation for short term capital gains like night follows day, and is going on today unabated since no "better ways of doing business post-bubble" have been put in place.

In fact, what Geithner has done is to make the way of doing business worse — for the economy . By making Goldman-Sachs, Citigroup and Bank of America into huge financial conglomerates, he is encouraging the leveraged speculation that caused the bubbles (with the inevitable "bust") that precipitated the changes in the important economic variables: output and employment.

For example, both Citigroup's and Goldman's "secretive" and "hidden" energy trading units make $667 Million last year. Last year Goldman was a broker/dealer that had to get the millions it was betting on oil futures from a bank. Now it is a bank — thanks to Geithner (and Paulson, the ex-CEO of Goldman!), so it will not have interest costs for the $ multi-million it regularly trades in the CFTC driving up oil prices. Goldman had to pay Mr. Hall, who ran this "hidden" operation $100 million last year, and he complained he was underpaid by $100 million! Identical (!) situation at Citigroup. AND THESE BASTARDS ARE BACK AT IT TODAY. Post-bubble way of doing business has been made worse by Mr. Geithner. (Dartmouth should rescind his degree.)

To stop the outrageous bonuses, stop these outrageous business practices that allow these Robber Barons to line their pockets at the expense of unemployed millions and destroyed savings.

We the people elected you to help the people (not Wall St.). Wasn't our government formed to "promote the health and welfare OF THE CITIZENS?

Here's how to stop the oil/gasoline bubble: Issue an Executive Order that margin trading on the CFTC is not allowed, and brokered transactions are allowed only for firms who have a legitimate business interest in future oil (commodities) prices.

With the stroke of a pen you will have created "a better way to do business post-bubble".

Similar opportunities exist in the stockmarket, housing and commercial real estate, bank regulation and control of the money supply. What all these areas have in common is that they are SRO,s; i.e., Self Regulated Organizations, and we know that self regulation does not work So, we say, you gave them the chance to clean up heir own houses and they did nothing. We know Machiavellian is not a nice way to go. But if the policies in place are not working, "benevolent dictator" approach is necessary to get badly needed changes in place,n'est-ce-pas?

We have written extensively to the SEC, Justice, CEA, Ben Bernanke, Tim Geithner and others, but all of these agencies and people are dominated by a conservative bias that by definition opposes change.

For example, Ben Bernanke is a conservative Republican, Brand X, Chicago School, Friedmanite macroeconomist. These people think Milton Friedman made some good additions to monetary theory, which are largely unknown to mainstream economists like us, and more importantly, according to them, sold the idea that "markets know best". That is, government regulation can not only not regulate markets, but such attempted regulation is a hindrance to our economic system. Alan Greenspan, a Friedmanite believed this to the end; But in the end had to admit, "I was wrong".

Larry Summers, Austan Goolsbee, C. Romer (?) are all of this persuasion. They willl never make a "better way to do business post-bubble". They are conservatives who like the status quo. In fact, Larry Summers makes $ millions from a hedge fund as a managing director, and hedge funds are another factor causing the stock market boom and bust cycle that triggered off the economic downturn AND WILL DO SO AGAIN if changes are not made.

Repeating (for emphasis): the stock market AND THE FED ARE SRO'S. Self regulation does not work. We need a SUPER REGULATOR. A new, difernt better Central Bank will go along way towards getting the necessary chngesmade. It will do want any good central bank does, AND THE FED DOES NOT DO :
  1. control the money supply, and
  2. supervise banking.

Proper supervision of banking would not have allowed "sub prime" mortgage lending, loans for bets in the stock market, highly leveraged spedculation, usurious credit card loans, world wide real estate bets and many other acitivites BAD FOR THE ECONOMY.

If the FED could control the money supply, there would not have been a "credit crunch". In fact, the FED decreases the money supply when it should be increased.. When banks do not lend, the money supply decreases. And "the FED" IS THE BANKS.

It would be real easy to have a good central bank: Just nationalize the 12 regional federal reserve banks that will be operated by the people for the people. We nominate Shelia Bair to run it; send Ben Bernanke back to the classroom to lick his wounds from the death of Friedmanite wrong-headed philosophy inre: money and banking.

POST SCRIPT

The "systemic risk" in the financial system is the Federal Reserve SYSTEM.
The current recession displayed this risk dramatically: It goes by the name "credit crunch". Credit crunch means that the banks are not making loans. The banks, which ARE THE FED, are privately owned businesses and they make money (the traditional commercial banks – there is no such thing as an " investment" bank) by only one means: making loans.
When borrowers do not look like good credit risks, they do not make loans. Therefore, the money supply shrinks. There is your "systemic risk". The financial system is always at risk from the profit seeking activities of the banks. They hurt the economy when it is down and they fuel inflation when it is over-heated. There is no way to fix this built-in deficiency of the Federal Reserve System, our central bank. WE NEED A NEW CENTRAL BANK.

Your place in history will be assured if you do this.
Only a strong leader with a majority behind him could do this.
STRIKE WHILE THE IRON IS HOT.

Copies : Rahm Emanuel, Ben Bernanke, SEC, Council of Economic Advisors

August 31, 2009   ADDENDDUM

It is now crystal clear that Treasury Secretary Geithner with FED Chmn Ben Bernanke's duplicity have not only made the financial industry into an oligopoly that is worse for the post-bubble economy, they have violated regulations and Antitrust Laws in doing so.

J.P. Morgan Chase, Bank of America and Wells Fargo each hold more than 10% of the nation's deposits despite regulations against doing so. And, in several metropolitan regions, they have market share well beyond what is allowed under Antitrust Laws.

We ask you to relieve Geithner and Bernanke of their duties for malfeasance.

By copy of this letter, we ask U.S. Attorney General Eric Holder to enforce the Antitrust Laws vs. the above named financial firms and prosecute all guilty parties to the fullest extent of the Law.

We also ask the U.S. Supreme Court to declare the Federal Reserve System null and void as the U.S. central bank for failure to perform its essential duties of bank supervision and control of the money supply.

Copies: U.S. Attorney General Eric Holder, U.S. Supreme Court Chief Justice Roberts

Frank DeFelice, Ph.D.

TO : U.S. ATTORNEY GENERAL ERIC HOLDER

FROM :
  Dr. & Mrs. Frank DeFelice
  222 Paradise Peninsula
  DeFelice Villa
  Lake Norman, NC
  Mail: Mooresville, NC 28117

DATE : August 25, 2009

SUBJECT : "WE NEED A BETTER WAY TO DO BUSINESS POST-BUBBLE," B. OBAMA
  GEITHNER HAS MADE IT WORSE
  JUSTICE HAS DONE NOTHING

President Obama "values (our) input", as he should since we are among the most
qualified economists trying to bring to fruition the President's solution to these recurring
boom-and-bust cycles that have plagued the U.S. economy for over 200 years.

We have carefully delineated with empirical evidence how the continuing failure of the
Antitrust Division has been a causal factor in these cyclical economic aberrations that
cause millions of Americans hard times needlessly.

An unsigned (!) letter from the Antitrust Division (copy enclosed) essentially dissed us as
"citizen complaint" nuts. Our enclosed credentials prove otherwise. We don't deal with
these low level apparatchiks (Russ.: bureaucrats); only people like you who can get
things done.

Background evidence goes back to the Reagan Administration when "supply side" and
other ultra conservative economists pushed Reagan into de-regulation and non-
enforcement of antitrust laws designed to preserve competition. Reagan's FED
chairman, Paul Volker (not an economist AND CURRENTLY in the Obama
Administration ?!) fought inflation with 16% interest rates on low risk loans and 10+%
unemployment. His successor, Alan Greenspan with the same mistaken philosophy that
"markets know best" did none of the regulation of banks necessary for the good of the
economy.', but at the end had to admit, "I was wrong".

But these Friedmanite economists like Larry Summers. Austan Goolsbee and Ben
Bernanke do not accept the fact that the "markets know best" philosophy died with
Greenspan and the current recession.
LAISSEZ FAIRE DOES NOT WORK.
MARKETS NEED TO BE REGULATED.
ANTITRUST LAWS NEED TO BE ENFORCED.

Congress of the Regan Administration is also responsible for a good part of the problem.
They passed the Garn-St. Germain Act that allows banks and brokers to get back together
since that was not allowed under Glassman-Steagall, which was a correction of that bad

148

situation in the Great Depression. The one-bank holding company with their brokerage, insurance, real estate, and all kinds of world wide businesses is a root cause of our present problems.

Geithner has made bigger, and therefore, fewer broker/dealers. Goldman-Sachs was made into a one-bank holding company and bigger by a $10 Billion infusion o f our money. Bank of America likewise made into a one-bank holding company conglomerate with Merrill Lynch in it along with $ Billions of U.S. money. Citigroup has been made bigger. Lehman Brothers and Bear- Stearns are gone.

The bigger the firms are in any industry, the fewer there are. The fewer there are, the less the competition. Geithner (a non-economist) thinks that financial firms have to be big to compete! He's got that "bass ackwards" inter alios.

The Clayton Antitrust Act limits a firm's acquisition of another firm's stock "where in any line of commerce in any section of the country, the effect of such acquisition may lessen competition.....". Acquisition by buying the assets loophole was closed by Celler-Kefauver in 1950. MANY MERGERS, CONSOLIDATIONS AND ACQUISITIONS HAVE BEEN DONE IN VIOLATION OF THESE LAWS.

Bank of America was forced to buy Merrill Lynch! This lessening of competition is bad for the economy: higher prices, less output and a mis-allocation of resources.

Hart-Scott-Rodino has required since 1979 mergers to be run by Antitrust, but even firms who admit publicly that their purpose is "to lessen competition", are approved. This has got to stop in order for there to be a " BETTER WAY TO DO BUSINESS POST-BUBBLE" as the President wants.

"Any industry in any section of the country"covers the financial services industry and Wall St. Goldman-Sachs now accounts for 25% of all short term capital gains speculation trading on the NYSE. The NYSE is no longer a competitive market place. Neither is the CFTC where Goldman and Citigroup each made $667 Million bidding up oil futures with highly leveraged trading. Supply and demand do not set oil prices. The Billions made in these rigged markets cost the U.S. economy$ Billions in high energy costs and when the bubbles burst (and they always do!) recession with millions unemployed and retirement savings for millions destroyed.

STOP THE BASTARDS, PLEASE.
WE THANK YOU.
THE PRESIDENT WILL THANK YOU.
THE AMERICAN PUBLIC WILL WORSHIP YOU IF (WHEN?) YOU BREAK UP THESE MODERN DAY ROBBER BARONS.

Copies: President Obama, our friend; Rahm Emanuel; Council of Economic Advisors

Frank DeFelice, Ph.D.

THE WHITE HOUSE
WASHINGTON

September 24, 2009

Dear Friend:

Thank you for taking the time to share your views. I appreciate hearing from you and value your input.

My Administration is working to address the serious challenges our Nation faces. Some say we are moving forward on too many issues too quickly, but given our unprecedented circumstances, swift, deliberate action is needed. I am committed to taking immediate steps that generate job creation and economic recovery, and I am determined to make investments that lay a new foundation for real and lasting progress.

To build this new foundation, I have called for health care reform—this year—that reduces costs, protects health care choices, and assures quality, affordable care for all Americans. I am committed to building a clean energy economy that creates millions of jobs, helps to achieve energy independence, and reduces pollution as we tackle the effects of global warming. To prepare our children to thrive in the global economy, we must guarantee every child a complete and competitive education. We need to secure our homeland against threats by preventing terrorist attacks and planning for and responding soundly to emergencies. We also have an obligation to rein in our budget deficit by cutting wasteful spending and ineffective programs. We can do all this, and change the way business is done in Washington, by building the most open, transparent, and accountable government in our history.

Ultimately, the only way to solve the problems of our time is to involve all Americans in shaping the policies that affect our lives. Thank you again for writing. I encourage you to explore www.WhiteHouse.gov, which is regularly updated and more interactive than ever before.

Sincerely,

150

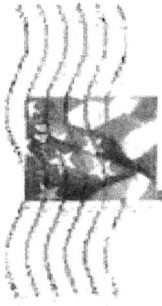

SOUTHERN MO 247

25 SEP 2009 PM 3 L

Dr. Frank DeFilice
3152 Jerod Harbor
Newland, NC 28657

28657+7926

THE WHITE HOUSE
WASHINGTON, DC 20500

Frank DeFelice, Ph.D.

THE WHITE HOUSE
WASHINGTON

October 9, 2009

Dear Friend:

Thank you for writing. I appreciate your perspective as my Administration works to fix our economy.

Our Nation's current recession has been caused by irresponsibility and poor decision-making that stretched from Wall Street to Washington to Main Street. It started with the housing market, where bets were made on risky loans wrongly marked with safe ratings. As property values declined and loans went into default, investors panicked. Banks stopped lending, businesses began to struggle and lay off workers, who then struggled with their own bills.

I understand that some people think we should let banks fail, while others support taking them over. I believe we need aggressive action to get credit flowing again. Credit sustains our economy; it allows families to pay for college education and small businesses to expand and hire workers. Without the flow of credit, we risk years of sluggish growth, low job creation, and anemic investment.

My Administration has taken bold action to help banks start lending again. We are pairing government resources with private investment to clear away bad loans and securities that prevent banks from lending—the so-called "toxic assets." We are also restructuring the auto industry so that America can preserve jobs and lead the world in building the next generation of clean cars. We are implementing regulatory reforms in the financial sector and increasing accountability in Washington to prevent another disaster. Each change protects the well-being of American workers and taxpayers above all. For more information, please visit: www.whitehouse.gov/issues/economy or www.financialstability.gov.

I will continue to do everything in my power to get our economy back on track. American families deserve nothing less. Thank you again for writing.

Sincerely,

UNITED STATES DEPARTMENT OF EDUCATION

OFFICE OF INNOVATION AND IMPROVEMENT

OCT 13 2009

Frank DeFelice, Ph.D.
2152 Land Harbor
Newland, NC 28657

Dear Dr. DeFelice:

Thank you for your letter to Secretary Duncan suggesting that all high school students must complete a Fundamentals of Economics Course as a requirement for graduation. Your letter was referred to the Office of Innovation and Improvement, and I am pleased to respond.

Please be aware that education is primarily a state and local responsibility in the U.S. In creating the Department of Education, Congress made clear its intention that the secretary of education and other Department officials be prohibited from exercising "any direction, supervision, or control over the curriculum program of instruction, administration, or personnel of any educational institution, school, or school system." (20 USC 3403) The establishment of schools and colleges, the development of curricula, the setting of requirements for enrollment and graduation -- these are responsibilities handled by states and communities, as well as by public and private organizations, not by the U.S. Department of Education. If you have not already done so, you may wish to contact state and local elected and appointed officials to inform them about your suggestion.

Again, thank you for sharing your suggestion with us. We appreciate your interest in education.

Sincerely,

Wanser R. Green
Management Analyst

400 MARYLAND AVE., S.W., WASHINGTON, DC 20202
www.ed.gov

Our mission is to ensure equal access to education and to promote educational excellence throughout the nation.

TO: ARNE DUNCAN, SECRETARY OF EDUCATION

FROM:
Dr. & Mrs. Frank DeFelice
Rainbow Resort
Lot 470
700 Co. Rd. 630A
Frostproof, FL 33843

DATE: OCTOBER 30, 2009

SUBJECT: REPLY TO YOURS OF OCT. 13 (by Wanser R. Green)
"WE NEED A BETTER WAY TO DO BUSINESS POST BUBBLE". OBAMA.
SEC HAS DONE NOTHING; FED HAS DONE NOTHING
GEITHNER HAS MADE THINGS WORSE.
ONLY EDUCATION REMAINS AS A MEANS TO EFFECT A
PERMANENT CURE FOR FINANCIAL FIASCOS THAT HAVE
PERIODICALLY DEBILITATED THE U.S. ECONOMY FOR
OVER 200 YEARS.

The eradication of economic illiteracy in the populus is what needs to done, and it needs to start in the public schools.
Your ideas that teaching kids about saving and personal finance is NOT economics education.
What the kids and all Americans need to understand starts with terminology and definitions: GNP, GDP, economic goals, National Income, Aggregate Demand, monetary policy, fiscal policy, economic competition, hypotheses, theory, scientific method, anecdotal data, comparative static analysis, dynamic analysis, economic fallacies, money & banking, money creation, the proper role of the stock market in the economy, "The Dow", risk and return, economic systems, real investment, financial investment, speculation, failures of the FED and the SEC, psychology in economics, and last, but not least, politics in economics.

We understand that curriculum reform is largely a state and local issue. However, the proper education of all Americans is your responsibility. Therefore, you have a political problem to solve in order to do our job. We do not solve political problems, but we know who does. Rahm Emanuel and David Axelrod are the Administration's "brilliant political strategists".

You alone are in a unique position to make virtually all high schools in the land require a course in Fundamentals of Economics because they all come to Uncle Sam for money. It's a fundamental financial principle the nobody gives anybody money without prior agreement as to what the money is to be used for. When they come for money, they know that you are going to exact certain conditions for its use. You can at that time, require this very important change in curriculum as a condition for the grant if you have solved the political problem.

If you do this, and it demonstrably reduces economic illiteracy to the extent that financial fiascos are significantly reduced, you will be a leading candidate for a Nobel Prize in economics. (The President will get another one when he establishes a good central bank, which is the long-run cure for these chronic AND UNNECESSARY debilitating economic boom-and-bust cycles hurting millions of Americans over and over again.)

This course – Fundamentals of Economics – needs a good textbook, which we are writing: WHAT ALL AMERICANS NEED TO KNOW ABOUT ECONOMICS,
Sub-title: The U.S. Recession of 2008-09: Causes and Cures.
Check out our credentials (enclosed) for this authoritative definitive text.

We are writing for easy understanding without the usual difficult-to-understand graphs and equations. No math pre-requisite is required.
We include an example of econometrics for those who may be inclined to consider the profession as a career. Only elementary Algebra and statistics (which should be taught in our public schools as it is in Japan) are used in econometrics.

We are what we are due to public funding: NDEA, NSF, Michigan, and North Carolina; and are honor bound to give back. This book , which is the distilled wisdom from over 50 years of study is our attempt to do so. But since we gave back with 23 years in college classrooms, starting at Chapel Hill in 1963, we do not have the funding necessary to efficiently prepare the manuscript for publication. We need professional work processing (typing) help. The book will be between 100 and 200 pages, and we'll have to edit and re-write 2 or 3 times. Word processing like typing, we assume, is done at $5 to $10/page(?). If we write only 100 pages and re-write only once, it will cost $1000. 200 pages with 2 re-writes will cost $6000 @ $10/page. Public funding should help us with this work because it is for the public good. All of our work to date has been pro bono.

Copies: President Obama, Rahm Emanuel, David Axelrod, CEA, SEC, Ben Bernanke

Post Script
   Since the SEC has a lawful obligation to do "investor education", they should support the publication of this very authoritative and sorely needed informative text. They blew their responsibility to maintain fair and orderly markets again: The mere fact that Goldman Sachs is making $100 million/ day trading is what lawyers call prima facie evidence of their abject failure.

TO: PRESIDENT OBAMA, OUR FRIEND

FROM: ————————————→

Dr. & Mrs. Frank DeFelice
222 Paradise Peninsula
DeFelice Villa
Lake Norman, NC
Mail: Mooresville, NC 28117

DATE: NOVEMBER 2, 2009

SUBJECT: REPLY TO YOUR FORM LETTER* OF OCTOBER 9, 2009
* (SO THAT EVERYBODY WILL KNOW WE KNEW)
THE REAL CAUSES AND CORRECT CURES FOR THE
CURRENT RECESSION THAT WILL LEAD TO :
"A BETTER WAY TO DO BUSINESS POST BUBBLE".

To say that the recession "started with the housing market", as you say, is fallacious economic reasoning known in economics as post hoc ergo propter hoc (remember your Latin?). It is also comparative static analysis because there is an implicit ceteris paribus assumption; and we all know the real world is mutatis mutandis; i.e., dynamic, not static.

The timing of the different boom-and-bust cycles is not important; one did not cause others., but they all have a single common cause: HIGHLY LEVERAGED SPECULATION FOR SHORT TERM CAPITAL GAINS.

Banks that provided the leveraging for the stock market, commodities futures market, real estate, LBO's, and hedge funds were themselves highly leveraged and also involved in the "pump and dump" strategies of all the above named speculators.

It was not just the decline in "property values", as you say, that precipitated the economic downturn. The stock market crash, the oil and gas bubble, commercial real estate, hedge funds and LBO's were all factors happening close enough together to cause public concern about what might follow.

Another important causal factor for the downturn is your use of the aforementioned negative news for political purposes; i.e., to repeatedly claim that the economy was in a "crisis", at the time your opponent, John McCain was CORRECTLY saying the "the fundamentals of the economy are in good shape, WHICH THEY WERE AT THAT TIME. When you kept hollering "crisis" and "worst recession since the Great Depression" the public always fears the unknown changes that may take place. Fear of the unknown raises the savings rate. When savings go up, consumption goes down. When consumption spending goes down, so too does business real investment spending. With both of these decreases in aggregate demand, unemployment increases. Also, government spending at the state and local level declines because of (stupid) balanced budget laws further aggravating the situation.

Banks stopped lending because borrowers were not in good enough shape for the banks to consider them as good borrowers; i.e., with low debt/equity ratios nor with good prospects to repay the loans. This was characterized as the "credit crunch".

Your statement inre: not letting banks fail is one of those that we in economics classify as "partially valid, but largely fallacious". 100 banks have failed this year. You bailed out several mega banks (the exact number is unclear because you make banks take money that did not want nor need it (Bank of America) with the idiotic rationale that you did not want the public to know which banks were bad). Government has a responsibility to tell citizens which banks are no good. Wasn't our government founded on the philodophy of "providing for the health and welfare * of the citizenry?

By "aggressive action to get credit flowing again", we assume you are referring to dumping $Billions into the banks coffers. That did not work. Neither did, or will, buying up banks' bad loans ("toxic assets") spur them to make loans. Having no bad loans on the books in not an incentive to lend.

Your (Geithner's?, Bernanke's?, your Friedmanite CEA's?) assumption that you had to "fix" the financial sector first to fix the economy was wrong. It works the other way around.: when the economy get gets going, banks benefit from that. Banks do not make the economy better; the economy makes the banks better.

When credit stops flowing, it's because banks are not making loans. Banks making loans increase the money supply. For banks to decrease the money supply in a recession demonstrates an abject failure of the FED, our central bank. The most important function of a central bank is to control the money supply for the benefit of the economy. The FED can not do this. It is because of a fatal flaw in the make-up of the federal reserve system: "You can't push a balloon up by a string". "You can't make them (the banks) do anything", Barney Frank. We,ve chewed this spaghetti too many times already. "ENOUGH IS ENOUGH!".

The single most important, paramount, sine qua non reformation of the financial sector is to eliminate SRO,s –SELF REGULATING ORGANIZATIONS. Self regulation does not work. The SEC delegates regulation to the regulated. The NYSE regulates the NYSE. The NASD regulates the NASD. When the regulated become the regulators this is a no-brainer conflict of interest.

THE FED IS ALSO AN SRO. THE BANKS REGULATE THE BANKS; NO GOOD; DOESN'T WORK FOR THE BENEFIT OF THE ECONOMY. There is virtually zero regulation of banking and when any of the so-called rules is broken, there is no enforcement. For example, currently Bank of America, JP Morgan Chase, and Citigroup are all over the 10% maximum of deposits allowed, but nobody does anything about it. They also have market shares in some markets exceeding ant-trust law limits.

THE FED CAN NOT BE FIXED. WE NEED A NEW GOOD CENTRAL BANK. IF AND WHEN YOU ESTABLISH ONE, YOU WILL GET A SECOND NOBEL PRIZE-FOR ECONOMICS.

Good luck and goodbye,   Your Friends, Frank & Ellie DeFelice

POST SCRIPT

Here's a multiple-choice question elementary school children can answer (Try it out on Sasha and Melita):

What one of the following does not fit in?

- A. The Bank of England
- B. The Bank of Canada
- C. The Bank of France
- D. The Bank of Japan
- E. The federal reserve system

If your kids get it, you do too. And it will be quite easy to do: just nationalize the regional federal reserve banks and designate them:

THE BANK OF THE UNITED STATES OF AMERICA.

This will not be the political problem of "socialism" because most Americans think the FED is already a government agency.

RECAP

The base cause of the recession was the boom-and-bust cycles caused by highly leveraged speculation by bankers, brokers, hedge funds, LBO's and individuals. The leveraging was supplied by federal reserve member banks that are not properly regulated because the federal reserve member banks ARE THE FED, which is an SRO and needs to be replaced because the regulated can not be the regulators and the FED can not control the money supply.

Another needed cure for the current problems is repeal of Garn-St. Germain and the break-up of the mega one-bank holding companies allowed by it and created by Geithner: Bank of America, Citigroup, Goldman-Sachs and JP Morgan Chase.

Copies: Rahm Emanuel, CEA, SEC, Ben Bernanke

ADDENDUM

New boom-and-bust cycles -- "bubbles" – are well underway presently. And why shouldn't they be? Nothing has been done to reduce leveraged speculation: margin accounts are still the "regular" accounts at brokerages; margins on the CFTC are still at 10% and lower; hedge funds and other speculators are getting all the money they want at very low interest rates from the $ Billions Geithner and Bernanke put in increase banks and brokers liquidity. There are more bigger one-bank holding companies now than before. In stead of curtailing speculation, financial sector finagling has made it easier and better. Interest rates are very low and big brokerage houses like Goldman Sachs and ML now have their own banks. Those banks within the firms can create all the money the brokers want for speculation and to engage in "pump and dump" trading to the extent that Goldman Sachs is now making $100 MILLION/DAY . Secretive and hidden energy trading units in these huge – bigger than allowed under antitrust laws – businesses have now got oil and gasoline prices almost to the top of the last bubble.

By executive order you could and should tell the CFTC that no margin trading is allowed in that market and only qualified traders with legitimate business interests are allowed. Similar executive orders could straighten out the SEC, which has devolved from providing essential services for capitalism – capital formation and corporate issues liquidity – to a legalized betting arcade run by Wall St entrepreneurs, who make $ Billions financing the betting. Warren Buffet, who just bought the nation's 2nd largest railroad for $3.4 Billion, characterized that transaction as " a bet".

TO PRESIDENT OBAMA, OUR FRIEND

FROM :   Dr. & Mrs. Frank DeFelice
          222 Paradise Peninsula
          DeFelice Villa
          Lake Norman, NC
          Mail: Mooresville, NC 28117

DATE : November 15, 2009

SUBJECT : HOW TO MAKE THE STIMULUS WORK : CORRECT MISTAKES

A. Terminology mistakes
   1. You oversold the idea of "jump starting" the economy, which is good politics
      but poor economics because it causes people to expect too much too soon.
      A much better analogy, in the same idiom, would be "slow charge".
   2. "Job creation" is wrong because it implies that by giving money and/or tax
      Breaks to businesses they will solve the problem. That's real good politics,
      Especially for all the conservatives, the business community generally,
      Geithner and the bankers, but not good economics. What you should say
      the policy goal is : "WORK CREATION", like what FDR did in the Great
      Depression (which we remember!) Those public works projects not only
created lots of work, but built up our social capital structure and enhanced our standard of
living until this day and are still doing so.

B. Incorrect calculations
   1. In modern macro-economics (which some of your advisors do not believe
      in!) you have to determine the amount of aggregate demand that will
      bring the total up to the full employment level. We see no evidence that
      you correctly calculated that figure.
   2. More than half of the first part of the stimulus went for tax cuts for
      businesses and others under the mistaken notion that if they had more
      money they would hire more workers. That's not why businesses hire
      workers. They hire them when they have work for them, when there is
      demand for their output. When individuals get a tax cut it goes to thnose
      who are working, and because of the bad economic conditions they spend
      much less of it than what the tax cut costs. In economic terms, the MPC
      goes down in recessions. For every dollar of tax cuts for individuals in
      these situations you might get 90 cents at best of increased spending, and
      for business nothing; they just put in the bank. Only if the stimulus is
      100% government spending increase do you get the full effect.
   3. Slowly putting in the stimulus over two years is perhaps good politics, but
      not good economics. Nobody knows the exact lag structure for the fiscal
      policies, but one thing is clear : the longer you wait to put it in, the longer
      it takes to take effect. In this game you have to go "all in".

C. Additional Responsible Steps

1. A balanced budget is good politics, but bad for the economy. Proof? Just look at what happened in the states with balanced budget laws: They had to cut services and raise taxes making the recession worse. The same policy at the federal level would lead to a real disaster. You are, therefore, irresponsible to be considering the budget at this time.

2. You have no idea of what the "limits of what the government could and should do" are. You have idiots telling you deficits could cause inflation, markets for our debt could dry up, and the "bigee": our children and grandchildren will be saddled with the debt and their standard of living will be much worse. (The demogogues that have to get elected every two years make a living with this crap, "bullshit" is what Rahm would call it).

3. Deficits should be financed with "Perpetuals", bonds that have no due dates. Nobody ever has to pay them off. There would then not be the huge amount of issues being refinanced weekly added to the new issues thereby abating the market-may- dry- up dummies.

4. Government finance should employ a carefully calculated very conservatively leveraged capital structure. Do not know if the economists that could not calculate the correct increase in aggregate demand to get back to full employment would be able to do this. Would you want us to supply the formulas to make that calculation?

Copies: Rahm Emanuel, Council of Economic Advisors

POST SCRIPT : Is Larry Summers still drawing $5 Million/yr as a managing director of a hedge fund?!

THE WHITE HOUSE
WASHINGTON

November 19, 2009

Dear Friend:

Thank you for expressing your thoughts on corporate responsibility and oversight. A handful of irresponsible corporations bear a great deal of responsibility for our economic crisis. I share the frustration of many Americans about their actions and the era of profound recklessness that spanned from executive suites to the seats of power in Washington.

My Administration values the entrepreneurial dynamism and innovation of American business that have defined this country since its founding. But this economic crisis has made clear that we cannot allow corporate excesses and abusive practices to undermine our economy. We must end the outrageous bonuses, risky transactions, and gross mismanagement that have hurt American workers and families, leading many to lose their jobs or life savings.

Fostering an environment that promotes corporate responsibility will allow businesses to prosper while protecting consumers. Markets work best when there is transparency, accountability, and fair, well-enforced rules. To achieve this, we will enhance oversight of large financial institutions to prevent systemic failure and fraud and to curb exorbitant executive pay. We will also create a new Consumer Financial Protection Agency with the sole responsibility of protecting ordinary consumers. It will oversee consumer products, including mortgage lending, credit cards, and student loans. This framework will help end the culture of narrow self-interest and short-term gain, and promote a new era of corporate responsibility and stewardship. Join me online to read more about my efforts at: www.whitehouse.gov/issues/economy and www.FinancialStability.gov.

Thank you again for writing.

Sincerely,

161

Frank DeFelice, Ph.D.

THE WHITE HOUSE
WASHINGTON, DC 20500

Mr. and Mrs. Frank DeFelice
222 Paradise Peninsula
Mooresville, NC 28117

162

TO : SECRETARY OF EDUCATION ARNE DUNCAN

FROM :   Dr. & Mrs. Frank DeFelice
        222 Paradise Peninsula
        DeFelice Villa
        Lake Norman, NC
        Mail: Mooresville, NC 28117

DATE : DECEMBER 12, 2009

SUBJECT : "RACE TO TOP" MONEY REQUIRES BOOSTING SCIENCE COURSE
          OFFERINGS
          ECONOMMICS IS A SCIENCE

The elimination of economics illiteracy is the key element to have "a better way to do business post-bubble" as President Obama wants and to permanently eliminate boom-and-bust cycles that have cost millions of Americans misery repeatedly for over 200 years.

What is presently being taught under the rubric of economics at the high school level is NOT economics. Information about personal finance and savings is NOT economics.

Please look at the subject topics in Chapters 1 and 2 of the text we are writing specifically for easy comprehension at the high school level (Table of Contents enclosed) to see what economics is all about.

Check out our credentials (enclosed) to write this authoritative definitive work.

We were National Defense Education Act (NDEA) Fellows financed by the federal government to get a Ph.D. in the science of economics, which we did. We became leading Western scholars of the Soviet economic system – because we learned Russian in order to be able to do primary research - which was what the government provided the Fellowship to accomplish. This and other economics wisdom garnered over 50 years of study of the science needs to be passed on to where it will do some good : in all public high schools in the land.

You would be doing a monumental service, not only for President Obama, but for the nation and even the entire world, to make deep inroads into this severely crippling illiteracy that allows such economic suffering as we are currently undergoing to be mightily mitigated.

We are not asking you to violate any law that leaves curriculum up to state and local decisions. The "Race to the Top" law REQUIRES those who want some of the money to boost science offerings.

ECONOMICS IS A SCIENCE.   Copies: Obama, Emanuel, CEA

We sure could use a small grant - $10,000 to expedite movememt grp. Our annuity + retirement savings "took a bath" like millions of Americas.

Frank DeFelice, Ph.D.

TO : FED CHAIRMAN BEN BERNANKE

FROM :
Dr. & Mrs. Frank DeFelice
222 Paradise Peninsula
DeFelice Villa
Lake Norman, NC
Mail: Mooresville, NC 28117

DECEMBER 19, 2009

SUBJECT : ACCOUNTABILITY TEST - SELF ADMINISTERED - OPEN BOOK

Hey Ben, here's an easy test of how well you are doing your job.

Q.1. Of the 125 banks that have failed so far this year, how many of them were Member Banks of the Federal Reserve System?
 a. none
 b. few
 c. most
 d. all
If your answer is any other than a., you have failed to regulate banking properly because a good central bank does not allow any bank to make bad loans nor engage in any other non-banking business such as trading or leveraged speculation in any market.

Q.2. Bank of America, Citigroup, and JP Morgan Chase are banks each with more than 10% of all deposits in violation of banking regulations. To which ones have you applied the rule?
 a. Bank of America
 b. Citigroup
 c. JP Morgan Chase
 d. All of the above
 e. None of the above
If your answer is any other than d, you have failed to enforce banking regulations.

Q.3 Bank of America and JP Morgan Chase each have a greater share of certain regional markets than allowed by Anti-trust Laws. To which ones have you down-sized to comply with Ant-trust Law?
 a. Bank of America
 b. JP Morgan Chase
 c. Both of the above
 d. Neither of the above
If your answer is any other than c, you have failed to regulate banking as required by Anti-trust Law.

Q. 4 The money supply should be increased, not decreased, in a recession. (Remember your promise to Milton Friedman?) In which of the following months did the money supply increase?
   a. November 2009
   b. October, 2009
   c. September, 2009
   d. All of the above
   e. None of the above

If your answer is any other than d, you have filed in the most important function of the central bank -- control of the money supply for the good of the economy (and broke your promise to Milton Friedman).

SINCE YOU ARE NOT PERFORMING THE ESSENTIAL FUNCTIONS OF THE CENTRAL BANK, WHY SHOULD YOU BE RE-APPOINTED?

We know (don't we, Ben) the reasons why you can not do the job:
   1. The Member Banks, where policies are supposed to be carried out, are independent businesses run for their own benefit regardless of what the economy needs.
   2. The FED is an SRO (=Self Regulating Organization) in which the regulated are the regulators. The banks regulate the banks. This is a no-brainer conflict of interests. Self regulation does not work
   3. Neither you, nor Barney Frank, nor Chris Dodd can make them (the banks) do anything.
   4. The Fed, therefore, IS the systemic risk. The federal reserve system has a fatal flaw in its make-up: private businesses can not be expected to carry out public policy when it is not in their best interests to do so.
   5. 5. Our economy is at risk because money and banking can not be controlled for the public good.

The FED can not be fixed. It needs to be replaced by a good central bank:

THE BANK OF THE UNITED STATES OF AMERICA,,OWNED AND OPERATED BY THE PEOPLE FOR THE PEOPLE..

This is quite easy to do actually. Just nationalize the regional federal reserve banks. There will be no political problem of "socialism" because most Americans think the FED is already a part of the government.

Copies: President Obama, Rahm Emanuel, CEA, Senator Dodd

Frank DeFelice, Ph.D.

THE WHITE HOUSE

WASHINGTON

January 28, 2010

Dear Friend:

Thank you for writing me. Each day, I hear from concerned Americans who are struggling in this economy, and I appreciate your perspective.

Far too many families are experiencing financial hardship in today's recession—falling behind on mortgage payments, losing a job without warning, or struggling to secure much-needed loans. My Administration is working tirelessly on policies to repair the damage from this economic crisis and get our economy back on track.

We are implementing plans that will generate economic growth. The American Recovery and Reinvestment Act is saving or creating millions of jobs in infrastructure and green industries. It also provides a tax cut to 95 percent of working families and extends unemployment benefits and health care coverage to the unemployed. We have also implemented several programs to ensure that banks restart lending and to help homeowners avoid foreclosure. In addition, we are working to make our auto industry more competitive so that these jobs stay in the United States. To follow developments and track projects in your community, visit: www.recovery.gov.

As we work for an immediate recovery, we must also make long-term investments that generate sustained prosperity. Sound investments in education, health care, and energy will lay a new foundation for economic growth. They will make our workforce more skilled and competitive, create new jobs and industries, and reduce the cost of health care for families and businesses throughout the country. To learn about my economic plans, join me online at: www.whitehouse.gov/issues/economy. Information on jobs, health benefits, housing assistance, and other public resources available to those in need can be found by calling 1-(800)-FEDINFO or by visiting: www.usa.gov.

I am working every day to strengthen our economy so that all Americans can reach their highest aspirations and potential. Thank you again for contacting me.

Sincerely,

166

28 JAN 2010

Mr. and Mrs. Frank DeFelice
Lot 470
700 County Road 630A
Frostproof, FL 33843

THE WHITE HOUSE
WASHINGTON, DC 20500

Frank DeFelice, Ph.D.

TO : PRESIDENT OBAMA, OUR FRIEND

FROM : Dr. & Mrs. Frank DeFelice
Rainbow Resort
Lot 470
700 Co. Rd. 630A
Frostproof, FL 33843

DATE : MARCH 11, 2010

SUBJECT : 21ST CENTURY MACRO-ECONOMICS
THEORETICALLY SOUND AND PRACTICAL

In an earlier memo, we suggested a new theory of government finance that embodies "very conservative leveraging", which can actually be done by doing nothing – without announcing any new policy – because that's the way government finance has been run for many years, is being run now, and should continue to be run.

Why? Because a balanced budget, which is great politics (everyone is for baseball, apple pie and a balanced budget, right?) is actually bad economics. To understand why this is so, check out our reply to the recent standard BS "balance-the-budget" editorial in the Orlando Sentinel, "Red Ink Alert" (copies of both enclosed).

We made the same argument in response to the same editorial in the Wall Street Journal in July, 1967 (43 years ago!) titled " Government and Debt"; both of which were re-printed in Glen Mills' Reason in Controversy, 2nd edition, Allyn and Bacon, when he was Dean of the School of Speech at Northwestern University.

At this point in time, we can up-date the argument using current OMB projections that show it will cost only 3% of National Income to carry our National debt. That is not a burden to anyone.

We are approaching 80 and have never been "burdened by" – had to pay – the National debt. Neither have our children, our grand-children nor our great grand-children. Neither will your children, your grand-children , nor their grand-children be "burdened by" – have to pay – it.

When John Maynard Keynes was asked about what happens in the long-run when contra-cyclical fiscal policy (deficit spending) debt comes due, he said, "In the long-run we are all dead", which is true but a bit glib of an answer to something the public INCORRECTLY perceives as a big problem. (We even saw David Gergen mouth the word "bankruptcy" on a TV talk show about government spending !)

A better explanation would be : we just keep doing what we have always done : sell re-funding issues of Treasuries as issues come due. (Just like WELL-RUN businesses do !)

A better solution would be to issue "Perpetuals", bonds that never come due, as they do in England.

You can keep talking "balanced budget", it's great politics, but you should tone down the rhetoric like Bill Clinton told you do with your "economic crisis" speeches (which probably was THE factor that got you elected). In both cases, you have made the problem worse than it really is. (In our book, What All Americans Need To Know About Economics (forth-coming), which will be the definitive work on the causes of the 2008-09 recession, such talk by you is cited as an important causal factor for the recession because John McCain was right when he said the economic fundamentals were fine when he said it.)

Financial leveraging in business has to do with the debt/equity ratio (D/E) on the balance sheet, but National Income accounting is not done like business accounting. Therefore, we need look only at debt-carrying capability to ascertain the risk involved.
Low risk, very conservative leveraging in personal finance is that debt can be 2 ½ times - 250% of - personal income, and in this calculation the debt has to be amortized (paid off). National debt, therefore, that costs only 3% of National Income to carry and never has to be paid off is miniscule – very low risk, very safe leveraging – and really not a problem at all.

We respectfully suggest that your (un-spoken) policy about the National debt be :
BENIGN NEGLECT. As the economy grows, and, therefore also National Income, what is incorrectly perceived by the public as a problem becomes less and less of one over time.

Copies: Rahm Emanuel, David Gergen, Michael Aronson, Larry Traidor, Jack Massey

Post Script : Don't listen to those conservative Republican Friedmanite economists like Ben Bernanke and Larry Summers inter alios that are stuck with worn-out defunct 20th century macro-economics nonsense.

THE WHITE HOUSE

WASHINGTON

April 29, 2010

Dear Friend:

Thank you for sharing your thoughts with me. I have heard from many Americans concerned about the Federal budget deficit and government spending, and I appreciate your perspective.

I am committed to making my Administration the most open and transparent in history, and part of delivering on that promise is hearing from people like you. I take seriously your opinions, and respect your point of view on this important issue. Please know that your concerns will be on my mind in the days ahead.

Thank you again for writing. I encourage you to visit WhiteHouse.gov to learn more about my Administration or to contact me in the future.

Sincerely,

THE WHITE HOUSE
WASHINGTON, DC 20500

30 APR 2010 PM 4 L

Mr. and Mrs. Frank DeFelice

8

Dr & Mrs Frank DeFelice
222 Paradise Peninsula
DeFelice Villa
Mooresville, NC 28117

TO : PRESIDENT OBAMA, OUR FRIEND

FROM :

Dr. & Mrs. Frank DeFelice
672 Windridge
Linville, NC
Mail: 2152 Land Harbor
Newland, NC 28657

DATE : July 10, 2010

SUBJECT : DO NOT SIGN FINANCIAL SECTOR SO-CALLED "REFORM" BILL.
IT IS NOT "BETTER THAN NOTHING"; IT IS WORSE THAN
NOTHING

The SEC has designated the NYSE and the NASD as SRO'S – Self Regulating
Organizations.

The Bill says the regulators will interpret and enforce the new rules.

That means that the regulatED are the regulaTORS !

Self regulation does not work –Madoff headed the NASD !

The FED is also an SRO; bankers regulate banking.

Correction of the financial sector must start with elimination of the basic cause of the
bubble : HIGHLY LEVERAGED SPECULATION FOR SHORT TERM CAPITAL
GAINS.

Such activities are evidence that the SEC is NOT running fair and orderly markets in
violation of its mandate.

Margin accounts are just one of the loans that are supposed to be controlled by the central
bank FOR THE GOOD OF THE ECONOMY; NOT WALL ST. Our central bank, the
FED, is completely remiss in its obligation to carry out this public service. But, of
course, it only a QUASI- public agency.

Quasi-public agencies like the FED, Fannie Mae, and Freddie Mac are a failed public
policy management models and must be replaced. That along with getting the SEC to do
its job is what is essential to avoid future financial bubbles and recessions, and is "A
BETTER WAY TO DO BUSINESS POST-BUBBLE" , whereas the "reform" Bill will
make things better for Wall St. and bankers, but worse for the economy. After all, the
entire financial sector – thousands of banks, thousands of brokerages, and thousands of
insurance companies and others constitute only 10% of the economy (in normal times).

THE WHITE HOUSE
WASHINGTON

August 24, 2010

Dear Friend:

Thank you for writing. I have heard from many Americans about financial reform, and I appreciate your perspective.

For too long, Wall Street firms were not held accountable, financial dealings were not transparent, consumers and shareholders were not given enough information and authority to make decisions, and Government did not have the appropriate tools to close down failing financial firms without bailing them out. That is why I went to Wall Street before this crisis hit and called for common-sense reforms to protect Americans and our economy, and that is why I am proud to have signed into law the most comprehensive package of financial reforms in decades, including the strongest consumer protections in our Nation's history.

Wall Street reform brings greater security to hardworking people on Main Street—from families looking to buy their first home or send their kids to college; to small businesses, community banks, and credit unions who play by the rules; to shareholders and investors who want to see their companies grow and thrive. By cracking down on abusive and deceptive practices, these reforms ensure that Americans are not unwittingly caught by overdraft fees or unfair rate hikes, that students who take out loans have clear information, and that lenders do not cheat the system. It also gives Americans free access to their credit score if they are denied a loan or insurance—or given a higher interest rate—because of that score.

Because of these reforms, the American people will never again be asked to foot the bill for the excessive risk-taking of some on Wall Street. There will be no more taxpayer-funded bailouts. By laying a foundation for a stronger, safer financial system that is innovative and competitive, our Nation will reach a more secure and prosperous future.

Thank you again for writing. For more information about how financial reform affects you, please visit: www.FinancialStability.gov.

Sincerely,

THE WHITE HOUSE
WASHINGTON. DC 20500

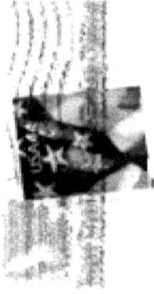

Frank DeFelice, M.D.
Mrs. Ellie DeFelice
2152 Land Harbor
Newland, NC 28657-7928

TO : REP. JOHN BOEHNER
SPEAKER OF THE HOUSE
U.S. CONGRESS
WASHINGTON, D.C. 20515

FROM :

Dr. & Mrs. Frank DeFelice
Lakemont Ridge Park
Lot 353
2000 Maine Avenue
Frostproof, Fl 33843

DATE : FEBRUARY 19, 2011

SUBJECT : SOLUTION OF THE GOVERNMENT AND DEBT PROBLEM .
OUR PLAN TO SAVE SOCIAL SECURITY AND MEDICARE
WITHOUT RAISING TAXES OR CUTTING BENEFITS

President Obama, our mutual friend, correctly said that there are Americans who can solve any problems we have as a nation.

We are among that very small group of economists with terminal qualifications in both Economics and Finance competent to solve government financing problems, which we have done for many years starting with "Gov't and Debt" back in July 1967 printed in the Wall Street Journal. Our solution stated then has stood the test of time and is even more compelling now. However, we have updated and up-graded the analysis to include the following FACTS :

1. Nobody's children or grand-children will ever have to pay off the National Debt.
2. We always pay all Treasuries in full when they come due.
3. The cost of carrying the National Debt is miniscule - less than one half of one percent of National Income ($242 Billion/$50 Trillion).

The "800 lb. gorilla" in the federal budget, we all agree, is the entitlements - Social Security (SS) and Medicare. But cutting benefits and/or raising taxes is not the best way to solve this problem. In five words, here it is : NO CAP ON TAXABLE EARNINGS.

The way the SS tax is imposed now is the most regressive tax we have. Like Leona Helmsley said, "Only the little people pay taxes". In this case the little people are all Americans - many millions - making less than $100,000/year because SS tax is capped at that level. This means that all those fat cat Wall Street folks getting $1 Million pay only one-tenth of what all Americans earning under $100,000 pay. This is very regressive, unfair and un-American. We believe, as all fair-minded people do, in progressive tax rates. The rich can afford to pay higher rates than the poor.

We also have a growing problem of in-equitable distribution of income in America, and making all the rich folks pay more tax will help ameliorate this problem.

By now, you must have done a little mental arithmetic that tells you that applying the SS tax to all income will not only generate so much revenue there will never again be a deficit, but benefits from the entitlements programs could be increased – earlier retirement with better payouts. We owe our seniors nothing less.

The Founding Fathers said that our government was formed for the purpose of promoting "THE HEALTH AND WELFARE" of the citizens. You are violating that duty and it is immoral when you decrease benefits for our senior citizens , and it is UN-NECESSARY.

The House is where all the spending and taxing policies originate, and you are the leader of that group. If you do this simple act : NO CAP SS TAXES, you will have not only solved what you and countless millions of Americans incorrectly think is a big problem – "We're broke" – but you will have made your mark in history. You would be eligible for a Nobel Prize in Economics (something President Obama would like to get!).

Before you file this in the "cylindrical file" beside your desk, check out our credentials on the enclosed sheet, "About Us".

Copies: President Obama, Gene Sperling, Michael O'Malley, Ph.D., M/M Jas. McKenna

TO : DR. ALAN B. KRUEGER, CHAIRMAN
      COUNCIL OF ECONOMIC ADVISORS
      THE WHITE HOUSE
      WASHINGTON, D.C. 20500

FROM :

Dr. & Mrs. Frank DeFelice
232 Paradise Peninsula
DeFelice Villa
Lake Norman, NC
Mail: Mooresville, NC 28117

DATE : SEPTEMBER 2, 2011

SUBJECT : HOW TO FIX THE ECONOMY

Now that all the Friedmanite, Chicago School, Brand X economists have gone off with their tails between their legs because none of their monetary policies worked, we can apply the only thing that will work : contra-cyclical fiscal policy that will increase aggregate demand to the full employment level. That's right – deficit spending, but it has to be correctly applied. The multiplier works only for increases in the Consumption and Government sectors ; not the Investment sector.

Economics education, one of our shared interests, is the key to un-locking the power of modern macro-economics to fix the economy. WHAT ALL AMERICANS NEED TO KNOW ABOUT ECONOMICS, a forthcoming E-book, contains theoretically sound approaches to solve all the pressing economics problems of the day. See the enclosed list, which was the first draft of our book cover. Also enclosed is the present front and back covers. Notice that we have moved "the entitlements problem" to the top, and we enclose that solution, which is on p. 12, Chapter1, which if applied, will not only solve funding for SS and Medicare forever, but will go a long way towards amelioration of our terribly in-equitable distribution of income.

And, though we rarely concern ourselves with the politics of applied macro-theory, this situation is so central to government finance that it required us to assess that it will "fly" politically because it can be done with no new taxes nor benefits cuts. And, currently, some of the world's super-rich – Warren Buffet for one – want to pay MORE taxes.

Even ultra-conservative tea party folks voted for a confiscatory 90% tax on Wall St/Bankers big bonuses at the time of the bailouts. And the public, generally, would like nothing better than to get some "skin" from all those Wall St. fat cats.

The super-rich's motivation for acceptance of higher taxes is to balance the federal budget, but we prove beyond any reasonable doubt that a balanced budget is ALWAYS bad economics. Those states (32) that have a balanced budget law hurt the economy in a recession; and, if the federal government had a balanced budget law, it would eliminate the possibility of contra-cyclical fiscal policy – THE ONLY WAY TO FIX THE ECONOMY. But you knew that, right?

So, deficit spending is good (now); a balanced budget is always bad, and the National debt is NOT a problem because the cost (interest) is only three tenths of one percent of National Income ($232B/$15T). And nobody's children or grand-children will ever have to pay it off. We heard President Obama, Our Friend, repeat that stupid remark (conservative "talking point"). He could not get much good economics education from Larry Summers; he's a Friedmanite, Hedge Fund manager. You can straighten the President out . We have been trying for 3 years; only heard him say one thing that maybe we taught him, "The stock market is not the economy". Here are the facts: Automatic re-financing of the National debt takes place every week with the demand for Treasuries at all time highs, (Wall St. loves this arrangement; underwriting fees and commissions get them $Billions. With current interest rates as close to zero as you can get, it costs us more for the Wall St.. fees than for interest on the debt!) What this automatic re-funding operation means is that we always pay in full every Treasury when it comes due. But you knew that, right, The President, the Congress and the public need to know that too, n-est-ce-pas?

We are Financial Economists (check Bio), and maybe that is the expertise that we bring to bear that you (?) and your pre-decessors are lacking.

Copies: President Obama, Gene Sperling

A PERSONAL NOTE : Turned down a scholarship at Cornell to take it at Michigan State because of a hockey connection between my high school (also LHS like yours) and MSU.: Our H.S. coach, Tom Moon, was the goalie on the 1936 U.S. Olympic team in Berlin and a teammate became MSU's coach. Therefore, LHS hockey players became the "Lexington line" at MSU; one of the best college hockey lines ever. Our two alma maters, MSU and UNC will play an historic basketball game on the deck of an aircraft carrier in San Diego, and it is real easy to remember the date : 11-11-11!
Good luck on your new job; hope you can shake off Geithner's bankers' bias.

TO : SENATOR BERNIE SANDERS (I)
     UNITED STATES SENATE
     WASHINGTON, D.C. 20510

FROM :
      Dr. & Mrs. Frank DeFelice
      232 Paradise Peninsula
      DeFelice Villa
      Lake Norman, NC
      Mail: Mooresville, NC 28117

DATE : SEPTEMBER 23, 2011

SUBJECT : HOW TO STOP THE GASOLINE PRICE RIP-OFF

Thank you for getting the CFTC data relevant to the $150/bbl run up of oil, and , therefore, $4-5.. gas prices, which was (incorrectly) reported in the Wall St. Journal. They did not list anything for Broker/Dealers, like Goldman-Sachs, Citigroup and others, just lumping them all together as "bankers"! Broker/Dealers and Hedge Funds were the biggest players in this illegal game, and when the bankers who were providing the margin money saw the $Billions being made by the Brokers, they got in on it for themselves. BANKS SHOULD NOT HAVE TRADING DESKS. This is one of the failures of the FED to regulate banking. And it is failure of the SEC that Hedge funds, which are mutual funds and therefore securities are allowed make securities markets unfair and disorderly. The SEC's primary mandate is to MAINTAIN FAIR AND ORDERLY MARKETS. That's the Law.
What's going on in the Commodities Futures Market is HIGHLY LEVERAGED SPECULATION FOR CAPITAL GAINS – THE CAUSE OF THE STOCK MARKET AND HOUSING SECTOR CRASHES that precipitated (but did NOT cause the recession) by hundreds of traders, most of whom do NOT have a legitimate economic interest in the future prices of commodities. Even those businesses – like oil and airlines – who do have a legitimate economic interest in future oil prices - do more than just hedge against future price increases. They are in the "pump and dump" trading game and make $Millions from trading…They even hedge their hedging by selling short ; so, no matter which way the price goes they will make money. (Congress characterizes this as "betting against yourself", but Wall St. rationalizes it as "reducing risk"!)
Short selling in commodities futures markets should not be allowed nor should trading by businesses with no legitimate economic interest - BANKS AND BROKERS - for their own account.
There is no theoretically sound reason for futures contracts to be bought on margin; i.e., with 95% of the money (Margins are only 5%!) borrowed from banks. And in the firms that are one-bank holding companies; e.g. Goldman Sachs and Bank of America – BOTH MADE SO BY GEITHNER! – they use the bank's capital to fund the trading. This is a classic example of why banks and brokers should be separated as they were under Glass-Stegall during the Great Depression. Margins in securities markets are set by the FED, but they will claim "no jurisdiction" over the CFTC. Likewise, the SEC that is required to maintain "fair and orderly markets". Insider trading IS ALLOWED BY THE CFTC –

a terrible mistake – but not by the SEC. So, there is a "turf war" that keeps regulators like the FED and the SEC at bay.

The CFTC is an SRO – Self Regulating Organization – which is the same way the SEC abrogates its responsibility to regulate the NYSE and the NASD.
When the regulated are the regulators, this is a no-brainer conflict of interests.
If there is one thing we should have learned from the 2008 financial fiasco it is : SELF REGULATION DOES NOT WORK. Example, par excellence, Bernie Madoff, who was the President of the NASD that the SEC has designated as an SRO!

All of these problems can be solved, as was pointed out in our April 23, 2011 letter to :

ATTORNEY GENERAL ERIC HOLDER and the
FINANCIAL FRAUD WORKING GROUP

HOW AND WHY GASOLINE PRICES RISE and
HOW TO STOP THE INFLATIONARY RISE

(copy enclosed, which is p. 76 in the Appendix of our forthcoming e-book:
WHAT ALL AMERICANS NEED TO KNOW ABOUT ECONOMICS.

If we can be of any further help in this monumental task you have undertaken to fix this problem that is very debilitating for the economy ("THE MARKETS" ARE NOT THE ECONOMY!) do not hesitate to call or write:

Email: DeFelice.Frank@yahoo.com

Cell Phone: 704-928-7660

TO : PRESIDENT OBAMA, OUR FRIEND

FROM :

Dr. & Mrs. Frank DeFelice
232 Paradise Peninsula
DeFelice Villa
Lake Norman, NC
Mail: Mooresville, NC 28117

DATE : OCTOBER 24, 2011

SUBJECT : TWEAKING CFTC WILL NOT STOP GAS PRICE RIP-OFF
BASIC DEFICIENCIES OF DODD-FRANK EXPOSED

Wall St Journal of Oct. 19, 2011 reports that, by PARTY LINE VOTE, the CFTC
has decided it will eventually try to implement some of the suggestions in the Dodd-
Frank so-called financial reform Act.
There is zero likelihood that whatever tweaking they do will stop the disgraceful,
unethical, immoral and greedy traders that make $ BILLIONS at the expense of all
Americans because nothing in Dodd-Frank stops the underlying cause of price
manipulation that occurs, not only in commodities futures markets, but also in the
NYSE, NASD and all securities markets and in the housing market: HIGHLY
LEVERAGED SPECULATION FOR SHORT TERM CAPITAL GAINS.
This is THE definitive explanation for the boom and bust "bubbles" in all markets, and
until you stop this, you will not have a "better way to do business post bubble" nor to
stop these recurring recessions that have plagued our democracy for over two hundred
years. (If you do it: maybe a Nobel prize!)
Speculation, per se, can not be stopped, but the leveraging and lack of regulation can.
Proper regulation will not happen from implementation of Dodd-Frank, because the
regulators are the regulated., The CFTC, LIKE THE NYSE,, NASD AND THE FED
are Self Regulated Organizations (SRO's); a no-brainer conflict of interests. Self
regulation does not work. Madoff was the NASD CEO!
The CFTC sets the margin for trading at 5%; that's 20:1, so a trader with one million
dollars can buy $20 Million of contracts, which is great for both the trader and CFTC that
does 20 times as much business than if there were no margin trading , which there should
not be. There is no legitimate economics rationale – in terms of what is good for the
economy – for margin buying of any securities including futures contracts.
Big brokerage firms like Goldman, Citigroup and hedge funds have $100 Million (and
more) cash and can therefore buy $2 Billion (and more) of contracts. When traders buy
and sell $2 Billion they can and do move the price. And what makes this real easy to do
is that INSIDER TRADING IS ALLOWED BY THE CFTC! This a classic example of
price fixing by collusion in an oligopoly, and is outlawed in the Anti-Trust Law of the
1890's,which have NOT been repealed, but they are NOT being enforced.
The CFTC also allows short-selling: so, if the prices goes down – WHICH THEY CAN
MAKE HAPPEN – the traders will make big profits whichever way the price goes.
The general public and Congress call this "betting against yourself", but it is common
practice in the securities business and is called "risk management". We call it

"racketeering" and implore you to stop it so that the negative effects of high energy prices on the economy will be mitigated.

Hedging the future prices of certain commodities is an important strategy FOR CERTAIN INDUSTRIES where the prices of certain commodities is a big part of their costs: e.g., airlines fuel costs and the oil industries basic input; but hedge funds, brokers and bankers do not have a legitimate economics rationale to be in the CFT market..

Therefore, the first thing to do is limit access to that market   to only those whose business needs to hedge future commodities prices. But this by itself will not solve the problem, because we know from data obtained by Sen. Bernie Sanders that the oil companies and the airlines inter alios not only buy contracts to hedge the price of important inputs in their business, but make big profits just trading – buying and selling the contracts. They do the same thing Enron traders did with electric power: driving up the price, then selling positions at the new higher price. This is called "PUMP AND DUMP" on Wall St. and is a real sickness in all our securities markets.

In an earlier communication to Attorney General Eric Holder and the Financial Fraud Committee – HOW AND WHY GASOLINE PRIES RISE AND HOW TO STOP THE INFLATIONARY INCREASES (enclosed) – we specified which Laws were being violated by the CFTC and the data to prove the case.

There are many Americans who think that the Democratic Party AND YOU are owned by Wall St.. We submit that the "Occupy Wall St" protesters are sending exactly this message. In fact, we heard Michael Moore, the award-winning documentarian, say that Goldman-Sachs was your "biggest campaign contributor". Is that so? If so, doesn't your promise of "transparency" require you to tell the people this fact? If you do, AND YOU STOP THE GAS PRICE RIP-OFF, you will get re-elected. If you do nothing, and it is true about Goldman, and the public knows it, you will NOT get re-elected.

But we are economists and don't really care whether you get re-elected or not (George Wallace was right when he said about politicians of both parties, "There ain't 15cents worth of difference between them".) ; we just want what is best for the economy.

Fixing the CFTC would help a lot.

Copies: Alan Krueger, Ph.D., Gene Sperling, Senator Sanders, John Thompson, Ph.D.

TO : READERS OF OUR E-BOOK WHAT ALL AMERICANS NEED TO KNOW
ABOUT ECONOMICS

FROM :

Dr. & Mrs. Frank DeFelice
232 Paradise Peninsula
DeFelice Villa
Lake Norman, NC
Mail: Mooresville, NC 28117

Email: DeFelice.Frank@yahoo.com

Cell Phone: 704-928-7660

DATE: NOVEMBER 15, 2011
SUBJECT : NANCY PELOSI EXPOSES A 4TH KIND OF INSIDER TRADING

In Chapter 1 we explained the insider trading done by insiders as defined by the SEC and reported regularly in the financial press. We also documented the "smelly" kind of insider trading as done by Mr. Stephen Friedman when he was on both the Goldman-Sachs and FED boards of directors.

Next we explained that insider trading is allowed by the Commodities Futures Trading Commission (CFTC), which makes it real easy for commodities traders to run their pump-and-dump operations to pocket $Billions every year as they drive up oil and gasoline prices to the detriment of all Americans and the economy.

Now we have an example of another kind of insider trading that really stinks. It takes place in the U.S. Congress when our elected representatives learn about pending legislation that will benefit a certain company. While the legislation was being worked out that would benefit Visa, Nancy Pelosi and her husband bought 5,000 shares of Visa. The legislation passed; Visa went up $20/share; the Pelosi's sold out, making $1,000,000. There was no quid pro quo between Pelosi and Visa, but this sort of insider trading THAT GOES ON IN CONGRESS ALL THE TIME is immoral, un-ethical and should be illegal. But guess what, Congress makes the rules for Congress. They have an ethics committee who decides what is or is not ethical. So here again we have a Self Regulating Organization (SRO) whereby the regulated are the regulators. This is a no-brainer conflict of interests. Self regulation does not work.

Nancy and all her Congressional friends get rich this way; so, it is almost a fair conclusion to say, "They are all rotten". (Possible exceptions might be those who went to Washington so rich they did not take their salaries, all of whom can be counted on the fingers of one hand.)

copies: President Obama, Nancy Pelosi

TO : THE OBSERVER FORUM
    THE CHARLOTTE OBSERVER
    P.O. BOX 30308
    CHARLOTTE, N.C. 28230

FROM :

Dr. & Mrs. Frank DeFelice
232 Paradise Peninsula
DeFelice Villa
Lake Norman, NC
Mail: Mooresville, NC 28117
704 664 2316

DATE : DECEMBER 5, 2011

Subject : "Expand (sic; extend?) payroll tax, but pay for it", Dec. 4, 2011, p. 28A
    CRITIQUE BY AN MBA, Ph.D.(UNC), FINANCIAL ECONOMIST

Your underlying assumption that we have a "dangerous (National) debt" is incorrect.
The National debt is only 70% of ONE YEAR'S NATIONAL INCOME, and it never has
to be paid off – just the interest, which is only three tenths of one percent (.003) of
National Income. National Income is going up every day and interest rates are very low.
Therefore there is no "danger".
But what is worse in your argument is that you ignore the fact that cutting taxes in one
place and adding them in another is a zero-sum game that will do the economy no good.
Insufficient aggregate demand is THE PROBLEM that can only be solved by decreasing
taxes overall and/or increasing government spending; all of which increase the deficit and
that is THE CORRECT THING TO DO TO FIX THE ECONOMY. (Cheney was right.
"Deficits don't matter".)

THE WHITE HOUSE
WASHINGTON

March 6, 2012

Dr. and Mrs. Frank DeFelice
232 Paradise Peninsula
Mooresville, North Carolina 28117

Dear Dr. and Mrs. DeFelice:

Thank you for writing. I have heard from many Americans about financial reform and the unfair practices of financial institutions, and I appreciate your perspective.

For too long, Wall Street firms were not held accountable, financial dealings were not transparent, consumers and shareholders were not given enough information and authority to make decisions, and Government did not have the appropriate tools to close down failing financial firms without bailing them out. That is why I went to Wall Street before this crisis hit and called for common-sense reforms to protect Americans and our economy, and why I am proud to have signed into law the most comprehensive package of financial reforms in decades, including the strongest consumer protections in our Nation's history.

Wall Street reform brings greater security to hardworking people on Main Street—from families looking to buy their first home or send their kids to college; to small businesses, community banks, and credit unions who play by the rules; to shareholders and investors who want to see their companies grow and thrive. One of the central aspects of reform was the creation of the Consumer Financial Protection Bureau, which will empower all Americans with the clear and concise information they need to make the best financial decisions for themselves and their families. This bureau will crack down on abusive and deceptive practices, ensuring that Americans are not unwittingly caught by overdraft fees or unfair rate hikes, students who take out loans have clear information, and lenders do not cheat the system. It also gives Americans free access to their credit score if they are denied a loan or insurance, or given a higher interest rate, because of that score. To learn more about the Consumer Financial Protection Bureau and how it can help you, or to file a consumer complaint, please visit www.ConsumerFinance.gov or call 1-855-411-CFPB.

These new consumer protections build upon the landmark Credit Card Accountability, Responsibility, and Disclosure Act (Credit CARD Act), which I signed during my first year in office. This law helps American families and businesses by requiring card issuers to give fair notice about payment due dates and changes in fees. It also bans most rate hikes within the first

TO : PRESIDENT OBAMA, OUR FRIEND
    THE WHITE HOUSE
    WASHINGTON, D.C. 20500

FROM :

Dr. & Mrs. Frank DeFelice
232 Paradise Peninsula
DeFelice Villa
Lake Norman, NC
Mail: Mooresville, NC 28117

DATE : MARCH 17, 2012

SUBJECT : RESPONSE TO YOURS OF MARCH 6 – FINANCIAL REFORMS

"YOU don't get it; you just don't get it!."

The financial fiasco of 2008 – failing banks and brokerage firms, the stock market crash, the housing market crash, and yes, $150/barrel oil = high gas prices, were all caused by the same thing : HIGHLY LEVERAGED SPECULATION FOR SHORT-TERM CAPITAL GAINS.

The so-called financial reforms do not address this problem at all, and unless and until you do, the same thing will happen again. In fact, gasoline prices are currently higher than they were in 2008.

In our memo of April 23, 2011 (enclosed) we explained how and why gasoline prices rise NOT BY SUPPLY AND DEMAND - and how to stop this atrocious rip-off of the American public with widespread detrimental effects to the economy.

The leveraging on the commodities futures exchanges is 20:1 – 5% margin - , and the regulators are the regulated – a no-brainer conflict of interests. They allow insider trading, short sales and allow market participants – bankers, brokers, hedge funds et cetera – with absolutely no legitimate economic interest in the future prices of commodities to engage in pump and dump trading that nets those people $BILLIONS annually at the expense of all of us. It is a huge zero-sum game : we all pay at the pump for their gains.

The next stock market bubble is currently being generated by these same tactics. Goldman-Sachs that accounts for 25% of all short-term trading on the NYSE is making $100 MILLION/day. In the third quarter of 2009 Goldman paid an average bonus of $691,000 to all of its 31,593 employees. 31,693 X $691,000 = $21.9 BILLION. Now do you get it?

Copies: David Axelrod, addendum (the big advantage of e-books) for
    WHAT ALL AMERICANS NEED TO KNOW ABOUT ECONOMICS
    (Amazon 9.99, Print Copy 19.99, signed 29.99)

THE WHITE HOUSE
WASHINGTON

April 25, 2012

Dr. and Mrs. Frank DeFelice
232 Paradise Peninsula Drive
Mooresville, North Carolina 28117

Dear Dr. and Mrs. DeFelice:

Thank you for writing. I appreciate hearing from you, and I share the vision of millions of Americans who want to take control of our Nation's energy future. My Administration's all-of-the-above energy strategy is about developing every source of American energy—a strategy aimed at saving families and businesses money at the pump by reducing our reliance on foreign oil, expanding oil and gas production, and positioning the United States as the global leader in clean energy.

Just like last year, gas prices are climbing across our country, and we are experiencing another painful reminder of why developing new sources of energy is so critical to our future. When gas prices go up, everyone is impacted, and Americans have to stretch their paychecks even further.

The hard truth is there are no overnight solutions to our energy challenges. The only way to deal with this problem is through a sustained, serious, all-of-the-above approach. Under my Administration, American oil production is at its highest level in 8 years, and we are now less reliant on foreign oil than in any of the past 16 years. We have more working oil and gas rigs than the rest of the world combined, and we have opened up millions of new acres for oil and gas exploration where appropriate and where it can be done safely. My Administration has also approved dozens of new pipelines to move oil around, including from Canada, which will help create jobs and encourage more energy production. Thanks to our Nation's booming oil production, more efficient vehicles, and a world-class refining sector that last year was a net exporter for the first time in 60 years, we cut net imports by 10 percent—or a million barrels a day—in the last year alone.

My Administration will continue to look for every way we can help consumers—from relieving distribution bottlenecks to ensuring speculators do not take advantage of volatility in the oil markets. To decrease our dependence on foreign oil, we established the toughest new efficiency standards for cars and trucks in history. These fuel economy standards will double

187

the fuel efficiency of our cars and light trucks by the middle of the next decade, which means filling up your car every two weeks instead of every week.

But as a country that has 2 percent of the world's oil reserves but consumes 20 percent of the world's oil, we cannot just drill our way to lower gas prices. The United States leads the world in natural gas production, with reserves that can last nearly 100 years—a supply that can power our cars, homes, and factories in a cleaner and cheaper way, and one that experts believe will support more than 600,000 jobs by the end of the decade. However, we must utilize this reserve without putting the health and safety of Americans at risk. That is why, for the first time ever, I am requiring all companies drilling for gas on public lands to disclose the chemicals they use.

Thanks in part to my Administration's investments in clean energy—the largest in American history—the United States has nearly doubled renewable energy generation from wind, solar, and geothermal sources, and thousands of Americans now have jobs as a result. By cooperating with the private sector, we have positioned our country to be the world's leading manufacturer of the high-tech batteries that will power the next generation of American cars. I have repeatedly called on Congress to stop giving away $4 billion a year in oil subsides to an industry that has never been more profitable, and instead to pass clean energy tax credits to cultivate a market for innovation in clean energy technology. And I have directed the Department of the Interior to allow the development of enough clean energy on public lands to power three million homes. The United States military—the largest energy consumer in the world—is also doing its part, making one of the largest commitments to clean energy in history.

Securing our Nation's energy future is one of the major challenges of our time, and will require the efforts of our brightest scientists and most creative companies. Americans must summon the spirit of optimism and the willingness to tackle tough problems that led previous generations to meet the challenges of their times. My Administration is making a serious, sustained commitment to tackling these problems, and I encourage you to learn more about our efforts at www.WhiteHouse.gov/energy.

Thank you, again, for writing.

Sincerely,

TO : PRESIDENT OBAMA, OUR FRIEND

FROM :   Dr. & Mrs. Frank DeFelice
            232 Paradise Peninsula
            DeFelice Villa
            Lake Norman, NC
            Mail: Mooresville, NC 28117

DATE : APRIL 29, 2012

SUBJECT : RESPONSE TO YOURS OF APRIL 25 – HIGH GAS PRICES

Your "all-of-the-above" energy strategy displays an implicit and INCORRECT
assumption that the underlying cause of high oil and gas prices is insufficient supply.
But the data in pp3 – "booming oil production and net exporter" put the lie to that
argument.
With "more efficient vehicles", lower real income, and lower "taste", there is no room to
argue that demand is pushing up prices.
The only valid conclusion is that supply and demand do NOT determine oil and gas
prices.
The explanation for this phenomenon is found in the 4th pp of your letter, in one word –
"SPECULATORS". They do not "take advantage of volatility"; they CAUSE it.

We are the "bright scientists" who have tackled AND SOLVED the problem, which is
not a "major challenge of our time". In our memo to Attorney General Eric Holder and
the Financial Fraud Enforcement Working Group , April 23, 2011 – copy enclosed – we
explained HOW AND WHY GASOLINE PRICES RISE and HOW TO STOP THE
INFLATIONARY RISE. There are "hidden and secretive energy trading units" (WSJ
description!) at Goldman, Citigroup, hedge funds et cetera who engage in pump-and-
dump trading that makes the $Billions annually that we all pay for at the gas pump. It is
huge zero-sum game for the economy, that can be stopped by enforcing laws on the
books and executive action; all of which is specified in that memo.
Q. Why are energy trading units "hidden and secretive"?
A. Because what they are doing is not only un-ethical and immoral but also unlawful!

Copies: David Axelrod, addendum (the big advantage of e-books) for
        WHAT ALL AMERICANS NEED TO KNOW ABOUT ECONOMICS
              (Amazon 9.99, Print Copy 19.99, signed 29.99)

TO : ATTORNEY GENERAL ERIC HOLDER and the
FINANCIAL FRAUD ENFORCEMENT WORKING GROUP
U.S. DEPARTMENT OF JUSTICE
950 PENNSYLVANIA AVE., N.W.
WASHINGTON, D.C. 20530-0001

FROM :
Dr. & Mrs. Frank DeFelice
222 Paradise Peninsula
DeFelice Villa
Lake Norman, NC
Mail: Mooresville, NC 28117

DATE : APRIL 23, 2011

SUBJECT : HOW AND WHY GASOLINE PRICES RISE and
HOW TO STOP THE INFLATIONARY RISE

Gasoline prices are a function of oil prices; and oil prices are NOT determined by supply
and demand. Oil prices are set on the Commodities Futures Trading Exchange, the New
York Mercantile Exchange, and other commodities trading facilities around the world by
hidden and secretive "energy trading units" at Goldman-Sachs, Citigroup, other big
brokerage firms and hedge funds.
These people have super-fast computers tied in to all the trading floors and computer
programs written by Ph.D. mathematicians that allow them to exploit in nano-seconds
miniscule differences between markets in $Billion trades.
With $Billion trades they can and do move up the price. Then they sell holdings at the
new higher price. This is called "pump and dump" on Wall Street, and generated such
great profits for John Henry's hedge fund, he bought the Red Sox "for change".
In 2008 , both Goldman-Sachs and Citigroup each made $667 Million from their "hidden
and secretive" energy trading units (data from the Wall Street Journal).
Their gains are a huge rip-off of the American people and bad for the economy and can
be stopped by doing the following things: (1) Do not allow traders like Goldman and
Citigroup or hedge funds in commodities markets because they do not have a legitimate
economic interest in the future prices of commodities; (2) Do not allow margin trading on
commodities exchanges; (3) Have an independent outside agency regulate these
exchanges instead of the Commodities Futures Trading Commission (CFTC), WHICH IS
MADE UP FROM THE TRADERS THEMSELVES, WHICH MAKES SUCH
EXCHANGES SELF REGULATING ORGANIZATIONS (SRO'S), which is the same
wrong way the SEC has set up the NYSE and NASD. SELF-REGULATION DOES
NOT WORK FOR THE GOOD OF THE ECONOMY, JUST FOR THE TRADERS!;
(4) enforce the Sherman Act because "pump and dump" is unlawful market manipulation,
and from "quick look" analysis it is obvious that prices are driven up by $Billion trades
that control the market to the detriment of consumers; (5) re-constitute the CFTC with
people who will set operating rules for the public good.
Further authority for action lies in the Employment Act of 1946 that requires the federal
government "to do everything within its authority to achieve stable prices".

Copies : President Obama, Gene Sperling, Alice Rivlin, Ph.D., Charlotte Observer